Pesach Haggadah / Shirat Miriam

FAMILY EDITION

CW01659064

Mosad Harav Kook
Founded by Rabbi Y.L. Maimom and Dr. Yitzchak Raphael

and Halacha Education Center

This edition of the haggadah is
an abridged version
of the original

PESACH HAGGADAH
SHIRAT MIRIAM
HAGGADAH MIMEKORAH

Which was dedicated in memory of

HYMAN AND MARION BESSIN ז"ל

Pesach Haggadah
Shirat Miriam
FAMILY EDITION

Haggadah MiMekorah

Rabbi Yosef Zvi Rimon

מרכז הלכה והוראה

MOSAD HARAV KOOK • JERUSALEM
HALACHA EDUCATION CENTER

מוסד הרב קוק

PRODUCTION: Kehat Ra'anan & Itay Levy
ENGLISH TRANSLATION: Rabbi Dr. Shmuel Himelstein
EDITING: Rabbi Yonatan Shai Freedman, Sara Daniel
TRANSLATION & EDITORIAL CONSULTANTS: Rabbi Dov Karoll, Rabbi Avishai Magence
PROJECT COORDINATION: Sefi Appel & Noam Rhein
TYPESETTING & LAYOUT: Raphaël Freeman, Renana
ILLUSTRATIONS: Binyamin Laukstein

PHOTOGRAPHS: of Judaica objects – courtesy of The Sir Isaac and Lady Edith Wolfson Museum of Jewish Art, Hechal Shlomo, Jerusalem
PHOTOGRAPHER: Shlomo Kashtan
The Nuremberg Haggadah – with the kind permission of Dr. David and Jemima Jeselsohn, Jerusalem – Zurich
Keter Aram Zova – with the kind permission of the Ben Zvi Institute, Jerusalem

ISBN 978-965-7513-14-9

"אהב ה' שערי ציון מכל משכנות יעקב - אוהב ה' שערים המצויינים בהלכה יותר מבתי כנסיות ומבתי מדרשות. והיינו דאמר רבי חייא בר אמי משמיה דעולא: מיום שחרב בית המקדש אין לו להקדוש ברוך הוא בעולמו אלא ארבע אמות של הלכה בלבד."

(תלמוד בבלי מסכת ברכות דף ח עמוד א)

This volume is dedicated with tremendous gratitude,
appreciation and love to our dear parents

David and Margie Zwiebel

May Hashem grant them good health, happiness
and joy for many years to come.

This volume is being published with great appreciation to

Rav Yosef Zvi Rimon and the Halacha Education Center

for paving a clear and accessible path for Am Yisrael to
understanding and appreciating the "four cubits of Halacha."
Your commitment and dedication to Torat Yisrael
and Am Yisrael are an inspiration to us all.

May G-d give you strength to continue to serve and lead Am Yisrael.

NOA & JAY ZWIEBEL

הרב אהרן ליכטנשטיין
ראש ישיבת הר עציון

Rabbi Aharon Lichtenstein
ROSH YESHIVAT HAR ETZION

ב"ה, עש"ק פ' זכור, י"ב אדר ב' תשע"א

לכבוד מרנן ורבנן
שוחרי תורה ולומדיה
השלום והברכה,

לשמחה ולנחת רוח לי לצרף בזה דברי הערכה והסכמה לספר נוסף מסדרת "הלכה ממקורה" של הרב יוסף צבי רימון שליט"א. הרב רימון תפס מקום נכבד כאחד מבחירי תלמידי ישיבת הר עציון, והועיד והכשיר עצמו מקדמת דנא להתמחות בתחומי הוראה; והינו ממשיך בעיסוק זה, הן במסגרת מעמדו כרבה של קהילת אלון שבות דרום, הן כר"מ, מדריך ומנחה קבוצת תלמידים מבוגרים בישיבת הר עציון השואפים ללכת בעקבותיו, והן כמחבר ספרים בהם משתלבים היקף, למדנות, בהירות, וזיקה לעולם הביצוע וההגשמה הלכה למעשה.

אתמחי גברא מזמן, וקנו להם ספריו תרומה של ממש בעולם התורה על רבדיו וגווניו, עבור יושבי בית המדרש בישיבות ובכוללים ועבור בעלי בית, שהעמקות וההיקף מחד, והבהירות והנגישות מכאן, נמצאים בחדא מחתא עם שפע של חומר השאוב ממקורות ומספרי פסיקה של קדמונים ואחרונים כאחד מעמיקות ומעשירות את לימודם.

חיל הרב י.צ. רימון שליט"א לאורייתא, ויהי רצון שימשיך ללמוד וללמד במסירות ובהצלחה לאי"ט.

ברכת התורה המצוה,
אהרן ליכטנשטיין

הרב זלמן נחמיה גולדברג
אב"ד בית ההוראה לדיני ממונות "הישר והטוב"
חבר בית הדין הרבני הגדול

Rabbi Zalman Nechemiah Goldberg
Head of the Bet Din for Financial Matters, *HaYashar VeHaTov*
Member of the *Bet Din HaRabbani HaGadol*

ב"ה יום כ"ו כסלו תשס"ז

הנני בזה להודיע שבחו של תלמיד חכם מופלג הרי הוא הרה"ג רבי יוסף צבי רימון שליט"א אשר גם משמש כרב בקהילת אלון שבות וגם כר"מ בישיבת הר עציון ונוסף לזה חיבר חיבורים חשובים מאוד לתועלת עם ישראל;

שמבאר יסודות ההלכה ואיך הגיעו הפוסקים מכח היסודות לפסוק הלכה למעשה וכעת חיבר חיבור יפה אף נעים בהלכות שבת וכתבם בלשון ובביאור הדברים למען ירוץ הקורא בהם.

ולא נצרכה אלא לברכה שהקב"ה יזכה להוציאו לאור עולם ולהמשיך לחבר חיבורים מועילים,

הכותב לכבוד התורה ולומדיה,
זלמן נחמיה גולדברג

Rabbi Ovadyah Yosef
The *Rishon LeTziyon* – The Chief Rabbi of Israel
President of *Mo'etzet Chachmei HaTorah*

הרב עובדיה יוסף
הראשון לציון
נשיא מועצת חכמי התורה

ירושלים כ"ט חשון תשס"ט Jerusalem

הסכמה

הובאו לפני גליונות הספר "**הלכה ממקורה**" חידושים לקוטים וביאורים בהלכות שבת ואשר מטרתו לבאר את הסוגיות ולהקל על הלומדים, ובאשר חיברו היקר והנכבד מזכה הרבים הרה"ג **יוסף צבי רימון** שליט"א, רב באלון שבות, וקיבץ כעמיר גורנה, ואסף חידושים וביאורים, רעיונות והגגים, ערוכים ומסודרים תפוחי זהב במשכיות כסף דבר דבור על אפניו, ולפעלא טבא אמינא איישר כחו לאורייתא.

ויהי רצון שחפץ ה' בידו יצלח לברך על המוגמר בקרב ימים, ועוד יפוצו מעיונתיו חוצה בבריאות איתנה ונהורא מעלייא לאורך ימים ימים ושנות חיים בטוב ובנעימים שובע שמחות וכל טוב "והיה כעץ שתול על פלגי מים, אשר פריו יתן בעתו ועלהו לא יבול, וכל אשר יעשה יצליח".

בברכה התורה
עובדיה יוסף
ראשון לציון
נשיא מועצת חכמי התורה

Rabbi Yitzchak Yosef
The *Rishon Letziyon* – Chief Rabbi of Israel
President of the *Bet Din HaRabbani HaGadol*

הרב יצחק יוסף
הראשון לציון הרב הראשי לישראל
נשיא בית הדין הרבני הגדול

כ"ה אלול תשס"ח

דברי ברכה

אני מכיר את ספריו של הרב הנכבד, מרביץ תורה, שוקד באהלה ש"ת, כש"ת הרה"ג ר' יוסף צבי רימון שליט"א רבה של אלון־שבות דרום, ור"מ בישיבת הר עציון.

חיבוריו מבוססים על דברי הפוסקים הקדמונים, מסודרים בסדר נפלא, מן המקורות בתלמוד, ראשונים ואחרונים, עד אחרוני זמנינו, בצירוף סברות ביאורים נאים, וטעמים. הדברים מסוכמים באופן שהדבר גורם לידיעת ההלכה בטעמיה ומקורותיה, והקפיד לציין בכל מקום אם יש חילוקי מנהגים בין הספרדים לאשכנזים, או חילוק בהלכה בין מרן השולחן ערוך לרמ"א, והדגיש זאת כדי שהספרדים ההולכים בעקבות הוראות מרן הש"ע, ידעו את ההלכה למעשה.

זכה המחבר להוציא לאור ספרים נאים ומסודרים, אשריו ואשרי חלקו, ולא נצרכה אלא לברכה, בידידות והוקרה, להרב המחבר שליט"א, שיזכה לחבר עוד חיבורים להפיץ מעיינותיו חוצה בעניני הלכה, יישר כוחו לאורייתא.

יצחק יוסף

הרב שלמה משה עמאר
הראשון לציון הרב הראשי לישראל

Rabbi Shlomo Moshe Amar
The Rishon Letziyon – Chief Rabbi of Israel

בס"ד, ב' אדר ב', תשע"א

534-18-1/ע"א

אגרת ברכה

הובאו לפני גליונות מהספר על הלכות פסח ליל הסדר שערך וחיבר הרה"ג יוסף צבי רימון שליט"א רבה של אלון שבות דרום ור"מ בישיבת הר עציון ואסף הלכות מספרים חדשים גם ישנים והביא מקורות לדברי, וכתב הכל בטוב טעם ודעת.

ויהי רצון שחפץ ה' בידו יצלח לברך על המוגמר, ועוד יפוצו מעיינותיו חוצה בבריאות איתנה ונהורא מעליא ויתקבלו דבריו בחן וחסד.

המצפה לישועת ה' ברחמים
שלמה משה עמאר
הראשון לציון
הרב הראשי לישראל

הרב שלמה דיכובסקי
אב"ד הרבני הגדול [לשעבר]
מנהל בתי הדין הרבניים

Rabbi Shlomo Dichovsky
Past head of the Bet Din HaRabbani HaGadol
Director of the Rabbinic Batei Din

בס"ד, בחמישי בשבת ששה ימים לחודש אדר הראשון התשע"א

מכובדי היקר
הרב יוסף צבי רימון שליט"א

נתכבדתי על ידו בשני ספרים חדשים: הלכות ברכת המזון והלכות צבא.

כבר כתבתי בזמנו ביחס לספרו על הלכות שבת והמדור ההלכתי הקבוע בעלון "שבת בשבתו", שכבודו הפליא לעשות בצירוף שני מקצועות הלכתיות: בירור הלכתי מקיף ופסיקת הלכה למעשה.

פסיקת הלכה תוך כדי בירור ממצה של המקורות – בקיצור נמרץ ובשפה ברורה ונעימה – אינה מן הדברים המצויים. החיבור בין השניים, ללא אריכות יתירה וללא הערות מפותלות, הוא חזון לא נפוץ בעולם ההלכה.

אני חסיד מובהק של דרך זו, וכל ספר גדול או קטן לא מש ממני, עד שעברתי עליו היטב. הרבה דברים התבררו לי והתלבנו לי בעקבות העיון במאמרים ובספרים, ועל כך, תודה רבה.

אני מתנצל שלא השתמשתי בתארי כבוד, שכידוע אינם מקובלים עלי.

בברכה מקרב לב,
הרב שלמה דיכובסקי
מנהל בתי הדין הרבניים

הרב אשר זעליג וייס

Rabbi Asher Zelig Weiss

כגן 8
פעיה"ק ירושלים ת"ו

Kagan 8
Jerusalem

בס"ד

כ"ה באדר א' תשע"א

הן ראיתי את סדרת הספרים "הלכה ממקורה" שחיבר איש מהיר במלאכתו, מלאכת שמים, ידידי הרה"ג ר' יוסף צבי רימון שליט"א. ספרים אלה תועלת מרובה יש בהם, בהיותם ערוכים בצורה ברורה ונעימה, בטוב טעם ודעת זקנים, ובאופן השוה לכל נפש.

בירור ההלכה הוא ממקורות הפוסקים ועד הוראה הלכה למעשה בבהירות מרובה.

ברכתי להרה"ג המחבר שליט"א שרבים יאותו לאורו, אור התורה, ויזכה תמיד להגדיל תורה ולהאדירה בשמחה, בשלוה ובנחת.

ביקרא דאורייתא,

אשר זעליג וייס

הרב שמחה הכהן קוק

Rabbi Simcha HaKohen Kook

הרב הראשי ואב"ד
רחובות

Chief Rabbi and Head of the Bet Din
Rehovot

ב"ה ד' אדר ב' תשע"א

דברי יקר!

הנה ברך ה' חילו של **הרה"ג יוסף צבי רימון שליט"א** ומן השמים זכוהו להגדיל תורה ולהאדירה, ולזכות את הרבים בכתיבת ספרים בהלכה, עריכה ומסודרת בצורה השוה לכל נפש הלכה למעשה.

וכל זאת ב"**הלכה ממקורה**" שציין את יסודי ההלכה במקורה, ובירור כל ההלכות ממקורות הראשונים והאחרונים עד גאוני זמנינו.

נברכהו בברכת התורה ובברכת כהנים באהבה, שיזכה רבות בשנים לנהל עדתו על מי מנוחות, לשבת באהלה של תורה, להפיץ מעינותיו חוצה על פלגי מים בין עדת צאן מרעיתו מתוך בריות גופא ונהורא מעליא ומתוך סייעתא דשמיא ושפע רב.

בברכת התורה
ובברכת כהנים באהבה
הרב שמחה הכהן קוק

Introduction

THE SEDER NIGHT IS A SPECIAL NIGHT, an exalted night of spiritual potential, commemorating the time when we gained our freedom. There is, however, certain difficulty in conducting the Seder night. The people present are of different ages, of different levels of understanding. It is night, and people are very tired. How can we succeed in transmitting the most important message of the year?

This volume of the Family Haggadah is designed to help conduct a Seder that will involve everyone present. It contains many of the sections included in the unabridged version, The Pesach Haggadah – Shirat Miriam, which are meant to be used before and during the Seder. For a more comprehensive review of the haggadah, please see that volume.

Sections included in this volume

A SUMMARY OF THE HALACHA: The practical halacha is mentioned within the text of the haggadah, for use on Seder night itself.

JEWISH THOUGHT: In adding sections of Jewish thought, we have tried to relate to the most central and crucial aspects of the haggadah, seeking to ask basic questions about the fundamental aspects of the Exodus from Egypt. Much thought has been devoted to our status as "free people," and what is defined as true freedom. We believe that this is the key point of the Seder night.

These passages are interspersed throughout the entire haggadah.

THE SOURCES OF THE HAGGADAH: In order to understand the principles of the haggadah in depth and where they are derived from, we have included these sources with brief explanations.

RIDDLES: In an attempt to deal with the difficulties of involving all the participants of the Seder, we have added numbered riddles throughout the haggadah. Corresponding answers to these riddles can be found at the end of the haggadah (some of the answers, as you will see, are only partial, as the riddle may have many possible answers!). These riddles will hopefully encourage everyone to participate, each on his own level. Riddles suitable for young children are colored green. Some riddles require some study – for example, the questions about the Ten Plagues require a look at the verses themselves.

TOPICS FOR DISCUSSION: Throughout the haggadah, we have added various topics for discussion, designed to encourage discussion of the haggadah's

◂ text

text in depth. At the end of the haggadah, there are answers to these discussions, which are, naturally, only partial answers to the topics raised. (These topics are marked with letters to match the corresponding answers at the end of the book.)

ACTIVITIES: There are a number of activities throughout the haggadah. The appropriateness of these varies from family to family, and of course each family can think of ways to add more and more suitable activities. One should choose activities that will involve the children but will nevertheless keep the Seder within the proper framework of relating the Exodus from Egypt and not transform the Seder into merely an entertaining fun family night without any meaningful content.

Another work that enhances this haggadah is "Halacha MiMekorah – Kinor David."

For each of the segments of the Seder there is a study section in Halacha MiMekorah – Kinor David. This chapter reviews all the laws related to that section, from the original sources down to the practical halacha today, along with explorations and discussions of major issues, rabbinical rulings of the greatest contemporary rabbis, etc. Although it is an in-depth study, it is clear and accessible.

I thank the Creator of the Universe, who enabled me to live in the tents of Torah, to learn and to teach – in Yeshivat Har Etzion, in the Halacha Education Center and in other places; who enabled me to serve as the rabbi of Kehilat Alon Shevut Darom, with its wonderful and pleasant people; who enabled me to be involved in acts of loving kindness with the former inhabitants of Gush Katif and others. I pray that, with the help of God, I will continue to learn and teach, to observe, do, and fulfill, all in love and joy.

Yosef Zvi Rimon
Alon Shevut, Adar 5772

Kaddesh

Urchatz

Karpas

Yachatz

Maggid

Rochtzah

Motzi Matzah

Maror

Korech

Shulchan Orech

Tzafun

Barech

Hallel

Nirtzah

The Pesach Haggadah

Kaddesh – RECITE KIDDUSH

Our aim: to sanctify! To sanctify the physical and mundane. To infuse our surroundings with sanctity. Our ultimate goal is revealed by our first act: to elevate the physical with the spiritual. With kiddush, we ascend the first step of the spiritual journey that is the Seder night.

קידוש

כולם מוזגים כוס ראשון, ומקדשים עליו.

יש נוהגים לומר לפני הקידוש:

הִנְנִי מוּכָן וּמְזֻמָּן לְקַיֵּם מִצְוַת קִדּוּשׁ וּמִצְוַת כּוֹס רִאשׁוֹן מֵאַרְבַּע כּוֹסוֹת. לְשֵׁם יִחוּד קוּדְשָׁא בְּרִיךְ הוּא וּשְׁכִינְתֵּיהּ עַל יְדֵי הַהוּא טָמִיר וְנֶעְלָם בְּשֵׁם כָּל יִשְׂרָאֵל. וִיהִי נֹעַם אֲדֹנָי אֱלֹהֵינוּ עָלֵינוּ וּמַעֲשֵׂה יָדֵינוּ כּוֹנְנָה עָלֵינוּ וּמַעֲשֵׂה יָדֵינוּ כּוֹנְנֵהוּ.

כשחל בשבת מתחילין כאן:

בלחש: **וַיְהִי עֶרֶב וַיְהִי בֹקֶר**

יוֹם הַשִּׁשִּׁי. וַיְכֻלּוּ הַשָּׁמַיִם וְהָאָרֶץ וְכָל צְבָאָם. וַיְכַל אֱלֹהִים בַּיּוֹם הַשְּׁבִיעִי מְלַאכְתּוֹ אֲשֶׁר עָשָׂה, וַיִּשְׁבֹּת בַּיּוֹם הַשְּׁבִיעִי מִכָּל מְלַאכְתּוֹ אֲשֶׁר עָשָׂה. וַיְבָרֶךְ אֱלֹהִים אֶת יוֹם הַשְּׁבִיעִי וַיְקַדֵּשׁ אֹתוֹ, כִּי בוֹ שָׁבַת מִכָּל מְלַאכְתּוֹ אֲשֶׁר בָּרָא אֱלֹהִים לַעֲשׂוֹת.

Halachic Summary

The four cups and kiddush

The four cups were instituted in order to signify freedom and to publicize the miracle, as well as to sanctify the mitzvot of the night with wine. One should use a cup that holds at least a *revi'it* (an 86 cc., or 2.9 fluid ounces, capacity. Others say it should have at least a 150 cc., or 5.07 fluid ounces, capacity, especially for the first cup). One should ideally drink the entire cup, or at least the majority of it, without removing the cup from one's mouth. One must drink while leaning to the left.

It is preferable to drink wine, but a person who does not like wine, gets a headache, or becomes tired from drinking wine can drink grape juice.

Women are required to drink the four cups. It is laudable for children to also drink the four cups, even though they are not obligated in the mitzvah. Children who are of educable age should be given a *revi'it* of grape juice, but all they need to drink is a mouthful.

Ashkenazic Jews recite a blessing over each of the four cups of wine. Sefardic Jews recite a blessing only on the first and third cups. Everyone agrees that the blessing after drinking wine

◄ is recited

KIDDUSH

The first cup is poured and kiddush is recited.
There are some who say before kiddush:

I am prepared and ready to recite kiddush and the mitzvah of the first cup of four cups. For the sake of the unification of the Holy One, Blessed be He, and His Presence, in the name of all Israel. And may the pleasantness of the Lord our God be upon us, and the work of our hands establish for us, and may the work of our hands establish it.

When the seder is on a Friday night, begin here:

Quietly: And it was evening and it was morning,

THE SIXTH DAY. And the heaven and the earth and all their hosts were completed. And on the seventh day, God finished His work that He had made, and He rested on the seventh day from all His work that He had made. And God blessed the seventh day and made it holy, for on it He rested from all His work that He, God, created to make.

---

is recited only after the fourth cup of wine.

One is not to recite kiddush until the stars appear. ▪

Food For Thought

Why drink four cups of wine? Are we drunkards?

The Sages decreed that one drink four cups of wine in order to show our freedom on the Seder night, as well as to correspond to the *four verbs regarding redemption* in the Torah (for further discussion, see *Halachah MiMekorah – Kinor David, Kaddesh* p. 37): "I will bring you out… I will deliver you… I will redeem you… I will take you." Why did the Sages insist specifically on wine? Firstly, free people drink wine, and drinking wine signifies freedom. In addition, drinking wine brings about special joy. This is explained by Sefer HaChinuch (Positive Mitzvah 31) regarding making kiddush on wine:

And the reason why we were com-

◂ commanded

כשחל בחול מתחילין כאן:
(בשבת מוסיפים את המילים שבסוגריים)

סַבְרִי מָרָנָן וְרַבָּנָן וְרַבּוֹתַי:

בָּרוּךְ אַתָּה יְהֹוָה אֱלֹהֵינוּ מֶלֶךְ הָעוֹלָם, בּוֹרֵא פְּרִי הַגָּפֶן:

בָּרוּךְ אַתָּה יְהֹוָה אֱלֹהֵינוּ מֶלֶךְ הָעוֹלָם, אֲשֶׁר בָּחַר בָּנוּ מִכָּל עָם וְרוֹמְמָנוּ מִכָּל לָשׁוֹן וְקִדְּשָׁנוּ בְּמִצְוֹתָיו, וַתִּתֶּן לָנוּ יְהֹוָה אֱלֹהֵינוּ בְּאַהֲבָה (שַׁבָּתוֹת לִמְנוּחָה וּ) מוֹעֲדִים לְשִׂמְחָה, חַגִּים וּזְמַנִּים לְשָׂשׂוֹן, (אֶת יוֹם הַשַּׁבָּת הַזֶּה וְ) אֶת יוֹם חַג הַמַּצּוֹת הַזֶּה, זְמַן חֵרוּתֵנוּ, (בְּאַהֲבָה) מִקְרָא קֹדֶשׁ, זֵכֶר לִיצִיאַת מִצְרָיִם. כִּי בָנוּ בָחַרְתָּ וְאוֹתָנוּ קִדַּשְׁתָּ מִכָּל הָעַמִּים, (וְשַׁבָּת) וּמוֹעֲדֵי קָדְשְׁךָ (בְּאַהֲבָה וּבְרָצוֹן) בְּשִׂמְחָה וּבְשָׂשׂוֹן הִנְחַלְתָּנוּ. בָּרוּךְ אַתָּה יְהֹוָה, מְקַדֵּשׁ (הַשַּׁבָּת וְ) יִשְׂרָאֵל וְהַזְּמַנִּים.

בָּרוּךְ אַתָּה יְהֹוָה אֱלֹהֵינוּ מֶלֶךְ הָעוֹלָם, שֶׁהֶחֱיָנוּ וְקִיְּמָנוּ וְהִגִּיעָנוּ לַזְּמַן הַזֶּה.

שותים הכוס בהסבת שמאל ואין מברכים ברכה אחרונה.

---

manded to perform this act over wine is that man's nature is greatly stirred by it, in that he drinks it and is joyful, and I have already said that according to one's being stirred up and his deeds he will affect matters in the world.

Wine makes a person rejoice, and when a person rejoices he can perform the mitzvot in a better way. Furthermore, the increased joy brought about by wine hints at the way the redemption will come. Usually, when a person eats, the first bite is the most delicious, the second less so, and the third even less so. In the case of wine, it is the exact opposite: with each cup one's joy increases. The same will be true of Israel's redemption, and thus we have the four verbs of redemption, with each stage higher than the previous

◄ one:

When the Seder night is on a weekday night, one begins here:
(The sections in square brackets are added on Shabbat.)

With your permission, gentlemen, my masters and teachers:

BLESSED are You, Lord, our God, King of the universe, who creates the fruit of the vine.

Blessed are You, Lord our God, King of the universe, who has chosen us from among all people, and exalted us above all tongues, and sanctified us through His mitzvot. You, Lord our God, have given us, with love, [Shabbat for rest and] festivals for happiness, festivals and seasons for joy: [this Shabbat and this] Festival of Matzot, season of our Freedom [in love], a holy convocation in remembrance of the Exodus from Egypt. For You have chosen us and sanctified us from all the nations, and You gave us [the Shabbat and] Your holy festivals [with love and favor], in happiness and joy, as a heritage. Blessed are You, God, Who sanctifies [the Shabbat and] Israel and the festive seasons.

BLESSED are You, Lord our God, King of the universe, who has granted us life, sustained us, and enabled us to reach this season.

The wine is drunk while one leans to the left, and there is no concluding blessing after it.

---

one: "I will bring you out" is the first stage, and this will be followed by "I will deliver you." That will be followed by "I will redeem you," and finally, "I

◂ will

Halachic Summary

One holds the cup in his hand and recites the blessing in joy and thankfulness to God for the miracles that He has performed for us. One should have the intention of fulfilling the mitzvah of four cups. Before the first cup, one should also have the intention of fulfilling the mitzvah of kiddush. When reciting the shehecheyanu blessing, one should have the intention to include all the other mitzvot of the night. ▪

קידוש ליל פסח שחל במוצאי שבת

סַבְרִי, מָרָנָן וְרַבָּנָן וְרַבּוֹתַי:

בָּרוּךְ אַתָּה יְהֹוָה אֱלֹהֵינוּ מֶלֶךְ הָעוֹלָם, בּוֹרֵא פְּרִי הַגָּפֶן:

בָּרוּךְ אַתָּה יְהֹוָה אֱלֹהֵינוּ מֶלֶךְ הָעוֹלָם, אֲשֶׁר בָּחַר בָּנוּ מִכָּל עָם וְרוֹמְמָנוּ מִכָּל לָשׁוֹן וְקִדְּשָׁנוּ בְּמִצְוֹתָיו, וַתִּתֶּן לָנוּ יְהֹוָה אֱלֹהֵינוּ בְּאַהֲבָה מוֹעֲדִים לְשִׂמְחָה, חַגִּים וּזְמַנִּים לְשָׂשׂוֹן, אֶת יוֹם חַג הַמַּצּוֹת הַזֶּה, זְמַן חֵרוּתֵנוּ, מִקְרָא קֹדֶשׁ, זֵכֶר לִיצִיאַת מִצְרָיִם. כִּי בָנוּ בָחַרְתָּ וְאוֹתָנוּ קִדַּשְׁתָּ מִכָּל הָעַמִּים, וּמוֹעֲדֵי קָדְשֶׁךָ בְּשִׂמְחָה וּבְשָׂשׂוֹן הִנְחַלְתָּנוּ. בָּרוּךְ אַתָּה יְהֹוָה, מְקַדֵּשׁ יִשְׂרָאֵל וְהַזְּמַנִּים.

בָּרוּךְ אַתָּה יְהֹוָה אֱלֹהֵינוּ מֶלֶךְ הָעוֹלָם, בּוֹרֵא מְאוֹרֵי הָאֵשׁ.

בָּרוּךְ אַתָּה יְהֹוָה אֱלֹהֵינוּ מֶלֶךְ הָעוֹלָם, הַמַּבְדִּיל בֵּין קֹדֶשׁ לְחֹל, בֵּין אוֹר לְחֹשֶׁךְ, בֵּין יִשְׂרָאֵל לָעַמִּים, בֵּין יוֹם הַשְּׁבִיעִי לְשֵׁשֶׁת יְמֵי הַמַּעֲשֶׂה, בֵּין קְדֻשַּׁת שַׁבָּת לִקְדֻשַּׁת יוֹם טוֹב הִבְדַּלְתָּ, וְאֶת יוֹם הַשְּׁבִיעִי מִשֵּׁשֶׁת יְמֵי הַמַּעֲשֶׂה קִדַּשְׁתָּ, הִבְדַּלְתָּ וְקִדַּשְׁתָּ אֶת עַמְּךָ יִשְׂרָאֵל בִּקְדֻשָּׁתֶךָ. בָּרוּךְ אַתָּה יְהֹוָה, הַמַּבְדִּיל בֵּין קֹדֶשׁ לְקֹדֶשׁ.

בָּרוּךְ אַתָּה יְהֹוָה אֱלֹהֵינוּ מֶלֶךְ הָעוֹלָם, שֶׁהֶחֱיָנוּ וְקִיְּמָנוּ וְהִגִּיעָנוּ לַזְּמַן הַזֶּה.

שותים הכוס בהסבת שמאל ואין מברכים ברכה אחרונה.

Havdalah goblet, gilded silver
The Wolfson Museum, Hechal Shlomo,
Max Grundt Collection

Kiddush when the seder begins on Saturday night:

With your permission, gentlemen, my masters and teachers:

BLESSED are You, Lord, our God, King of the universe, who creates the fruit of the vine.

Blessed are You, Lord our God, King of the universe, who has chosen us from among all people, and exalted us above all tongues, and sanctified us through His mitzvot. You, Lord our God, have given us, with love, festivals for happiness, festivals and seasons for joy: the Festival of Matzot, season of our Freedom, a holy convocation in remembrance of the Exodus from Egypt. For You have chosen us and sanctified us from all the nations, and You gave us Your holy festivals, in happiness and joy, as a heritage. Blessed are You, God, who sanctifies Israel and the festive seasons.

BLESSED are You, Lord our God, King of the universe, Creator of lights of fire.

Blessed are You, Lord our God, King of the universe, who distinguishes between holiness and secular, between light and darkness, between Israel and nations, between the seventh day and the six days of activity. You have made a distinction between the holiness of the Shabbat and the holiness of the festivals; and You have sanctified the seventh day above the six days of labor. You distinguished and sanctified Your nation, Israel, with Your holiness. Blessed are You, God, who distinguishes between holiness and holiness.

BLESSED are You, Lord our God, King of the universe, who has granted us life, sustained us, and enabled us to reach this season.

The wine is drunk while one leans to the left; there is no concluding blessing.

---

will take you" – where we will enter under the wings of the Divine Presence. (For further discussion of this idea, see *Halachah MiMekorah – Kinor David, Kaddesh* p. 37, in the name of Rav Shlomo Zalman Auerbach.)

This, however, needs clarification. Am Yisrael is generally opposed to the

◂ drinking

drinking of wine. It is true that we drink a cup of wine for kiddush, but drinking four cups seems to be somewhat excessive. Is it appropriate for us to use a symbol that seems to imply drunkenness, and at the seder of all times? (Even on Purim, there are guidelines for how much one ought to drink!)

The answer is that drinking wine on Seder night expresses *our freedom*, our ability to use the material for a higher purpose. Wine, alcohol, is one of the most dangerous threats to a person's sense of control, one of the most widely abused substances in humanity's history.

Rather than abusing wine for lowly matters, we harness its potency through kiddush *and use it to achieve spiritual elevation and holiness.* Freedom signifies control! A free person knows how to control his passions and his body. The freedom of the Seder night teaches us to be free people the entire year, and certainly not to lose control and indulge in drinking wine (as mentioned above, one can also drink grape juice). However, on the Seder night itself we drink four cups. On the Seder night our souls are free and, therefore, four cups of wine will not threaten our freedom. Rather, *the four cups allow us to channel our spirituality towards expressing our joy and gratitude to God.*

Kaddesh or *Kiddush*?

The list of stages of the seder begins with a command: Kaddesh! – Recite kiddush! What is the significance of the fact that this is phrased as a command? After all, we make kiddush every Shabbat. This change can be explained in light of the difference between the conclusion of the Friday night kiddush and the conclusion of the festival kiddush. On the Shabbat we conclude with, "He who has sanctified the Shabbat," whereas on festivals we conclude with, "He who has sanctified Israel and the seasons." The Talmud in Tractate Beitzah (17a) explains that it is Am Yisrael that sanctifies the seasons, and that is why we conclude kiddush on the festivals in this fashion. Am Yisrael *was given special sanctity, in order that we may sanctify the seasons* (based on Rav Avraham Yitzchak Kook, *Olat Re'iyah*, II:225–254, and so too in the name of Rav Zvi Yehudah Kook).

As opposed to Shabbat, which was ordained at Creation, the festivals have a direct influence on Am Yisrael. Am Yisrael sanctifies the months, thereby determining when the festivals will occur. That is why on the Shabbat, we merely *reveal* the sanctity of the Shabbat and join it, whereas with kiddush of the festivals, we *create* the sanctity. (Nonetheless, according to Ramban (Exodus 20:8), there is a certain degree of added sanctity in kiddush of the Shabbat, as in the sanctification of the jubilee year.)

The festivals reveal to us our purpose in the world: *To sanctify!* Am Yisrael was given its sanctity in order to spread it to the world. On each festival, we must remember this goal and

◂ *remember*

remember our mission: to sanctify the world, to sanctify the mundane.

On Pesach this is especially appropriate: "who has chosen us from among all people… and sanctified us through His mitzvot. You, Lord our God, have given us… this Festival of Matzot, season of our freedom… and sanctified us from all the nations, and You gave us Your holy festivals, in happiness and joy, as a heritage. Blessed are You, God, Who sanctifies [the Shabbat and] Israel and the festive seasons." The holiness of Am Yisrael requires us to sanctify the seasons, which is true for all the festivals. However, on the festival of Pesach, which is the first of the holy convocations, the first and foremost of all the festivals, it becomes clear that the ability to sanctify stems from the special *freedom* that we received.

Do you wish to be free? Sanctify your existence!

A slave lives merely to serve and to survive. A free person knows how to change, to develop – to raise his or her circumstances to a higher plane. A free person knows how to bring sanctity into the mundane world! This is the first mitzvah of the Seder night – *kaddesh*! Lift up your existence and with it be lifted up to the source of sanctity, the Holy One, Blessed be He. ▪

Riddles

1. Which mitzvot do we fulfill during kiddush of the Seder night?
2. Generally, we do something immediately after kiddush, but at the Seder night we are lenient. What is this thing? Why are we lenient on the Seder night?
3. What is the difference between kiddush of every other festival and kiddush of the Seder night?

Urchatz

The first step in attaining holiness is purification. “Wash yourselves, make yourselves clean!” (Isaiah 1:16). The readiness to remove our barriers, to allow our negative desires to wash away.

נוטלים ידים לאכילת הכרפס, אך אין מברכים על הנטילה.

We wash our hands before karpas, but we do not recite a blessing.

Halachic Summary

We wash our hands in the regular fashion (with a utensil, and using a *revi'it* of water), but do not recite a blessing, for immediately afterwards we will eat a vegetable that is wet. Ideally, everyone present should wash their hands. At large seder gatherings, where this is problematic, only the head of the household need wash his hands. If a person accidentally recites the blessing on this washing, he should be sure to eat at least a *kezayit* of karpas. ▪

Food For Thought

Why do we wash our hands specifically on the Seder night?

At first glance, it would seem that this washing has nothing to do with the Seder night. A person is required to wash his hands before he eats any food that has been dipped in liquid. That is why, before eating karpas that was dipped in salt water, one must wash his hands without reciting a blessing on the washing. However, throughout the year most people are lenient regarding this matter, whereas on the Seder night all adopt the more stringent view on this issue (see *Halachah MiMekorah – Kinor David, Urchatz* p. 60). Why?

The primary aim of this washing is to sanctify and purify ourselves, as the

Vessel for hand washing, copper
The Wolfson Museum, Hechal Shlomo, Golnitzki Collection

◂ kohanim

kohanim sanctify themselves before eating terumah (see *Halachah MiMekorah – Kinor David, Urchatz* p. 57). The rabbinic authorities differ regarding the degree of obligation of this hand washing in our time (even though it is preferable to be stringent in this regard). However, on the Seder night, we all aspire to be pure and holy. On this night God redeemed us, and when we come to the point in time of the peak of our freedom, we strive to be pure and holy, to be like the kohanim before the eating of terumah. ▪

Food For Thought

Four cups of tea…

Pesach 5704 (1944) Bergen-Belsen

A few days after Purim, the question arose: what should we eat during the eight days of Pesach? Could we refrain from eating the bread portions throughout Pesach and live only on the soup and unpeeled potatoes that were distributed at lunchtime? The rabbis of the camp ruled that the prohibition against eating bread on Pesach was suspended because of the mitzvah of "and you shall live by them." The rabbis composed a special prayer to be recited before eating chametz:

> Our Father in heaven, it is clear and apparent to You that it is our desire to do Your will and to celebrate the festival of Pesach by eating matzah and by observing the prohibition of chametz, but our hearts grieve that our enslavement prevents this, as we are in mortal danger. We are hereby ready and prepared to fulfill Your mitzvah of "and you shall live by them" – "and not die by them" and to heed the warning of "guard yourself and guard your life carefully." Therefore, it is our prayer to You that You keep us alive and enable us to exist and redeem us soon, in order that we may observe Your laws, do Your will and serve You with a full heart. Amen.

Without questioning the validity of this ruling, we decided that we would try, as much as possible, to refrain from eating chametz on Pesach…

For about three weeks before Pesach, I set aside potatoes each Monday from the food we all received. I was able to set aside ten potatoes a day…

It is obvious that the food we received was not "strictly" kosher for Pesach, but we managed not to eat any chametz…

Before Pesach, Baruch obtained a small amount of flour from Jews who had reached the camp from Benghazi in Libya. We prepared to bake enough matzah so that there would be a *kezayit* for each one [of us] for the Seder night. Elchanan left a bottle of water out for three days and, on the night before the

◂ baking,

baking, he prepared *mayim shelanu* – water that had been stored in advance. While my mother arranged utensils for preparing the dough, we "organized" wood and checked that the oven in the hut could be used for baking. A few people joined us to bake the matzah. A young man named Yosef Adler, may God avenge his blood, was in charge of the oven. Rabbi A.I. Davids, may God avenge his blood, supervised my mother as she kneaded the dough. Each person helped in his or her own way. We placed the dough that had been prepared carefully and according to all the laws onto a metal sheet in the oven. As we baked, other people in the hut brought additional flour, and soon, the *mayim shelanu* became insufficient.

Rabbi Davids ruled that plain water could be added to the bottle as long as long as some *mayim shelanu* remained in it. Baruch and Yaakov Yehoshua stood outside and guarded. Suddenly the cry was heard, "Achtung!" ("Attention!"). The door opened and – to the astonishment of all – an S.S. officer entered and asked what we were doing. My mother managed to hide some of the utensils while the others told the German that we were preparing a birthday cake! Luckily, this Nazi soldier was one of the oldest of the camp staff. He turned and left.

The Seder night passed without any disturbances. We observed the mitzvah of the Four Cups by drinking four cups of tea. We read the haggadah, and each of us ate a small amount (a *kezayit*?) of the matzah.

At the end of the meal, we said with great feeling: "*Pour out Your wrath upon the nations that do not acknowledge You… Let Your wrath overtake them. Pursue them with wrath and annihilate them from beneath the heavens of the Lord.*" ▪

[Source: *Yesupar LaDor* – Rabbi Yonah Emmanuel, pp. 122–124]

Riddles

4. Why do we wash our hands before eating karpas?
5. What are the seven liquids and how are they linked to the Seder night?
6. How is washing the hands for karpas different from the regular washing of the hands?

Karpas

The first stage in acquiring freedom. An appetizer to the meal of freedom. This is just a small taste, with a long interlude of Torah thoughts and the story of the Exodus from Egypt. A free person is able to wait and prefers the spiritual to the material.

לוקחים כרפס או פרי אדמה אחר, טובלים במי מלח, מברכים ברכת "בורא פרי האדמה" ומכוונים לפטור גם את המרור שיאכלו אחר כך.

בָּרוּךְ אַתָּה יְהֹוָה אֱלֹהֵינוּ מֶלֶךְ הָעוֹלָם, בּוֹרֵא פְּרִי הָאֲדָמָה.

ואוכלים פחות מכזית בלי הסבה (ויש נוהגים להסב), ואין מברכים ברכה אחרונה (אפילו אם אכל כזית).

Food For Thought

Why do we eat karpas?

Some say that we eat karpas so that the children will ask why there are two dippings, as we say in the Mah Nishtanah: "On all other nights we need not dip even once, but on this night we do so twice!" Bach explains that karpas signifies special freedom by stimulating one's appetite before the meal (see *Halachah MiMekorah – Kinor David, Karpas* p. 68).

This explanation is profound. For Am Yisrael, food is a *means* and not merely an *end*. The only aim we have when eating is to strengthen our bodies, as Tur (155) and Mishnah Berurah (155:11) wrote regarding the morning meal: "It is a positive mitzvah to act properly (to eat breakfast) and to guard one's health, in order to be healthy and strong, in order to serve the Creator, may He be blessed."

Why, then, do we eat karpas? Why, at the seder, do we have an "appetizer," and attempt to whet our appetite? Is that proper behavior for a free person? Do truly free people enslave themselves to food and transform their enjoyment of food into an aim in itself by trying to whet their appetites?

We will see that this is indeed a case of true freedom. It is true that we eat

Riddles

7. May one use a cucumber for karpas?
8. What is the meaning of the word "karpas?"
9. Why do we eat less than a *kezayit* of karpas?

Topic for Discussion:

a. Are we really free people on the Seder night? Does a free man not eat even though he wishes to, and remain hungry for such a long a time until the meal? What is the definition of freedom? Is a person who does whatever he wants really free?

◂ "appetizers"

One takes parsley or another vegetable and dips it into salt water. He then recites the blessing of "*who creates the fruit of the earth,*" having in mind the maror he will eat later.

BLESSED are You, Lord our God, King of the universe, who creates the fruit of the earth.

One eats less than a *kezayit* without leaning (some have the custom to lean) and does not recite the concluding blessing, even if one ate a *kezayit*.

Halachic Summary

One takes a vegetable of any kind (many have the custom to take parsley or celery, while others use potatoes or other vegetables), dips it in salt water, recites the blessing on eating vegetables ("*borei peri ha'adamah*"), and eats it.

It is the custom to eat less than a *kezayit* (a quantity smaller than the size of a common matchbox), so as not to be faced with the question of whether to recite a concluding blessing. However, if one ate a *kezayit*, he should not recite a concluding blessing. There are those whose custom it is to make sure to eat at least a *kezayit* and then to recite the concluding blessing of "*borei nefashot.*" One who wishes to do so is permitted to, especially if he is hungry and finds it difficult to concentrate on the haggadah.

There is a dispute whether one must lean while eating karpas, and many people have the custom of leaning. In any event, if one did not do so, it is still valid. ▪

Decorative Pesach platter, Hungary, 19th century The Wolfson Museum, Hechal Shlomo

"appetizers" – karpas is meant to whet our appetites – but we do not eat the meal immediately thereafter. We wait for a considerable period of time before we actually get to the meal. Meanwhile, we discuss Torah thoughts, read the haggadah, and tell of the Exodus from Egypt. That is true freedom! A free person is able to wait for his meal, even if he is hungry. *A free person can immerse himself in feelings of thanks to God and concentrate on the Exodus from Egypt, even after eating "appetizers" that whet the appetite.*

◄ The

The commentators found an allusion to the slavery in Egypt in the word karpas; they rearranged the four letters, *chaf, resh, peh, samekh*, to stand for *samekh* (sixty) *ribo* (ten thousand = 600,000) who worked *befarech* (*peh, resh, chaf*), in hard labor. When free people eat it, they declare: the spirit rules over the body.

Our spirits govern our bodies' courses. Karpas whets one's appetite, but – unlike slaves who devour everything they can when it becomes available – we, as free people, are not enticed by it. Although we can smell the food, we choose to engage in discussing Torah thoughts instead. We choose to be servants of God, nourishing our spirits, and only afterwards do we address our bodily needs.

"Only one who serves God is truly free."

(Rabbi Yehudah Halevi)

■

Yachatz

The moment of crisis, of rupture. Things fall apart – all seems broken and beyond repair. Yet, our faith lives on – the faith that destruction will eventually lead to progress and renewal; sometimes things must be broken in order that they may be rebuilit. In the darkest times, we must recall the greater process at hand. Already at yachatz, we await the afikoman. *At the moment of crisis, as the "bread of affliction" is broken in two, we recognize this rupture as a stage in the redemption process, and we anticipate eating the matzah of freedom.*

בוצעים את המצה האמצעית לשניים. את החלק הקטן מניחים בין שתי המצות השלמות, ואת החלק הגדול מצפינים לאפיקומן.

Halachic Summary

The middle matzah is broken into two pieces. The larger piece is put aside for the afikoman, and the smaller piece is placed between the two whole matzot before the haggadah is recited. Thus, we recite the haggadah over bread that is appropriate for a poor person, who is used to having a broken matzah rather than a whole one. ▪

Food For Thought

Why is the matzah broken?

The Torah (Deuteronomy 16:3) refers to matzah as lechem oni, and the Sages (*Pesachim* 115b) interpreted this phrase in different ways. One explanation is that it is *"lechem she'onim alav devarim harbei"* – "bread over which many words are recited," for the haggadah is read over it. Another explanation is derived from the word *aniyut*, "poverty." Just as it is normal for a poor person to eat only part of a loaf, here too the matzah is broken up. Why do the poor eat only broken, rather than whole loaves? The simple answer is that they don't have enough money to buy a whole loaf, and are therefore forced to buy only part of a loaf. Some also explain that a poor person eats only part of a loaf rather than eating the whole loaf at once, because he needs to leave some of the bread for later – for difficult times. We, too, break the matzah and hide part of it for later for the afikoman, in order not to eat this piece of the matzah accidentally before its time (Tur and Beit Yosef, 473). Another answer is that just as the poor man wants to prolong his meal as long as possible, we want to fulfill the mitzvah of eating matzah for as long as possible, until the end of the seder.

Why is the matzah broken at this time, and not at the beginning of the seder?

Various explanations have been given for this (see *Halachah MiMekorah – Kinor David, Yachatz* p. 88), but it appears that the explanation of Kolbo (Section 50) is the most logical. Kolbo explains that this is done now, before maggid, so that we will say *ha lachma anya* – "this is the bread of affliction" – on a broken matzah, a matzah of the poor. In this way, we will be able to

◂ feel

One breaks the middle matzah into two. The smaller piece is placed between the two whole matzot, and the larger piece is hidden for the afikoman.

feel the distress of our forefathers in Egypt as we recite the haggadah: "and the custom is to break it before we read the haggadah, so that one can say ha lachma anya over it – just as the poor man has a broken piece, here, we too have a broken piece."

The purpose of 'yachatz' – afikoman

The *Orchot Chaim* brings an interesting explanation for yachatz (*Seder Leil Pesach*, 17): "There are those who give a different explanation for the breaking: a reminder of the splitting of the Sea of Reeds." What connection is there between the two?

Riddles

10. Why do we break the matzah?
11. Why do we hide the larger part for the afikoman? After all, the mitzvah to eat matzah is more important than that of eating the afikoman (at least according to most of the Rishonim).

Topic for Discussion:

b. Is matzah a symbol of slavery or of freedom? On the Seder night, do we attempt to emphasize the slavery or the freedom? Try to explain your answer.

Yachatz expresses poverty, "*ani darko biperusah*" – a poor person is accustomed to eating part of a loaf. The afikoman, on the other hand, reflects how a rich person eats for pleasure at the end of the meal, although he is no longer hungry.

The transition from yachatz to afikoman allows us to progress through the different stages of the redemption. At first, in sympathy with Am Yisrael's suffering, we break the matzah. The splitting of the sea was preceded by crisis, with *Bnei Yisrael* trapped between the sea and the Egyptians, and this crisis is symbolized by *yachatz. Already now, at the moment of crisis, we are aware that destruction is an inherent part of redemption. Sometimes, we must destroy in order to rebuild.* We know that God looks after *Am Yisrael*, that the slavery in Egypt, too, had a purpose, and that is why we immediately hide the second part of the matzah for the afikoman.

Over the course of the seder we will attempt to shake off our enslavement to the superficial, to the material, to escape our base desires, our pettiness, to repair what is broken and divided within us. Over the course of the seder, we reenact a process of redemption and purification, a process in which our souls will be true to themselves and true to the Creator.

To us, yachatz symbolizes the

◂ beginning

beginning of our path this night, and our ultimate goal: *the transition from slavery and poverty to freedom. From yachatz to afikoman, we will progress, stage by stage, until we succeed in emerging as free people.* ▪

Food For Thought

Why do the children "steal" the afikoman?

The Talmud (109a) states, "R' Eliezer says: 'The matzot are grabbed on the night of Pesach so that the children will not sleep.'" There are many interpretations by the Rishonim of "grab" (see Rashi and Rashbam ibid.; Ra'avad 7:3, and others). Rambam writes, "They grab this matzah immediately so that the children will see and ask." According to Rambam, grabbing the matzot is done by the adults, so as to keep the children awake. This custom probably evolved into the present one, where the children themselves grab the afikoman (and the adults have to hide it to "prevent" the children from grabbing it), to involve the children so that they will not fall asleep during the seder (see *Chok Yaakov* 472:2). As "Israel's customs become the law," it appears that one can give another reason for this custom and for the significance of keeping the children awake by means of the afikoman.

As we explained, the afikoman is an expression of redemption; hiding it is preparation for the redemption, expressed already at the time of the breaking. The custom of hiding the afikoman and having the children search for it ensures that even if we do not remember the afikoman at the end of the meal, or that we simply are too tired at that point, the children will come and remind us. The redemption can sometimes be delayed because of the weariness and waning strength of the traditional adult leadership. At that point, the young ones must come and arouse the adults to act and bring about the redemption. In every generation, the transmission of power and responsibility from the old generation to the new is marked with difficulty; old leaders are often loath to acknowledge the rising powers of the young. *There is no shame in waking up and being refreshed by the vital voices of the children at the Seder night and in life itself. We hide the afikoman, encouraging the children to be active partners in what goes on around them, and at the same time, we can draw new strength from the power of their youth.* ▪

Maggid

We are privileged to fulfill the Torah mitzvah of telling the story of the Exodus from Egypt! Through its retelling, we learn about both slavery and freedom. Through understanding slavery, we will understand the greatness of our redemption, and we will also understand the purpose of our slavery: through it, we were transformed into a nation. The Divine process of the Exodus did not only bring freedom to our nation, but introduced the concept of physical and spiritual freedom to the entire world. *Through the redemption of Israel, freedom came to the world!*

Retelling our past will help us rediscover our own personal freedom. We will attempt to progress from the mindset of the slave, who thinks only of himself, to the mindset of a free person who thinks about others (*ha lachma anya* – inviting in guests). We will attempt to progress from the state of the slave, who is governed by his body, to the state of a free person, who is governed by his spirit. *Internalizing the story of the Exodus from Egypt will bring us to thank, praise, and extol the One who performed all these miracles for our forefathers and us.*

MAGGID

A Torah mitzvah	The Torah commands us to tell the story of the Exodus from Egypt on the Seder night.
What is the difference between the mitzvah to remember the Exodus every day and the mitzvah to relate the story of the Exodus on the Seder night?	The *Acharonim* noted many differences between the two mitzvot. We will mention the main ones:

ALL YEAR ROUND	ON THE SEDER NIGHT
To remind oneself	To tell one's child
To tell the story of the Exodus	To tell the story through questions and answers
Focus on the outcome: we left Egypt	Focus on the process: we were slaves and God took us out
A story that mentions only the event	To retell it by means of the mitzvot of the night: Pesach, Matzah and Maror
To tell the story without props	A story that is meant to bring us to respond with praise
To tell the story of the past	To tell it with the goal of experiencing it, to feel the Exodus, both as a continuation of the Exodus from Egypt and as a reawakening of our freedom and our subservience to God on this night each year. *Our goal is to tell the story in an attempt to free ourselves, to abandon our external enslavement and to return to our natural state, subservient only to our Father in Heaven.*

Why do we not recite a blessing on relating the story of the Exodus from Egypt?	There are those who hold that we do in fact recite a blessing, albeit in a different form: the "*emet ve'emunah*" text of the Ma'ariv (evening) prayer (*Me'iri*), "*zecher leyetzi'at Mitzrayim*" that is recited in kiddush (*Rabbenu Yerucham*), or in the "*ge'ulah*" blessing that we recite at the end of maggid (*Shibolei HaLeket*). Alternatively, some hold that one is substantively unable to recite a blessing on the haggadah because the main element of the mitzvah is an internal act rather than an external act. The recitation of the haggadah helps us to internalize these matters, and one does not recite blessings on "matters of the heart" (*Maharal*). Even without a specific mitzvah we would have needed to thank God, and one does not recite a blessing on mitzvot that we would have performed rationally even without any specific mitzvah (*Sefat Emet*). In practice, *one must have the intention to perform the positive mitzvah of relating the story of the Exodus from Egypt, but must also try to experience gratitude to God as a natural result of recounting the Exodus.*
What is the most important section of the maggid, which one must recite even if very pressed for time?	The main purpose of the haggadah is to remember our dire straits and how God saved us: "We were slaves to Pharaoh in Egypt, and the Lord, our God, took us out from there," and "In the beginning, our ancestors were idol worshipers; but now God has brought us close to His service." In addition, we must mention Pesach, Matzah and Maror and the reason for each, and conclude with words of praise and thanks.
Must one recline for maggid?	Mishnah Berurah and Shulchan Aruch HaRav write that one does not lean, whereas Me'iri writes that one does lean. In practice, one should recite the maggid in whichever way will be most enjoyable for the entire family.
Who recites the haggadah?	There are those who state that only the head of the household recites the haggadah (Shulchan Aruch HaRav, Gra). Others hold that everyone recites the haggadah (Aruch HaShulchan), and there are those who divide up the segments (and even then many have the custom of reading along with the reader in an undertone).
Involving the children!	One should make sure that children participate through various means: gifts, activities, etc., so that the children will play a central role in the story of the Exodus from Egypt.

MAGGID

Every night there is a mitzvah to remember the Exodus from Egypt ("'The days of your life' means only the days; the additional word 'all' indicates the inclusion of the nights!"). ***What, then, is special about the Seder night?***

- Throughout the year the mitzvah is to remind oneself. On the Seder night the mitzvah is to tell it to others (*Minchat Chinuch*, 21). Additionally, on Seder night the story must be told through questions and answers (R' Chaim of Brisk).
- Throughout the year we mention only the end result, that we left Egypt, whereas on the Seder night we recount the entire process, from beginning to end (R' Chaim of Brisk).
- On the Seder night there is a special mitzvah to tell the story through the mitzvot of the night: Pesach, Matzah and Maror (R' Chaim of Brisk). The mitzvah might be to tell and to fulfill the mitzvot of the night as part of the story.
- Throughout the year it is enough to mention the Exodus, without any response on our part. On the Seder night the story is meant to cause a reaction, to move us to offer praise and thanks to God (Rabbi Yosef Dov Soloveitchik, and possibly Rambam in *Sefer HaMitzvot* Positive Mitzvah 157).
- Throughout the year we tell the story of the past. On the Seder night we must experience the story as if it is happening right now, "as if he were leaving Egypt" (based on *Maharal, Gevurot Hashem*, ch. 62 and implied by Rambam 7:6). The story of the Exodus has special significance on this night, as the quality of freedom was instilled into the Seder night when the world was created.

For further discussion, see *Halachah MiMekorah – Kinor David, Maggid* p. 93.

Why don't we recite a blessing on the mitzvah of relating the story of the Exodus from Egypt?

Some have the custom to recite a special blessing before the haggadah (cited in *Me'iri, Berachot* 12b). It is our custom not to make such a blessing. Why?

- This is a rational mitzvah, one that we should have observed even without a mitzvah, and, therefore, one does not recite a blessing. Performing the mitzvah without reciting a blessing shows our natural, inner desire to thank and praise God.
  Sefat Emet, Pesach 5640 (1880)

- The primary component of the mitzvah is in one's heart. Reading it aloud helps one to internalize these messages. One does not recite a blessing on a mitzvah of the heart that has no external action.
  Maharal, Gevurot Hashem, ch. 62

- The blessing of "*Asher ge'alanu*"–"who has redeemed us" – is the blessing of the haggadah. Why do we say it at the end? Because we must begin with the slavery.
  Shibolei HaLeket in the name of R' Binyamin

- One fulfills his obligation in kiddush with the words, "*zecher leyetzi'at Mitzrayim*" – "a reminder of the Exodus from Egypt."
  Rabbenu Yerucham quoting Rabbenu Peretz

- One fulfills his obligation at the Ma'ariv prayer when reciting the blessing, "*ga'al Yisra'el*" – "redeemer of Israel."
  Me'iri

יש נוהגים לומר לפני ההגדה:

הִנְנִי מוּכָן וּמְזֻמָּן לְקַיֵּם הַמִּצְוָה לְסַפֵּר בִּיצִיאַת מִצְרַיִם. לְשֵׁם יִחוּד קוּדְשָׁא בְּרִיךְ הוּא וּשְׁכִינְתֵּיהּ עַל יְדֵי הַהוּא טָמִיר וְנֶעְלָם בְּשֵׁם כָּל יִשְׂרָאֵל. וִיהִי נֹעַם אֲדֹנָי אֱלֹהֵינוּ עָלֵינוּ וּמַעֲשֵׂה יָדֵינוּ כּוֹנְנָה עָלֵינוּ וּמַעֲשֵׂה יָדֵינוּ כּוֹנְנֵהוּ.

Halachic Summary

One of the central mitzvot of this night is to relate the story of the Exodus from Egypt, which is a *Torah-mandated mitzvah.* It is a mitzvah to recount the story in all its depth and length, mentioning both the difficulties that we endured in Egypt ("We were slaves") and our redemption ("and God took us out of there"). The story of the Exodus from Egypt is meant to move us *to thank, praise, and extol God,* who performed these miracles for our forefathers and for us.

We have to try *to experience the Exodus from Egypt, to feel as if we left Egypt, to attempt to be free men who are subservient only to God and to divorce ourselves from any external enslavement. The haggadah should be said slowly, joyfully, and respectfully, in fear of God and with a tremendous feeling of gratitude to God.*

The children must be involved throughout the haggadah through provocative questions and other stimuli, so as to make them major partners in the story of the Exodus from Egypt. ▪

Food For Thought

What is so special about the story of the Exodus from Egypt?

On the Seder night there is a special mitzvah to talk about the story of the Exodus from Egypt (Exodus 13:8): "And you shall tell your son on that day, saying, 'It is because of this that the Lord did [all these miracles] for me when I left Egypt.'" However, we are commanded to mention the Exodus every day – so what is so special about retelling the story of the Exodus on the Seder night?

There are a number of unique elements in telling the story of the Exodus on the Seder night. One should tell it in the form of questions and answers (and it is important to include the children, addressing them on their appropriate level). One should talk about the entire process, and not only about the end result, how we left Egypt. On the Seder

◂ night

There are those who have the custom of reciting this passage before the haggadah:

Behold, I am prepared and ready to fulfill the mitzvah of relating the Exodus from Egypt. For the sake of the unification of the Holy One, Blessed be He, and His Presence, in the name of all Israel. And may the pleasantness of the Lord our God be upon us, and the work of our hands establish for us, and the work of our hands establish it.

---

night we speak of how "We were slaves to Pharaoh in Egypt, and the Lord, our God, took us out from there." We must also retell the story through the mitzvot of the festival, "Pesach, Matzah and Maror" (R' Chaim of Brisk, *Chiddushim al HaShas*, 40). According to Rabbi Yosef Dov Soloveitchik (*Shiurim LeZecher Abba Mari*, Part I, p. 2), what is unique about this night is that the obligation is not to tell and remember that which occurred, but to thank God for it.

Another special element of its retelling on the Seder night is the fact that the Exodus occurred on this very night. Ramchal (*Derech Hashem* Part IV, ch. 7, paragraph 6) explains that significant events leave an imprint on the time they occurred, so that Seder night itself has a special quality of freedom. *Relating the story of the Exodus on the Seder night we are not dealing with history – we are connecting to the spiritual potency of this special time.*

On this night each year, this quality of freedom is aroused across the world: restoring our capacity for natural independence; to establish the world under the sovereignty of God; to uproot evil from the world; to fulfill the special mission of God in the world.

On the seder night we attempt to rediscover our personal freedom. The Seder night is the night when we reenact our Exodus from Egypt; each person is required to see himself "as if he himself had left Egypt." This is an opportunity to utilize the special potential freedom of this night, to undertake a process of purification, of the removal of our enslavement and lusts. *On Seder*

◄ *night*

Riddles

12. Which Torah mitzvot do we fulfill on the Seder night and which rabbinic ones?
13. Why does one not recite a blessing on telling the story of the Exodus from Egypt?

Topic for Discussion:

c. Each night we are commanded to tell of the Exodus from Egypt (as we say in the haggadah, "'The days of your life' would mean only the days; the additional word 'all' indicates the inclusion of the nights!"). If that is the case, what is special about the mitzvah to relate the story of the Exodus from Egypt on the Seder night?

מגביהים את הקערה כשהמצות המונחות בה מגולות, ואומרים:

הָא לַחְמָא עַנְיָא דִי אֲכָלוּ אַבְהָתָנָא בְּאַרְעָא דְמִצְרָיִם. כָּל דִכְפִין יֵיתֵי וְיֵכוֹל. כָּל דִצְרִיךְ יֵיתֵי וְיִפְסַח. הָשַׁתָּא הָכָא לְשָׁנָה הַבָּאָה בְּאַרְעָא דְיִשְׂרָאֵל. הָשַׁתָּא עַבְדֵי לְשָׁנָה הַבָּאָה בְּנֵי חוֹרִין.

Seder plate, Israel, 1993, ceramic, artist: Eran Grebler, The Wolfson Museum, Hechal Shlomo

night we try to be faithful to the pure and special independence wthin each and every one of us.

The retelling of the Exodus on Seder night is not only a reminder of a significant historical event, like the daily mention of the Exodus. Evoking the Exodus on Seder night itself is an active and creative deed that connects to the special potency of this time, one which reconstructs our own inner freedom. ▪

Halachic Summary

When reciting *Ha lachma anya, it is customary to lift the seder plate with the matzot uncovered* (Responsa of Rosh, *Kelal* 14, Shulchan Aruch 473:6). Some lift up only the matzot (Maharil, Laws of the Haggadah, quoting Maharash). The custom of Chabad is to uncover a little of the matzot, without lifting anything (*Haggadat Chabad*).

The lifting up of the seder plate is designed to draw the children's attention (see Rashbam 115b), to express joy, like raising one's cup (Ra'avyah 525; Responsa Maharshal 88), and to display the matzah over which we recite the haggadah (*Hagahot Minhagim* 96. See also *Leket Yosher* p. 84).

The seder plate is held up until the start of the following passage (Mah Nishtanah). ▪

The seder plate is raised up with the matzot uncovered, and one says:

THIS IS THE BREAD OF AFFLICTION that our fathers ate in the land of Egypt. Whoever is hungry, let him come and eat; whoever is in need, let him come and celebrate the Pesach festival. This year we are here; next year may we be in Eretz Yisrael. This year we are slaves; next year may we be free people.

When we invite those in need to come and celebrate the Pesach festival with us, we express our hopes that the final redemption will come soon, and we will be able to offer the Pesach sacrifice. (One explanation is that whoever needs can come and receive the provisions of the festival – *Mateh Moshe* Part III, Section 631). This year we are here; next year may we be in Eretz Yisrael – "here" refers to Jews who do not live in Eretz Yisrael at present, and we pray that their time in exile will end soon. This year we are slaves; next year may we be free people. ▪

Halachic Summary

One replaces the seder plate and covers the matzot

At the time of the Talmud (Pesachim 115b) they would *remove* the small tables before the meal, in order to arouse the children's curiosity.

Based on this, Shulchan Aruch (473:6) writes that after *ha lachma anya* the seder plate is to be placed at the edge of the table (and so does Eliyahu Rabbah and the Gra in *Ma'aseh Rav* 191; Mishnah Berurah 473:65). Most places do not follow this custom today, presumably because children know that we do not eat the food on the seder plate (see Magen Avraham 473:25; *Shulchan Aruch HaRav,* who do not mention this custom; and the author of Mishnah Berurah did not practice this custom – see *HaSeder HaAruch* 1, p. 391). *Aruch HaShulchan* (473:21) writes that to us covering the matzot is equivalent to removing the tables. ▪

Food For Thought

What is the significance of inviting guests when no one hears the invitation?

Perhaps in the past, when people would open their doors, poor people would actually enter at that point, but this was stopped when non-Jews began to take advantage of this practice. (Avudraham p. 221, quoting Rav Matatiyah). It appears that the basis for this custom is the Pesach sacrifice, about which the Torah states (Exodus 12:4), "he and his neighbor who is nearest to his house shall take [a lamb] according to the number of people." The Pesach sacrifice was not an individual but a group sacrifice (Rambam, *Korban Pesach*. 2:2, based on the verse, "*they* shall do it"). What is the significance of this statement nowadays, when we are sure that no one will take up this invitation (nor do we say it at the very beginning of the seder).

In order to understand this, we must first understand the difference between a slave and a free man (for other explanations of the significance of freedom, see the end of the haggadah, p. 285). Rabbi Yosef Dov Soloveitchik (Festival of Freedom, p. 22, and see *Haggadat Si'ach HaGrid*) explains:

> Hesed is the characteristic mark of the free man. The bondsman is not spiritually capable of joining the hesed community, because he is too much concerned with himself... Only free and proud people think of others and share with others. The birth of the hesed community... is symbolized by the paschal sacrifice. God... simply wanted the people – slaves who had just come out of the house of bondage – to emerge from their isolation and insane self-centeredness into the hesed community....

If so, the distinction between the slave and the free person is that the slave thinks only about himself, about his own personal survival. A free person, who is full of vigor and strength, shakes off his own personal concerns and thinks of others and how to help them. One of the characteristics of the slave is that he is unable to help others: "whatever is acquired by a slave belongs to his master" (*Pesachim* 88b). Thinking about others is the mark of a free man!

At the beginning of the seder, we proclaim, "*Do you want to be free? Think about others.*"

It is likely that it is already too late to invite guests. Everyone is already in the place where they will be celebrating the seder, and an invitation at this time is meaningless. Nonetheless, we announce for ourselves and our families: we are leaving for freedom, and the first expression of this is that we are free to look beyond ourselves and to help others: "Whoever is hungry, let him come and eat." This task will accompany us throughout the year, but

◂ we must

The Source of the Hagaddah

The Rishonim differ as to whether *Ha lachma anya* was found in the ancient haggadah text. It is not found in the Mishnah, nor the Talmud. Indeed, Ritva (on the haggadah) writes that the haggadah begins with "We were slaves," and not with *ha lachma anya*. Some explain that it was a later addition that was added when we were already in exile, and that is why it is in Aramaic (Netziv of Volozhin, *Haggadat Imrei Shefer*). On the other hand, Rambam (in his haggadah text) states that this section is part of the haggadah itself (and the fact that the words invite others to share in the Pesach sacrifice indicates that this is an ancient passage, introduced at the time that the Pesach sacrifice was offered), and this passage already appears in the works of the Geonim (for example, the siddur of Rav Sa'adiah Gaon). ▪

---

we must remember that giving to others is not done only through food; it is done through every area in which God gave us powers and abilities. *Our goal at the seder is to become free, to be aware of others, to become people who influence others, and give to them as only truly free men can.*

Ha Lachma Anya – Remember your past!

It is normal for a person who has difficulties to feel that if he could only fill a certain void in his life, he would take great pains to ensure that no one else would suffer as he suffers now. If only he had money, he would make sure to supply the needs of others; if only he were only married, he and his wife would help their single friends. However, once that particular problem is solved, the person tends to forget the other people whom he had planned to help, who are in the same position he once was.

At the beginning of the haggadah, we announce and remember: "Our forefathers ate the bread of affliction!" Even though our circumstances are much improved since those times, *we*

Riddles

14. What is the meaning of "ייתי ויפסח" and what problem does this present?
15. What is *"kimcha d'pis'cha?"*

Activities

It is possible to stage a play to make the Exodus from Egypt more real. The father or another family member can dress up, go outside, knock on the door, and say that he has arrived with those who have just left Egypt. Similarly, one can ask the children to prepare a play a few days before the Seder night, and in this way involve them in preparation for the seder.

◂ *remember*

מניחים את הקערה ומכסים את המצות (ויש הנוהגים להניח את הקערה בקצה השולחן עד סוף מה נשתנה). מוזגים כוס שני, והבן שואל "מה נשתנה".

מַה נִּשְׁתַּנָּה הַלַּיְלָה הַזֶּה מִכָּל הַלֵּילוֹת.

שֶׁבְּכָל הַלֵּילוֹת אָנוּ אוֹכְלִין חָמֵץ וּמַצָּה, הַלַּיְלָה הַזֶּה כֻּלּוֹ מַצָּה.

---

remember the previous condition of our nation, and that gives us the power and desire to help all those who are still living in poverty. We will always remember our suffering – "this is the bread of affliction" – and by remembering it we will be sure to help all those who suffer still. ▪

Food For Thought

Why ask questions?

The Talmud in Tractate Pesachim (115b) tells us that Abaye, who was then a small child, saw that the table was being removed from before him. He said to them: "We have not yet eaten, and you are removing the table from before us?" Rabbah said to him, "You have exempted us from needing to ask the Mah Nishtanah."

Abaye's question had nothing to do with the Exodus from Egypt, yet Rabbah ruled that "You have exempted us from needing to ask the Mah Nishtanah." From this we learn that there is special importance in questions,

Decorative Pesach platter, England, end of 19th century, porcelain, The Wolfson Museum, Hechal Shlomo

The seder plate is put down and the matzot are covered (there are those who place the seder plate at the edge of the table, until the end of Mah Nishtanah). The second cup is poured, and the son asks Mah Nishtanah.

WHAT MAKES THIS NIGHT DIFFERENT
from all other nights?

ON ALL OTHER NIGHTS we eat chametz or matzah, but on this night only matzah.

The Source of the Hagaddah

This section is found in the Mishnah (116a): "They fill a second cup for him, and at this stage the son asks his father." The Mishnah does not limit itself to this, but then lists the actual questions. The Mishnah, unlike our own haggadah, asks: "Why do we eat roast meat, as they used to do when the Pesach sacrifice was offered?" This question was replaced by our question regarding leaning.

One should note that Rambam (8:2) lists five questions (including both "leaning" and "roast"), and the text of the Jerusalem Talmud lists only three questions (dipping, matzah, roast). It is possible that the version of the Jerusalem Talmud reflects the one used in the Bet HaMikdash. There, at the beginning of the meal they did not eat plain matzah, but rather "rich" matzah, (*matzah ashirah*, made, for example, with eggs or fruit juices, with which one cannot fulfill the mitzvah of eating matzah), and afterwards they ate maror dipped in charoset, in accordance with the verse (Exodus 12:8), "roasted over the fire, and unleavened cakes; *with bitter herbs they shall eat it*," and therefore the first question was about dipping. Afterwards they would eat matzah, and finally they would eat the Pesach sacrifice, which is to be eaten when one is sated, which explains the order of the questions in the Jerusalem Talmud (for further discussion, see Rabbi D.Z. Hoffman, *Beit Va'ad LaChachamim*, II, 5662 – 1902). ▪

---

questions, even questions that have nothing to do with the Seder night. Questions cause children to remain alert, and as a result they will listen to those topics that are related to the Exodus from Egypt. When a child is encouraged to ask, he will also learn to ask questions that are important to us.

◂ As we

שֶׁבְּכָל הַלֵּילוֹת אָנוּ אוֹכְלִין שְׁאָר יְרָקוֹת, הַלַּיְלָה הַזֶּה מָרוֹר.

שֶׁבְּכָל הַלֵּילוֹת אֵין אָנוּ מַטְבִּילִין אֲפִילוּ פַּעַם אֶחָת, הַלַּיְלָה הַזֶּה שְׁתֵּי פְעָמִים.

שֶׁבְּכָל הַלֵּילוֹת אָנוּ אוֹכְלִין בֵּין יוֹשְׁבִין וּבֵין מְסֻבִּין, הַלַּיְלָה הַזֶּה כֻּלָּנוּ מְסֻבִּין.

As we saw, it is possible that this a fundamental aspect of relating the story of the Exodus from Egypt: to ask and answer. From this we can extrapolate that children are the center of the night: (Exodus 13:18), "And you shall tell your son." We encourage them to ask so that our children will be *active participants in the Seder night.*

However another reason is stated in the Talmud (116a) – and it is the ruling in Shulchan Aruch 473:7 – if one does not have children, other adults must ask the seder leader the questions, and even Torah scholars must ask one another. Even if a person is by himself – he must ask himself (see Rambam 8:2, that the one conducting the seder repeats the questions). While this focus on asking questions emphasizes the need to arouse the curiosity of each individual, another aspect of the importance of asking questions is raised here.

To ask questions means not to accept the situation as it is. The ability to ask, clarify, and delve into topics also opens the possibility for *change! A person who asks in sincerity, in order to receive a true answer, opens himself up to change! He is willing to accept new answers, to strive for new spiritual achievements; he asks with the aim of absorbing, with the aim of ascending and changing.*

Why specifically Mah Nishtanah?

The Mishnah (10:4) teaches us that one must ask: "at this stage the son asks his father." The Mishnah does not limit itself to this statement, but then lists the actual questions, even though other questions might better serve the purpose of telling the story of the Exodus from Egypt. However, there is special importance in using the text of the Mishnah, and we should study the significance of this formulation of questions closely. The questions are phrased in a surprising way, for they

◂ would

ON ALL OTHER NIGHTS we eat any kind of vegetable, but on this night we eat maror.

ON ALL OTHER NIGHTS we need not dip even once, but on this night we do so twice!

ON ALL OTHER NIGHTS we eat sitting upright or reclining, but on this night we all recline.

---

would have more logically be phrased: "Why on the Seder night do we eat matzot? Why on the Seder night do we eat maror?" However, the Mishnah asks: Mah Nishtanah – "What makes this night different from all other nights?" Why is this?

This formulation may well reflect the *underlying concept of the entire Seder night.* What is the difference between a slave and a free man? A free man is able to change, to believe in change, and even to change reality. A slave, on the other hand, is bound to his work, is unable to change, and is sometimes even afraid to change (when Am Yisrael was in the desert, they preferred the slavery of Egypt and all its hardships, rather than accept an unfamiliar freedom).

Through the Exodus, God made a change in the world: a nation of slaves went free. The Seder night celebrates the power to change, the power to be changed.

Every Jew must ask himself on the Seder night: how is this night different from all other nights? How did the Exodus from Egypt revolutionize the concept of freedom for Am Yisrael and the entire world? What unique inner qualities am I able to unleash? How can I emerge from the Seder night on a higher, more spiritual plane – with a soul that is free, not enslaved to any external cravings?

How can I change my body to best channel God's will? How can I make the world around me a better place, with a cleaner and purer reality?

We ask, "What makes this night different from all other nights?" We explore the powers granted to us on this night – the power to change and the power to be changed, and attempt to clarify to ourselves: what makes this night different? What is the change that will lead our souls to freedom?

How exactly is this night different?

Rambam writes (7:1):

> It is a positive Torah-mandated mitzvah to tell of the miracles and

◂ wonders

Riddles

16. Where does the question end and where does the answer begin in Mah Nishtanah?
17. On Seder night, many things related to the number 4. How many can you think of?
18. "But on this night only matzah" – when is it a mitzvah to eat matzah, and when is it an obligation?
19. Examine the text of the Mishnah of Mah Nishtanah (10:4; Talmud 116a):

   What makes this night different from all other nights?
   On all other nights we eat chametz or matzah, but on this night only matzah. On all other nights we eat any kind of vegetable, but on this night we eat maror. On all other nights we eat meat roasted, stewed, or boiled, but on this night only roasted. On all nights we dip once, but on this night we dip twice.
   What is in the Mishnah that we do not have in our haggadah? What is in our haggadah that is not in the Mishnah? Why?

Topic for Discussion:

d. As we saw, one of the differences between our version of Mah Nishtanah and that of the Mishnah is the question of roasted meat, which we do not have because in our times there is no Pesach sacrifice. What is the importance of the Pesach sacrifice? Is it something we are missing in the course of our seder? What, in general, is the importance of sacrifices?

Torah case, Iraq, 20th century, wood and cloth, The Wolfson Museum, Hechal Shlomo, Golnitzki Collection

wonders that were performed for our forefathers on the night of the fifteenth of Nissan, as it states (Exodus 13:3): "Remember this day, when you went out of Egypt" just as it says, "Remember Shabbat day."

Why does Rambam equate the story of the Exodus from Egypt with the mitzvah to remember Shabbat? Rabbi Yosef Dov Soloveitchik (*Haggadat Si'ach HaGrid*, pp. 24–25) understood that what Rambam meant is that just as the basis for the mitzvah to remember Shabbat is the division between Shabbat and weekdays (Rambam Sefer HaMitzvot, Positive Mitzvah 155), so too the mitzvah to remember the Exodus is meant to separate this night from all the other nights of the year. When we recite Mah Nishtanah, we learn of the unique quality of this night that sets it apart from all other night – its capacity for potential freedom. The Torah mandates us to recognize the special qualities of this night of freedom, the night that commemorates the Exodus from Egypt. God willing, we will channel these special qualities to advance our own spirituality. ▪

Activities

We learned that questions and answers are the method we should employ in telling the Exodus from Egypt, as expressed in Mah Nishtanah. Below are three possibilities for involving the family by means of questions and answers:

1) Before the festival, the one who will be conducting the seder asks each of the participants to write a question related to Pesach on a piece of paper, and on another piece of paper to write the answer. On the Seder night, the questions and answers are mixed up separately. Each of the participants draws a single question and a single answer. The aim of the game is to match the right question and its answer. Each person in turn reads the question he drew, answers it, and tries to find who is holding the correct answer.
2) One of the children begins by asking the participants a question related to Pesach. The person who answers it correctly must then ask the next question, and so on. The winner is the one who answered the greatest number of questions correctly.
3) Going around the table at the seder, each person in turn must ask a question related to Pesach. At the end of the round of questions, each person chooses one of the the questions to answer.

מחזירים את הקערה למקומה, מגלים את המצות על מנת לומר את ההגדה על המצות:

עֲבָדִים הָיִינוּ לְפַרְעֹה בְּמִצְרָיִם, וַיּוֹצִיאֵנוּ יְהֹוָה אֱלֹהֵינוּ מִשָּׁם בְּיָד חֲזָקָה וּבִזְרֹעַ נְטוּיָה. וְאִלּוּ לֹא הוֹצִיא הַקָּדוֹשׁ בָּרוּךְ הוּא אֶת אֲבוֹתֵינוּ מִמִּצְרָיִם, הֲרֵי אָנוּ וּבָנֵינוּ וּבְנֵי בָנֵינוּ מְשֻׁעְבָּדִים הָיִינוּ לְפַרְעֹה בְּמִצְרָיִם. וַאֲפִילוּ כֻּלָּנוּ חֲכָמִים, כֻּלָּנוּ נְבוֹנִים, כֻּלָּנוּ זְקֵנִים, כֻּלָּנוּ יוֹדְעִים אֶת הַתּוֹרָה, מִצְוָה עָלֵינוּ לְסַפֵּר בִּיצִיאַת מִצְרָיִם. וְכָל הַמַּרְבֶּה לְסַפֵּר בִּיצִיאַת מִצְרַיִם הֲרֵי זֶה מְשֻׁבָּח.

The Source of the Hagaddah

The Mishnah (116a) explains that the structure of the haggadah is that "commences with shame and concludes with praise." According to the Talmud (*ibid.*), Rav and Shmuel dispute how to interpret this statement in the Mishnah. According to Shmuel, we start with, "We were slaves to Pharaoh in Egypt…" being the shame, and "the Lord, our God, took us out from there" is the praise. According to Rav, "In the beginning, our ancestors were idol worshipers" is the shame, and "now God has brought us close to His service" is the praise. In the Jerusalem Talmud (10:5), only the view of Rav is cited. The Rishonim argue about whether the dispute between Rav and Shmuel is about the text in the haggadah, and that according to each side one only has to use its text and ignore the other, or whether they both agree that both texts are to be said, but differ in the order in which they are to be said. We say both texts, beginning with Shmuel's version – "We were slaves to Pharaoh in Egypt…"

This passage is the focal point of the haggadah, encapsulating the entire story of the Exodus: "We were slaves to Pharaoh in Egypt, and the Lord, our God, took us out from there." Therefore, a person who for whatever reason is unable to recite the haggadah should say just this passage (with a number of other passages – see *Halachah MiMekorah – Kinor David, Maggid* p. 96). From this we learn that the retelling of the Exodus from Egypt must revolve around our slavery and redemption.

◂ The

The seder plate is returned to its place and the matzot are uncovered in order to recite the haggadah with the matzot visible.

WE WERE SLAVES TO PHARAOH IN EGYPT, and the Lord, our God, took us out from there with a mighty hand and with an outstretched arm. If the Holy One, Blessed be He, had not taken our fathers out of Egypt, then we, our children and our children's children would still be enslaved to Pharaoh in Egypt. Even if all of us were wise, all of us understanding, all elders and versed in the knowledge of the Torah, we would still be obligated to discuss the Exodus from Egypt; and everyone who discusses the Exodus from Egypt at length is praiseworthy.

The following passage that begins, "Even if all of us were wise," is a different topic. In Siddur Rav Sa'adiah Gaon this passage does not appear, and nor does "It happened that Rabbi Eliezer...". Indeed these sections have a different focus: "We were slaves" is a brief recounting of the Exodus from Egypt, whereas "Even if all of us were wise" and the subsequent sections deal with the limits of the mitzvah of relating the Exodus from Egypt: who is obligated, what the mitzvah encompasses, and the relationship between this mitzvah and the daily mitzvah of remembering the Exodus from Egypt (which is different from the mitzvah of telling the Exodus from Egypt on the Seder night – see *Halachah MiMekorah – Kinor David, Maggid* p. 96).

These passages, however, *are* found in other ancient sources, such as in Siddur Rav Amram Gaon (which chronologically precedes Siddur Rav Sa'adiah Gaon) and in the version of Rambam.

Food For Thought

This night we are going free!

The Mishnah (116a) states: "he commences with shame and concludes with praise." In the Talmud (*ibid.*), Shmuel explains that this is the reason why we say, "We were slaves to Pharaoh in Egypt and the Lord, our God, took us out from there." The part of the sentence, "We were slaves to Pharaoh in Egypt," discusses our shame. Afterwards "the Lord, our God, took us out from there" is the praise.

◂ Why

Why is there need to begin with our shame? We do so in order to feel the full force of the freedom that we attained. Sometimes, because of our fortunate circumstances, we take our freedom for granted. It is important to remind ourselves of the terrible past in which we lived – our slavery, the bitterness, and the sorrow – so we can appreciate our freedom.

However, it appears that there is an additional reason for beginning with our shame – *shame played an important role in our Exodus to freedom.* There is an overall Divine plan for the world, and just as our deliverance from Egypt was carried out by God, so too were our exile and slavery part of that same Divine process.

Why were exile and slavery necessary? What role did they play? Rav Kook (*Olat Re'iyah* p. 20) offers an explanation (a somewhat similar explanation can be found in *Shelah, Torah Shebichtav,* Part 2, *Torah Or, Parashat Beha'alotecha,* 14: "the yoke of Egypt preceded the receipt of the Torah, so that they would be used to a yoke"):

> One begins with the shame of "We were slaves." There is no doubt that slavery caused a number of negative things, a number of depraved qualities… but it also [enhances] the trait of submission to the One to whom it is appropriate to submit as true servants of God; [thereby] setting aside one's personal desire and tendency in favor of accepting the yoke of the kingdom of Heaven…One can gain this ability through the submission that accompanies enslavement, because after [one's] impurities are expunged… one can willfully channel his submission to its proper address, with the understanding that slavery [to God] is true freedom.

The slavery in Egypt, which was clearly a terrible thing, also brought good to Am Yisrael. That slavery built within Am Yisrael the ability to accept servitude, the ability to submit. These attributes, which were terrible in Egypt, were transformed into positive and significant ones when we became free, and we used these same attributes to accept our servitude to God. Servitude in Egypt was slavery indeed, but servitude and worship of God is *true freedom.*

In our present state we are often slaves: slaves to money, slaves to fashion, slaves to advertising, slaves to bodily cravings, slaves to jealousy. When we left Egypt we received the power to be free men, not to be enslaved to people, but rather to use the power of servitude in regard to God, servitude that expresses our freedom.

The haggadah says that "We were slaves," and not "Our forefathers were slaves," because slavery and freedom relate to every single one of us. We were all slaves, and we all have the power to set ourselves free.

Tonight we choose freedom - by rechanneling the capacity we received through our slavery to Pharaoh, we choose to become true servants of God!

◂ What

What is the answer to the Mah Nishtanah?

We ask many questions in the Mah Nishtanah, but where are the answers? In one sense, the entire haggadah is an answer to these questions. However, the passage of "We were slaves" also offers an answer of sorts.

In general, all the changes on the Seder night are made because of the special reality of the Exodus from slavery on this night (see Rashbam 115b: "as they were enslaved in Egypt, we do all these things").

However, it is possible that there is a more detailed explanation (see haggadah of Abarbanel on "we were slaves"):

> "We were slaves" – therefore we have items symbolizing slavery – maror, bread of affliction...
>
> "The Lord, our God, took us out from there" – and that is why we have items that symbolize freedom – matzah, dipping, leaning.

How do we know that "If the Holy One, Blessed be He, had not taken our fathers out of Egypt, then we, our children and our children's children would still be enslaved to Pharaoh in Egypt?"

Maharal (Gevurot Hashem, ch. 61, p. 274) states that some ask what we gained by our Exodus from Egypt, for afterwards we have been enslaved by many other kingdoms. This question is even stronger given the fact that Am Yisrael has always celebrated the Seder night throughout all the years of our exile, even under the most terrible of regimes.

Maharal answers: when we left Egypt, we gained our freedom, and this instilled freedom in our very being. Even if we were subsequently enslaved, in our essence we are free men and our slavery is merely external. It is with this understanding that we can appreciate the fact that God took us out of Egypt.

Freedom is not only an absence of slavery. Freedom is a higher inner state. If we had managed to leave Egypt by ourselves, it is true that we would no longer be slaves, but we would not have attained the special spiritual level that we attained when we left Egypt.

Through the Exodus, we gained the privilege of becoming servants of God. When God freed us, we became subservient to Him alone. Now, we no longer submit to human will, but are free to walk along a Divine path, one which elevates our souls, one which leads to true independence.

"If the *Holy One, Blessed be He,* had not taken out our fathers" – that was not merely being taken out to freedom; that was a Divine Exodus! *The Exodus from Egypt had a unique influence on Am Yisrael and on the entire world.* The Exodus left an imprint of Divine freedom on Am Yisrael, changing its very nature. Ever since, even in times of slavery, we have been free. Ever since, we have been servants of God, even when our external freedom has been compromised.

Many of us are privileged to live in

◂ Israel,

Israel, where we live free of the yoke of foreign nations (even though, unfortunately, the yoke of other nations breathes heavily down our neck). We must remember: freedom is not only an absence of slavery. Even while we enjoy external, physical freedom, we must strive to maintain the freedom of our soul, a soul that recognizes that true freedom is attained by clinging to God's mitzvot, by always being under the wings of the Divine Presence.

We were never slaves to Pharaoh!

The expression "slaves of Pharaoh" (*avdei Par'oh*) in the Torah only refers to Pharoah's Egyptian slaves, but never to Am Yisrael. Therefore, in the haggadah too, we say, "We were slaves to Pharaoh," but never "Pharaoh's slaves."

What is the difference? Rabbi Yosef Dov Soloveitchik (Festival of Freedom, pp. 47–48) explains:

> The Jews in Egypt were slaves... but they did not completely lose their love of freedom and their spiritual heritage. Had they been totally "Pharaoh's slaves" and not just "slaves to Pharaoh," they would never have been liberated. They would have lost their personality and their quest for freedom.

Even in the most difficult times, when they were subjected to the cruelest slavery, Am Yisrael never lost their identity and their faithfulness to their nation. They remained dedicated descendants of their holy forefathers, members of the Jewish nation. They still had the ability to be servants of God!

Moshe was afraid that Am Yisrael was not worthy of redemption. Before he received God's mission to take them out of Egypt, the burning bush symbolized that they were worthy: from the outside, it looked like any other bush in the desert, but internally it burned with fire, burned with the desire to draw closer to God. This was also the case with Am Yisrael when they were enslaved in Egypt. The slavery was external – they were slaves of Pharaoh, but not Pharaoh's slaves. The entire time, their innermost soul yearned to serve God! (Based on Rabbi Soloveitchik, ibid.).

Why retell the story each year if we already know it?

The story of the Exodus from Egypt is not merely a historical description, a retelling of events. Rather, it is meant to move us to internalize our belief in God, who performed all these miracles for our forefathers and us; to internalize our transition from being slaves of Pharaoh to being servants of God. The story is meant *to strengthen the internal freedom within each of us, to strengthen our bond with God.* We each need to enhance our internal freedom. We each need to examine the areas in which we still are not free. This is why the story of the Exodus from Egypt is important to every single one of us – whoever and wherever we are.

Furthermore, there is another

◂ Furthermore,

purpose in telling the story of the Exodus from Egypt: *To express our thanks to God!* "Therefore it is our duty to thank, praise, hail, glorify, exalt, honor, bless, extol…." Through retelling the story of the Exodus, we are moved to feel that we too are being set free from Egypt, and with that feeling we – children, adults, and great Torah scholars alike – must all thank God.

The whole night is devoted to the children and their questions. When do the adults learn about the Exodus from Egypt?

The question and answer exchange is not only for the child's sake. The child understands the answers according to his level, but the parent also internalizes the story of the Exodus from Egypt through his explanations to the child. When a person is required to teach and transmit a message, the topic is understood more fully by the one who is teaching it, and he grows through his own teaching. *The children help the adults gain a greater understanding.* Children's questions are sometimes very direct and sincere, and the questions themselves can be of great value to everyone present, old and young.

There is no doubt that there are suitable times around the table for the adults to study and explore topics in depth. There are opportunities for people of every age and level to study by themselves around the table. Beyond the actual learning and the personal development of the adults, there is tremendous educational value in having the children see the adults themselves learning and discussing the story of the Exodus from Egypt. ▪

Riddles

20. "We were slaves to Pharaoh in Egypt." Which part of the verse was omitted by the author of the haggadah? Why? (See Deuteronomy 6:21.)
21. How many years were we slaves in Egypt?

Topic for discussion

e. "We were slaves." Why is it important to know that we were slaves? How does our slavery at that time affect us today? How does our having been slaves affect our national history?

מַעֲשֶׂה בְּרַבִּי אֱלִיעֶזֶר וְרַבִּי יְהוֹשֻׁעַ וְרַבִּי אֶלְעָזָר בֶּן עֲזַרְיָה וְרַבִּי עֲקִיבָא וְרַבִּי טַרְפוֹן, שֶׁהָיוּ מְסֻבִּין בִּבְנֵי בְרַק, וְהָיוּ מְסַפְּרִים בִּיצִיאַת מִצְרַיִם כָּל אוֹתוֹ הַלַּיְלָה, עַד שֶׁבָּאוּ תַלְמִידֵיהֶם וְאָמְרוּ לָהֶם: רַבּוֹתֵינוּ, הִגִּיעַ זְמַן קְרִיאַת שְׁמַע שֶׁל שַׁחֲרִית.

The Source of the Hagaddah

This passage does not appear in the **Mishnah**, **Talmud** or **Siddur Rav Sa'adiah Gaon.** However, it is found in **Siddur Rav Amram Gaon** and the version of Rambam. The Tosefta (10:8) mentions a similar story:

It happened that Rabban Gamliel and the Elders sat reclining in the home of Boethus ben Zunin of Lod and they discussed the laws of Pesach the entire night until the cock crowed. They got up and went to the study hall. ▪

Food For Thought

Why specifically in Bnei Brak?

The Talmud in Tractate Sanhedrin (32b) lists where some of the Sages in our story live:

> *Our rabbis taught: "Justice, justice shall you pursue." Follow the Sages to their academies – Rabbi Eliezer to Lod, Rabbi Yochanan Ben Zakkai to Beror Chayil,*
>
> *Rabbi Yehoshua to Peki'in, Rabban Gamliel to Yavneh, Rabbi Akiva to Bnei Brak…*

Rabbi Eliezer lived in Lod, Rabbi Yehoshua in Peki'in, and Rabbi Akiva in Bnei Brak (Rabbi Elazar was the *nasi* in Kerem B'Yavneh, and he evidently lived there – *Berachot* 27b; afterwards he lived in Zippori – *Tosefta Kelim* 2:1. Rabbi Tarfon evidently lived in Lod – Kiddushin 40b). *Why did all the Sages come to Bnei Brak?* Why didn't each one celebrate the festival in his own town? Moreover, Rabbi Eliezer and Rabbi Yehoshua were the teachers of Rabbi Akiva (Rambam, introduction to his commentary on the Mishnah) – wouldn't it be more logical for a student to come to the home of his rabbi?

The key to the answer may well lie in a Mishnah in *Pesachim* (10:6), in which

◂ Rabbi

IT HAPPENED THAT RABBI ELIEZER, Rabbi Yehoshua, Rabbi Elazar ben Azaryah, Rabbi Akiva and Rabbi Tarfon sat reclining [at a seder] in Bnei Brak. They were discussing the Exodus from Egypt all night, until their students came and told them: "Our Masters! The time has come to recite the morning shema!"

Rabbi Tarfon and Rabbi Akiva argue where the blessing of Redemption ends:

> *One concludes with [a formula of] redemption. Rabbi Tarfon used to say, "Who redeemed us and redeemed our fathers from Egypt," but he did not conclude [with a blessing]. Rabbi Akiva used to say, "So may the Lord our God and the God of our fathers enable us to reach other seasons and festivals in peace, rejoicing in the building of Your city and joyful in Your service, and there we will partake of the sacrifices and the Pesach sacrifices..." up to "who has redeemed Israel."*

According to Rabbi Tarfon, the blessing of redemption on the Seder night deals only with *the redemption from Egypt*. On the other hand, Rabbi Akiva holds that the blessing deals with *the future redemption*, in which we express our hopes that we will yet rejoice at the building of Jerusalem and the renewal of the Bet HaMikdash service.

This is typical of Rabbi Akiva. *Rabbi Akiva always radiated optimism, even in the most difficult of times.* In a famous story in Tractate *Makkot* (24b), the Sages saw a fox emerging from the Holy of Holies. The other Sages cried, while Rabbi Akiva laughed. The other Sages said to Rabbi Akiva, "Why are you laughing?" He told them, "Now that Uriah's prophecy was fulfilled, that Zion was ploughed as a field, I am sure that the prophecy of consolation, 'Old men and women will yet sit in the broad places of Jerusalem' (Zechariah 8:4) will also be fulfilled." The Talmud concludes that the other Sages said to him: "Akiva you have consoled us. Akiva you have consoled us."

Rabbi Akiva had the power of consolation. Rabbi Akiva understood that destruction also has a role to play; that the *churban* is preparation for the rebuilding of Jerusalem and the Bet HaMikdash (see Maharal, *Netzach Yisrael*, ch. 23, and elsewhere). The same is true of the Mishnah quoted above: Rabbi Akiva understood that even when we are in exile, we must talk of the joy of the redemption and of the rebuilt Bet HaMikdash – "rejoicing in the building of Your city and joyful in Your service."

This story takes place in a generation when the Romans persecuted the

◂ Jews;

Jews; a generation where those who studied Torah were pursued. The nation was broken; the circumstances in which they lived were simply unbearable. *On the Seder night, the national festival of freedom, all the rabbis wanted to come to the one who would offer them encouragement and strengthen their resolve, one who saw their suffering as the prelude to the redemption. That is why they came to Rabbi Akiva.*

What did the Sages do at that seder?

In the previous section, we considered why the Sages came to Bnei Brak, Rabbi Akiva's city, for the seder, and specifically why Rabbi Eliezer and Rabbi Yehoshua, both Rabbi Akiva's teachers, came to him rather than the opposite.

There are other puzzling elements in this story. Rabbi Eliezer said that he praised the lazy ones who do not leave their homes for the pilgrimage festivals (*Sukkah* 27b). If that is so, why did he leave his home? And another puzzling aspect: a very important person was absent from the seder, Rabban Gamliel, the Nasi. He is generally mentioned along with these Sages, but here he was absent from the seder.

And another question: why did they talk about the Exodus from Egypt "the entire night"? The Talmud (*Berachot* 9a) brings a dispute between Rabbi Elazar ben Azaryah and Rabbi Akiva as to whether the Pesach sacrifice must be eaten by midnight (Rabbi Elazar ben Azaryah) or until dawn (Rabbi Akiva), and this dispute also applies to telling the story of the Exodus from Egypt. If some of the Sages ruled that the mitzvah to tell the story is only until midnight, then why did they discuss it the whole night? While it is possible that as the seder took place in Bnei Brak, Rabbi Akiva's town, they followed his ruling in this question, there might be another, more fundamental answer to these questions.

The era in which this particular seder took place was a very difficult time for the Jewish People. Great Sages died *Al Kiddush Hashem* – sanctifying God's name. Many had already been killed; later, Rabbi Akiva himself would be killed by the Romans. Jews were put to death for practicing ritual circumcision, for reading the Torah, and for eating matzah (see *Midrash Eichah Rabbati* 2:5; *Yoma* 78b; *Tosefta Chullin* 2:6; *Mechilta d'Rabbi Yishmael, Yitro*, 6).

At that time, they had to clarify *how to express their freedom despite the harsh decrees, how to study Torah despite the difficulties, and how to continue observing the mitzvot.* Many matters had to be discussed regarding the meaning of the freedom of Israel with regard to all the difficulties they faced. It is possible that they even had to discuss whether to rebel against the Romans.

This Seder night could not be held in any other place. The Romans were evidently keeping an eye on Rabbi Eliezer in Lod (see *Tosefta Eiruvin* 9:2 on the investigators stationed in that city), and the same was true for Rabbi Yehoshua's city (*Genesis Rabbah* 2:8)

◂ and

Torah pointer, Persia, 19th century, silver
The Wolfson Museum, Hechal Shlomo

and in Zippori (*Shabbat* 145b). Rabban Gamliel was absent so as not to draw attention to the secret meeting that was to take place.

That is why all came to Rabbi Akiva. *There they could conduct the Seder night without the Roman spies. There they could discuss the Exodus in the past, and could discuss its significance for their own time* (this general idea, phrased somewhat differently, is found in Rabbi Maimon, Rabbi Zvi Yehudah Kook, and others).

They may well have discussed the Exodus from Egypt until midnight (because according to all views, it is a mitzvah to discuss the Exodus from Egypt until midnight), and then later plotted an "Exodus" for their own time. This story teaches us how the Sages joined forces to deal with the oppression of their own generation, and of the importance of linking the Exodus from Egypt to the struggle for freedom in every time and in every place. ▪

Riddles

22. In whose city was the seder of the Sages conducted?
23. All the names of the Sages listed here appear in the same format, except for one. Who is that one?

Topic for Discussion

f. Why do the Sages of Israel need to tell the story of the Exodus from Egypt? They surely know the story already. Also, why do we, who already know the story well, have to continue to tell it every year anew?

אָמַר רַבִּי אֶלְעָזָר בֶּן עֲזַרְיָה: הֲרֵי אֲנִי כְּבֶן שִׁבְעִים שָׁנָה וְלֹא זָכִיתִי שֶׁתֵּאָמֵר יְצִיאַת מִצְרַיִם בַּלֵּילוֹת, עַד שֶׁדְּרָשָׁהּ בֶּן זוֹמָא, שֶׁנֶּאֱמַר: לְמַעַן תִּזְכֹּר אֶת יוֹם צֵאתְךָ מֵאֶרֶץ מִצְרַיִם כֹּל יְמֵי חַיֶּיךָ (דברים ט״ז, ג). ״יְמֵי חַיֶּיךָ״ - הַיָּמִים, ״כֹּל יְמֵי חַיֶּיךָ״ - הַלֵּילוֹת. וַחֲכָמִים אוֹמְרִים: ״יְמֵי חַיֶּיךָ״ - הָעוֹלָם הַזֶּה, ״כֹּל יְמֵי חַיֶּיךָ״ - לְהָבִיא לִימוֹת הַמָּשִׁיחַ.

Food For Thought

The mitzvah to remember, the mitzvah to tell the story

This section is tangent to the Seder night itself, discussing the daily mitzvah to mention the Exodus from Egypt. This presents a question about the entire Seder night, for if we have to mention the Exodus from Egypt every night, what is special about its retelling on the Seder night?

Many explanations have been given about this (see *Halachah MiMekorah – Kinor David, Maggid* p. 95) among them: on the Seder night the mitzvah is to tell the story at length, not only the actual Exodus from Egypt but the entire process; on the Seder night one must tell it through questions and answers (with the children participating); on the Seder night one is not commanded only to tell the story, but also to thank God as a result of that telling.

As this section is only tangent to the Seder night, we can ask why it is even quoted here. It seems that this section comes to teach us that the story of the Exodus from Egypt is meant to affect the entire year. It is through the special power of freedom that we attain on Seder night that we are able to recall the Exodus throughout the entire year (see *Sefat Emet*, Pesach 5641, *Bemidrash Shir Hashirim*; and Pesach 5639, *Yachol*). Therefore, after we have

◂ mentioned

Riddles

24. Why does Rabbi Elazar ben Azaryah state, "I am *like* a seventy-year-old man," rather than saying, "I am a seventy-year-old man?"

RABBI ELAZAR BEN AZARYAH SAID: "I am like a seventy-year-old man, yet I did not succeed in proving that the Exodus from Egypt must be mentioned at night – until Ben Zoma explained the verse: 'In order that you may remember the day you left Egypt all the days of your life' (Deuteronomy 16:3). 'The days of your life' would mean only the days; the additional word 'all' indicates the inclusion of the nights!" The Sages, however, say that "the days of your life" would mean only the present world; the additional word "all" includes the days of the Mashiach.

---

mentioned the Sages who discussed the Exodus, we quote the law of remembering it throughout the year, and by doing so we are saying that we want the seder night to cause a substantive change in our lives throughout the entire year!

Mentioning the Exodus from Egypt at Night

What is the dispute between Rabbi Elazar ben Azaryah and the other Sages? Night symbolizes darkness, crisis, and exile. Is that an appropriate time to speak of the Exodus from Egypt? According to the Sages, one should wait for better times, ones that are brighter. The Exodus from Egypt will prove most significant in our final redemption, in Mashiach's time. Then, Israel's freedom will be complete, the entire world will know that God's kingdom fills the earth, and "The Lord will be King over all the earth" (Zechariah 14:9).

As opposed to this, according to Rabbi Elazar ben Azaryah, there is significance in the Exodus from Egypt even at a time when we are in exile and in servitude. Exile is also part of redemption, part of the Divine process of the Exodus from Egypt. Every exile is a step in the process that Am Yisrael must undergo to reach the ultimate redemption. In a sense, we act in accordance with both views: we mention the Exodus at night and understand that there is significance and importance for each of the stages of the redemption, but at the same time we understand that the entire process – the Exodus from Egypt, the terrible exiles that we have endured and the stages of the redemption that we have merited to experience – leads to the time of the Mashiach, when our true freedom, whose seeds were planted in Egypt, will finally be blossom in full glory. ▪

בָּרוּךְ הַמָּקוֹם, בָּרוּךְ הוּא.
בָּרוּךְ שֶׁנָּתַן תּוֹרָה לְעַמּוֹ יִשְׂרָאֵל. בָּרוּךְ הוּא.

כְּנֶגֶד אַרְבָּעָה בָנִים דִּבְּרָה תוֹרָה: אֶחָד חָכָם, וְאֶחָד רָשָׁע, וְאֶחָד תָּם, וְאֶחָד שֶׁאֵינוֹ יוֹדֵעַ לִשְׁאוֹל.

חָכָם מַה הוּא אוֹמֵר: מָה הָעֵדֹת וְהַחֻקִּים וְהַמִּשְׁפָּטִים אֲשֶׁר צִוָּה יְהֹוָה אֱלֹהֵינוּ אֶתְכֶם (דברים ו׳, כ). וְאַף אַתָּה אֱמָר לוֹ כְּהִלְכוֹת הַפֶּסַח: אֵין מַפְטִירִין אַחַר הַפֶּסַח אֲפִיקוֹמָן.

Food For Thought

The main point – to be thankful!
What is the aim of telling the story of the Exodus from Egypt? Rav Yosef Dov Soloveitchik (*Shiurim LeZecher Abba Mari*, Vol. 1, new edition, p. 14) explains that our main obligation of the Seder night is to be moved to thank God through the story:

> *The duty of remembering does not impose on a person an obligation to recite praise and thanks, whereas the mitzvah to tell the story obligates one not only to relate the wonders and miracles that God did for us, but also to praise and thank Him, "Therefore, it is our duty to thank, praise, hail, glorify, exalt, honor, bless..." and that is the basis for the obligation of hallel on Pesach night.*

We begin maggid with Mah Nishtanah, which is meant to excite the children – and us as well – *to make a change, and to change ourselves.* Afterwards (according to Shmuel, as discussed above) we tell the story of the Exodus: "We were slaves to Pharaoh in Egypt, and the Lord, our God, took us out from there." We then explain the dimensions of the obligation: who is obligated (everyone, including Torah scholars), how much one must say ("everyone who discusses the Exodus from Egypt at length is praiseworthy"), and we also tell of the Sages who spent the Seder night together and spoke about the Exodus from Egypt the entire night.

Now, the time has come to thank God: "Blessed is God, blessed be He!

◂ *Blessed*

Blessed is God, blessed be He! Blessed is He who gave the Torah to His people Israel, blessed be He!

Concerning four sons, the Torah speaks: one is **WISE**, one is **WICKED**, one is **SIMPLE** and one **WHO DOES NOT KNOW HOW TO ASK.**

THE WISE SON – what does he say? "What are the testimonies, the statutes and the laws that the Lord, our God, has commanded you?" (Deuteronomy 6:20). You, in turn, shall instruct him in the laws of the Pesach offering: one may not eat dessert after the Pesach offering.

Blessed is He who gave the Torah to His people Israel, blessed be He!"

This praise marks the end of the section which relates Am Yisrael's physical redemption, concluding the first of the four stages of the haggadah, which is characterized by a cyclical retelling of the Exodus followed by praise.

Do we exclude the wicked son from Am Yisrael?

If we read the verses closely, we will see that there is a linguistic difference between our answer to the wicked son and the other sons. The answer to the other sons is direct, while the answer to the wicked son refers to him in the third person: "It is because of this that the Lord did [all these miracles] for me when I left Egypt"; 'for me' – but not for him! Had he been there, he would not have been redeemed!" That said, it does not say explicitly, "for me but not for you. Had you been there, you would not have been redeemed." What is the reason for this?

The wicked son is an inseparable part of us. In Egypt, before we became a single nation, the wicked were not saved, and, therefore, the midrash states that the wicked ones among us did not leave Egypt (Midrash Tanchuma, *Beshalach*, 1). However, after the Exodus and the giving of the Torah, Am Yisrael received the power of unity and mutual responsibility. The perfect expression of this was at the giving of the Torah, "they encamped in the desert, and Israel encamped there opposite the mountain" – and Rashi comments, "as a single person with a single heart" (Rashi, Exodus 19:2).

Nowadays, the *wicked* are also a part of Am Yisrael. Therefore, the words

◂ were

רָשָׁע מַה הוּא אוֹמֵר: מָה הָעֲבֹדָה הַזֹּאת לָכֶם (שמות י״ב, כו). ״לָכֶם״ - וְלֹא לוֹ. וּלְפִי שֶׁהוֹצִיא אֶת עַצְמוֹ מִן הַכְּלָל כָּפַר בָּעִקָּר. וְאַף אַתָּה הַקְהֵה אֶת שִׁנָּיו וֶאֱמָר לוֹ: בַּעֲבוּר זֶה עָשָׂה יְהֹוָה לִי בְּצֵאתִי מִמִּצְרָיִם (שמות י״ג, ח). ״לִי״ - וְלֹא לוֹ. אִלּוּ הָיָה שָׁם לֹא הָיָה נִגְאָל.

were stated in the third person: the wicked person in Egypt would not have been redeemed, but you, the wicked person who lives among us, are considered as part of us. We want you with us, despite your wickedness (compare *Eiruvin* 19a – "the wicked of Israel – gehinnom has no power over them"). Rav Zadok HaKohen of Lublin similarly explains: "'Had he been there, he would not have been redeemed,' however, as he is a descendant of one who *was* redeemed, he is assured that he will remain with us and will repent."

That is why on the Sukkot festival we take the Four Species together, knowing that if a person does not have aravot (willow branches) – the willow is likened to the wicked – he is unable to recite the blessing on the Four Species. Am Yisrael is composed of various types of people, and only when all are together can we reach the full potential ofthe Four Species.

We do not, at the time, try to answer the question of the wicked son. We do not attempt to argue with him, for it won't yield any productive results, right now. He is still not prepared to listen and pay attention. However, we do say one thing to him: *Take care not to leave Am Yisrael!* Even if you commit many sins, the hand is still stretched out to receive you back, as long as you are still with us around the table. However, one who removes himself from the community indeed denies the basic principle of our faith.

Teach a child according to his nature

The answers to all the sons begin with *ve'amarta* or *ve'amartem* – "you shall say" – with the exception of the one who is unable to ask, which begins with vehigadeta – "you shall tell" using a different verb root (see *Or HaChaim*, Exodus 13:8). What is the difference between the verb **אמר** and the verb **הגד**? Rashi (on Exodus 13:5) explains that "*vehigadeta le'vincha*" refers to the son who does not know how to ask, and the verse teaches us that one must speak to him "in words of aggadah, which draw him in." With this, Rashi teaches us that one must employ different educational approaches, according to the

◂ child's

THE WICKED SON – what does he say? "What is this service to you?!" (Exodus 12:26). He says "to you," thereby excluding himself. By excluding himself, he denies the basic principle of our faith. You, in turn, shall blunt his teeth and say to him: "It is because of this that the Lord did [all these miracles] for me when I left Egypt" (Exodus 13:8); "for me" – but not for him! Had he been there, he would not have been redeemed!

---

child's nature. Sometimes, a parent or educator should take an intellectual approach (the wise son), and sometimes one ought not to answer the child at all (the wicked son). Again, one might use stories or other imaginative approaches (the aggadah "draws him in") so that the child will be eager to listen and accept our words.

From this we learn an important rule: *one should not give the same answer to all children,* nor should one attempt to give the same education to all children. Each must be given an education suited to his or her own needs. Some parents who try to create equality among their children, to approach each of them the exact same way. This method is liable to be detrimental to their children's education, for each must receive what is best for him or her. A parent or educator should take care to address, teach, and even play with each child in a way that is best suited to their child's character.

The son who does not know how to ask is not wicked. Sometimes, however, this type of child is the most difficult to teach. The wicked son, at least, reacts to what he sees. The fourth son's inability to ask, however, may stem from indifference. Even a negative response is at least a response. In fact, it might eventually lead the person to examine matters more closely, and even to reject his wicked lifestyle. (Many of our great rabbis were individuals who in their younger years had rebelled and fought against religion). This is why it is so difficult to teach the child who does not ask. A child who is indifferent to the Exodus and our redemption from slavery may have a deep flaw in his character, perhaps even a certain tinge of the wicked son's attitude. This is why both of these sons are linked to the same verse in the Torah. The son who does not know how to ask is not opposed to anything; he is simply indifferent to what happened. That is why, while we do not answer the wicked son, we try to involve the son who does not know how to ask by drawing him in through stories.

◂ The

תָּם מַה הוּא אוֹמֵר: מַה זֹּאת (שמות י"ג, יד). וְאָמַרְתָּ אֵלָיו: בְּחֹזֶק יָד הוֹצִיאָנוּ יְהֹוָה מִמִּצְרַיִם מִבֵּית עֲבָדִים (שם).

וְשֶׁאֵינוֹ יוֹדֵעַ לִשְׁאוֹל אַתְּ פְּתַח לוֹ. שֶׁנֶּאֱמַר: וְהִגַּדְתָּ לְבִנְךָ בַּיּוֹם הַהוּא לֵאמֹר, בַּעֲבוּר זֶה עָשָׂה יְהֹוָה לִי בְּצֵאתִי מִמִּצְרָיִם (שמות י"ג, ח).

The Four Sons within each of us

Sefat Emet (Pesach 5634, *Keneged*), has an innovative insight. He states that within each of us there are elements of all of the Four Sons: "and these questions are within each Jew." Every person has to contend with internal questions, urges, and inclinations. These internal questions come from different directions, from different places of the soul – some are wise questions, some wicked questions, some simple questions, and sometimes there is even the need to uncover different questions that are not apparent. Based on this, we can see that no one is perfect, and that each of us are driven by different factors. That is why we appreciate every question and do not reject any of them.

The Mishnah in Tractate Avot (1:12), states, "Be of the disciples of Aaron,

◂ loving

Amulet ring, Morocco, 19th century, silver
The Wolfson Museum, Hechal Shlomo

THE SIMPLE SON – what does he say? "What is this?" Tell him: "With a strong hand did the Lord take us out of Egypt, from the house of bondage" (Exodus 13:14).

As for the one **WHO DOES NOT KNOW HOW TO ASK** – you must prompt him, as it says: "You shall tell your child on that day: 'It is because of this that the Lord did [all these miracles] for me when I left Egypt'" (Exodus 13:8).

Riddles

25. The wise son and the wicked son say similar things, and yet we are angry at the wicked son and do not answer him. Why? What is the difference between them?

    Read the verses in the Torah: Exodus 12:26 (for the wicked son) and Deuteronomy 6:20 (for the wise son). Look at what each son says and then answer the question!
26. Where does the midrash of the Four Sons end?

Topic for discussion

g. In the end, was the wicked son redeemed? In the final analysis, is the wicked son part of Am Yisrael?

h. What is the message of the midrash of the Four Sons? Why does the haggadah mention the midrash?

loving peace and pursuing peace, loving your fellow creatures and bringing them close to the Torah." Rav Zvi Yehudah Kook explains that the Mishnah commands us to do two inherently separate and different acts: to love; and to bring close. We are not commanded to love people in order to bring them close to the Torah. We have to love people because they are all God's creatures, to love Am Yisrael because we are all one. It is this love that will bring about a time when even those who are far away will draw closer to the Torah; that they too, will feel the pleasant and warming fire of a person who radiates love of the Torah and the mitzvot, and will want to warm themselves by that same fire. ▪

יכול ד

יָכוֹל מֵרֹאשׁ חֹדֶשׁ, תַּלְמוּד לוֹמַר: בַּיּוֹם הַהוּא (שם).
אִי בַּיּוֹם הַהוּא יָכוֹל מִבְּעוֹד יוֹם, תַּלְמוּד לוֹמַר:
בַּעֲבוּר זֶה (שם), בַּעֲבוּר זֶה לֹא אָמַרְתִּי אֶלָּא בְּשָׁעָה שֶׁיֵּשׁ מַצָּה
וּמָרוֹר מֻנָּחִים לְפָנֶיךָ.

Food For Thought

Matzah and maror – the unity of opposites

The Rishonim differ concerning the significance of the interpretation of the Sages that "the expression 'It is because of this' can only be said when matzah and maror are placed before you." Do the matzah and maror have to be actually in front of us, or does that interpretation only mean that this is to be said *at the time* that one fulfills the mitzvot of matzah and maror, without them necessarily being in front of us? The basis for the disagreement is how one understands the words of the Talmud in Pesachim.

The Talmud (116b) discusses whether a blind person is obligated to tell the story of the Exodus from Egypt. According to Rav Acha bar Jacob, a blind person is exempt, because the Torah states, "It is because of *this*," implying that the person must be able to indicate what he sees before him, and a blind person cannot see the matzah and maror when the story of the Exodus from Egypt is told.

On the other hand, Rav Yosef and Rav Sheshet (both of whom were blind) hold that a blind person is obligated in the telling of the story of the Exodus from Egypt. Why? Rashbam (on that verse, *ba'avur*) and Rambam (*Sefer HaMitzvot*, Positive Mitzvah 157) explain that one must tell the story at the time of matzah and maror, but matzah and maror do not have to be physically present. The same was written by Minchat Chinuch (Mitzvah 21). There is also another interpretation offered by Me'iri (116b), who explains that a blind person can also fulfill the mitzvah of "It is because of ◂ this,"

Torah finials, Germany, silver
The Wolfson Museum, Hechal Shlomo, Max Grundt Collection

ONE MIGHT THINK THAT FROM THE beginning of the month there is an obligation to discuss the Exodus. The Torah therefore says: "On that day" (Exodus 13:8). "On that day," however, could be understood to mean only during the daytime; therefore, the Torah specifies, "It is because of this" (ibid.) The expression "It is because of this" can only be said when matzah and maror are placed before you.

---

this," by *lifting* the matzah and maror. From this, we see that according to Me'iri, the two have to be physically present, but that it is enough just to lift them without seeing them.

The mitzvah of telling the story of the Exodus from Egypt depends on the mitzvot of matzah and maror – both in terms of the time and in terms of their actual presence. Matzah is the symbol of freedom, while maror is the symbol of servitude. The Seder night is the night that can handle contradictions, the night that deals with questions. This is the night when "matzah and maror" can exist side by side, when one can understand that the different contradictions and questions that exist in the world do not diminish the greatness of our faith in any way. It is God who directs and rules the world, and God's perspective can encompass contradictions, even extending to matters that the limited human eye and mind deem impossible. In a sense, it is precisely these contradictions, precisely those matters that are beyond human comprehension, which show the presence of God in the world (this view is reinforced daily in modern science, and especially in modern physics, which indicates vast "contradictions" within the world of science itself). ▪

Activity

Before the festival, one can prepare paper crowns with the names of all the important people in the haggadah and the story of the Exodus from Egypt – Rabbi Elazar, the wise son, Pharaoh, Lavan, etc. One at a time, one of the members of the seder puts the crown on his head, and one of the names is to be attached to the crown with a paper clip, so that the others can see it but he cannot. Using questions and answers, the person wearing the crown must try to guess the name of the person whose name was attached to the crown. The winner is the one who guesses the name on his slip of paper with the fewest questions.

מִתְּחִלָּה עוֹבְדֵי עֲבוֹדָה זָרָה הָיוּ אֲבוֹתֵינוּ, וְעַכְשָׁיו קֵרְבָנוּ הַמָּקוֹם לַעֲבוֹדָתוֹ, שֶׁנֶּאֱמַר: וַיֹּאמֶר יְהוֹשֻׁעַ אֶל כָּל הָעָם, כֹּה אָמַר יְהֹוָה אֱלֹהֵי יִשְׂרָאֵל, בְּעֵבֶר הַנָּהָר יָשְׁבוּ אֲבוֹתֵיכֶם מֵעוֹלָם, תֶּרַח אֲבִי אַבְרָהָם וַאֲבִי נָחוֹר, וַיַּעַבְדוּ אֱלֹהִים אֲחֵרִים. וָאֶקַּח אֶת אֲבִיכֶם אֶת אַבְרָהָם מֵעֵבֶר הַנָּהָר, וָאוֹלֵךְ אוֹתוֹ בְּכָל אֶרֶץ כְּנָעַן, וָאַרְבֶּה אֶת זַרְעוֹ, וָאֶתֶּן לוֹ אֶת יִצְחָק. וָאֶתֵּן לְיִצְחָק אֶת יַעֲקֹב וְאֶת עֵשָׂו, וָאֶתֵּן לְעֵשָׂו אֶת הַר שֵׂעִיר לָרֶשֶׁת אוֹתוֹ, וְיַעֲקֹב וּבָנָיו יָרְדוּ מִצְרָיִם (יהושע כ"ד, ב-ד).

Food For Thought

What is the shame?

"He commences with shame and concludes with praise" says the Mishnah (116a). In the Talmud (ibid.) there is a dispute between Rav and Shmuel as to what the shame and praise refer to. According to Shmuel, the shame is that "We were slaves," and according to Rav it is that "In the beginning, our ancestors were idol worshipers." We began the haggadah with Shmuel's view, and now we go on with Rav's view.

What is the dispute between Rav and Shmuel? It seems that they differ as to what the main emphasis of the night should be – whether it should be on our *physical shame*: "We were slaves"; or our *spiritual shame*: "In the beginning, our ancestors were idol worshipers." The spiritual shame may seem the greater of the two, but the physical oppression was more obvious, and we therefore begin with the physical shame, but immediately afterwards we emphasize that the main liberation was our exodus from our spiritual shame. We stress that the goal of the Exodus was that "Now God has brought us close to His service."

Why begin with Abraham? When we look at things with a spiritual eye, we are able to see beyond the fleeting physical aspects of the event (i.e., the time and place). This spiritual eye allows to put events in perspective, to see them as part of a bigger picture. The focus is not only on the Exodus from Egypt, but begins all the way back with Abraham,

◂ see

IN THE BEGINNING, OUR ANCESTORS were idol worshipers; but now God has brought us close to His service, as it says: "Joshua said to all the people: 'Thus said the Lord, the God of Israel: Your fathers used to live on the other side of the river – Terach, the father of Abraham and the father of Nachor – and they served other gods. And I took your father Abraham from beyond the river, and I led him throughout the whole land of Canaan. I increased his seed and gave him Isaac, and to Isaac I gave Jacob and Esau. To Esau I gave Mount Seir to inherit, and Jacob and his sons went down to Egypt'" (Joshua 24:2–4).

---

from when Am Yisrael was first chosen, until the giving of the Torah. The process of the Exodus from Egypt was but a part of the formation of Am Yisrael, of the transformation of Bnei Yisrael into a nation that worshipsGod. ▪

Riddles

27. Why is our language called "Ivrit" – "Hebrew?" (hint: "ever" in Hebrew means "across"). How does this answer connect with the section in the haggadah about "In the beginning, our ancestors were idol worshipers?"
28. Do the verses quoted in the haggadah from the book of Joshua speak about the Exodus from Egypt? Look at Joshua 24:2–6. Which verses are not quoted in the haggadah? In your opinion, should they have been quoted? If so, why aren't they not quoted?
29. Who was Nachor?
30. What is the connection between Mount Seir and the name of Esau?

Topic for Discussion

i. Why do we begin the story of the Exodus from Egypt with Abraham and not from the time they were made slaves or when they first went down to Egypt?

בָּרוּךְ שׁוֹמֵר הַבְטָחָתוֹ לְיִשְׂרָאֵל, בָּרוּךְ הוּא. שֶׁהַקָּדוֹשׁ בָּרוּךְ הוּא חִשַּׁב אֶת הַקֵּץ לַעֲשׂוֹת כְּמָה שֶׁאָמַר לְאַבְרָהָם אָבִינוּ בִּבְרִית בֵּין הַבְּתָרִים, שֶׁנֶּאֱמַר: וַיֹּאמֶר לְאַבְרָם יָדֹעַ תֵּדַע כִּי גֵר יִהְיֶה זַרְעֲךָ בְּאֶרֶץ לֹא לָהֶם וַעֲבָדוּם וְעִנּוּ אֹתָם אַרְבַּע מֵאוֹת שָׁנָה. וְגַם אֶת הַגּוֹי אֲשֶׁר יַעֲבֹדוּ דָּן אָנֹכִי וְאַחֲרֵי כֵן יֵצְאוּ בִּרְכֻשׁ גָּדוֹל (בראשית ט"ו, יג-יד).

Food For Thought

God's calculations

In the simple sense, the expression, "the Holy One, Blessed be He, calculated the end," refers to the Covenant between the Pieces, where God *determined the end* of the stay in Egypt, which was to be four hundred years. However, a number of interpretations were given by the Rishonim about this expression.

Shibolei HaLeket on the haggadah writes that God "calculated the end" in such a way as to minimize the number of years. Thus, the Sages tell us in the midrash (Yalkut Shimoni, Shir Hashirim 986):

> *"The sound of my beloved! Behold, he is coming!" This refers to Moshe. When he came and said, "In this month you will be redeemed," they said to him: "Our teacher, Moshe, how are we to be redeemed? Did not the Holy One, Blessed be He, say to Abraham, that 'they will enslave them and oppress them, for four hundred years' and only 210 years have passed?!" He said to them, "As God wishes to redeem us, He will not look at the calculations but will be skipping over the mountains, jumping over the hills... and this month you will be redeemed."*

Shibolei HaLeket offers another interpretation. The word for "end" (that we say that God "calculated the end") is *keitz* in Hebrew, and the gematria value of the word *keitz* is 190. Thus God subtracted 190 years from the original 400 years, and that was why we were only in Egypt for 210 years (see the solutions to the riddles, in explaining the calculation, p. 268).

When we look at the different textual versions of the haggadah, we will see that there are two different versions of this text here. Many haggadot have the words, "*mechashev et hakeitz*" – He

◂ calculates

BLESSED IS HE WHO KEEPS HIS PROM-ise to Israel, blessed be He! For the Holy One, Blessed be He, calculated the end [of the bondage], in order to do as He had said to our father Abraham at the "Covenant between the Pieces," as it says: "And He said to Abraham, 'Know for certain that your seed will be strangers in a land that is not theirs, and they [the Children of Israel] will serve them and they [the Egyptians] will oppress them for 400 years. But I shall also judge the nation that they shall serve, and after that they will come out with great wealth'" (Genesis 15:13–14).

Amulet case, silver
The Wolfson Museum, Hechal Shlomo

calculates the end (Rav Amram Gaon, Rav Sa'adiah Gaon, and others), while others have the version, "*chishev et hakeitz*" – He calculated the end (Rambam, Avudraham on the haggadah, and that is our version). Our version is that God *calculated* (in the past) the time for the redemption from Egypt. The other version is in present tense, "which God *calculates*" – God is constantly calculating when the redemption is to come. That is the interpretation of Shibolei HaLeket: that when we speak of the Exodus from Egypt, we must be consoled by it, for in the future God will again redeem us, "as He kept His word in the past."

The fact that God is constantly calculating the redemption teaches us that everything depends on Divine Providence. Everything is calculated, both our troubles and our consolations. In reading the haggadah on the Seder night, we must remember that we are not only speaking about the past, but that this is also a description of the present and the future to come, with God's help, as the prophet Micah said to us (7:15), "As in the days of your Exodus from the land of Egypt, I will show him wonders!"

◂ Why

Why through trickery and theft?

"Afterwards they will go forth with great wealth." God promised Abraham at the Covenant between the Pieces (Genesis 15:13–14) that after the slavery of Egypt, Am Yisrael would go out with great wealth, which was justified after slaving for the Egyptians for 400 years. Thus, the Sages tell us in Tractate Sanhedrin (91a), that many years later the Egyptian people came to demand from Am Yisrael all the gold and silver that their ancestors had taken when they left Egypt. In response to the Egyptians, Gebiha ben Pesisa said, "pay us for the toil of… 430 years."

> On another occasion the Egyptians came in a lawsuit against the Jews before Alexander of Macedon. They said to him: "Is it not written, 'And the Lord gave the people favor in the sight of the Egyptians, and they lent them [gold and precious stones, etc.]?' Then return to us the gold and silver that you took!" Thereupon Gebiha b. Pesisa said to the Sages, "Give me permission to go and plead against them before Alexander of Macedon: should they defeat me, then say, 'You have merely defeated an ignorant man among us'; while if I defeat them then say, 'The Law of Moshe has defeated you.'" So they gave him permission, and he went and pleaded against them. "From where do you bring your proof?" he asked. "From the Torah," they replied. "Then I too will bring you proof only from the Torah," he said, "for it is written, 'Now the sojourning of Bnei Yisrael, who dwelled in Egypt, was four hundred and thirty years.' Pay us for the toil of six hundred thousand men whom you enslaved for four hundred thirty years." Then Alexander of Macedon said to them, "Answer him!' "Give us three days' time," they begged. So he gave them time; they sought but found no answer.

However, we would have expected that the money would be received in a more honest way. Am Yisrael should have approached the Egyptians and demanded the silver and gold utensils as

◂ wages

Riddles

31. "They [Bnei Yisrael] will serve them and they [the Egyptians] will oppress them for 400 years." Were Bnei Yisrael indeed slaves for 400 years?
32. How can one calculate the number of years Am Yisrael was enslaved in Egypt (see Rashi on Genesis 15:13)?
33. How do we calculate the years from the birth of Isaac until the Exodus from Egypt?
34. "After that they will come out with great wealth." How did Am Yisrael acquire this great wealth? How did the plague of Darkness help them?

wages for their work. It is obvious that the Egyptians would have done so, because they were afraid of more plagues. Why, then, did Bnei Yisrael need to borrow these utensils, with the implication that they would return them at some point, when they knew they had no such intention?

Ibn Ezra (*HaAroch*, Exodus 3:22), asks this very question, and he answers:

> *There is no reason to ask why, because God created everything, and He gave wealth to whomever He wished, and He will take it from one person and give it to another, and that is not wicked, because all is His.*

Everything belongs to God, and since He commanded this, it is not unjust. However, we still have to understand why God wanted this to happen in such a manner.

Rashbam (Exodus 3:22; 11:2), explains that the word "*she'elah*" (generally translated as "to borrow") means asking someone to *give* something to you, as in the verse, "Request ("*she'al*") of Me, and I will *give* ("*va'etnah*") you nations as your inheritance" (Tehillim 2:8). Rav Sa'adiah Gaon (*ibid.*) also explains it thus. In other words, Am Yisrael did not ask to borrow these vessels, but asked to be given them, *and the Egyptians knew that they would not be returned to them.*

What is the significance of the fact that Bnei Yisrael left Egypt with a great number of possessions? The nation was meant to leave Egypt as royalty, and not as slaves – not as refugees. Am Yisrael was about to cause a revolution in the world, the revolution of freedom. That was why they had to leave Egypt in style, with a great number of possessions. This was not done because of any avarice – Heaven forbid. Silver and gold utensils are a sign of royalty for the nation chosen to perfect the world under the Kingdom of God (for further explanations of this topic, see the commentary on "Had He given us their wealth," on p. 104). ▪

Torah pointer, Persia/North Africa, 19th century, silver
The Wolfson Museum, Hechal Shlomo

מכסים את המצות, מגביהים את הכוס ואומרים:

וְהִיא שֶׁעָמְדָה לַאֲבוֹתֵינוּ וְלָנוּ, שֶׁלֹּא אֶחָד בִּלְבָד עָמַד עָלֵינוּ לְכַלּוֹתֵנוּ, אֶלָּא שֶׁבְּכָל דּוֹר וָדוֹר עוֹמְדִים עָלֵינוּ לְכַלּוֹתֵנוּ, וְהַקָּדוֹשׁ בָּרוּךְ הוּא מַצִּילֵנוּ מִיָּדָם.

Food For Thought

Why do we cover the matzot when we raise the cup?

Generally, the matzot are meant to be uncovered when the haggadah is read (Rama, 413:7; Mishnah Berurah, subsection 76). When we say Mah Nishtanah, we cover the matzot rather than remove the table, as the latter custom is no longer observed. Similarly, we cover the matzot each time we raise our cups. The reason for this is that on Shabbat we cover the challah loaves when we recite kiddush, as according to halacha one makes a blessing on bread before making one on wine (the blessing on bread is more important, and takes precedence over the blessing on wine). Therefore, when we give precedence to the wine (when we recite kiddush), we cover the challah out of respect for the bread. The same is true here: when we wish to show the importance of the wine by raising our cup, we cover the matzot, while at all other times the matzot are uncovered (Responsa Maharil, 58b; Mishnah Berurah, 473:73,78).

This [promise] has sustained us – in all generations

The Rishonim dispute whether the text should read "*vehi*" – "*and* this" – like our version – or whether it should read "*hi*' – "this" (the version of Rambam in the Frankel edition). "And," "*vehi*," implies that this passage is a continuation of the promise made to Abraham at the Covenant between the Pieces, which was mentioned earlier. If the version is "*hi*," this is a new passage, which describes how God has saved Am Yisrael throughout history, although "*vehi*," which specifically refers to God's covenant with Abraham, can also be understood in this sense nonetheless (for further discussion, see the riddles on this section and their answers).

Weeping in the middle of the haggadah – Seder night in the Holocaust

The story of Rabbi Yonah Emmanuel – Pesach within the bitter reality of the Holocaust (as told at the brit of his grandson):

I would like to tell you what happened forty years ago today. I was unable to tell this story until now. I never told it to my wife, I never told it to my children, I never told it to anyone – I was unable to. For the first time I feel

◂ that

We cover the matzot, raise the wine cup, and recite:

THIS [PROMISE] HAS SUSTAINED OUR fathers and us! For not only one enemy has risen against us to destroy us, but in every generation they rise against us to destroy us; and the Holy One, Blessed be He, saves us from their hand.

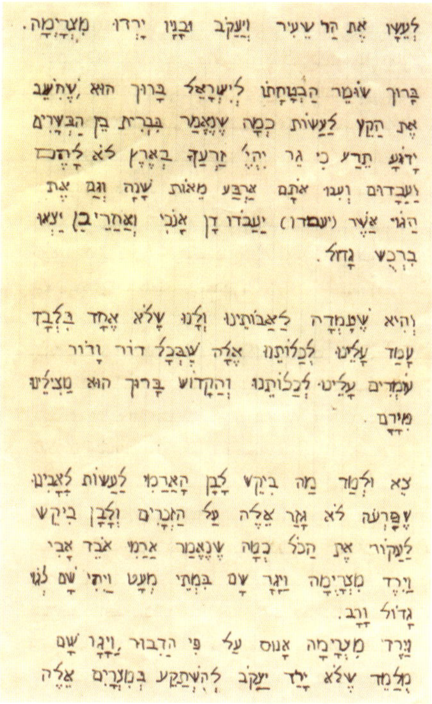
לעשו את הר שעיר ויעקב ובניו ירדו מצרימה.

ברוך שומר הבטחתו לישראל ברוך הוא, שחשב
את הקץ לעשות כמה שאמר בברית בן הבתרים
ידע תדע כי גר יהיה זרעך בארץ לא להם
ועבדום ועִנו אתם ארבע מאות שנה וגם את
הגוי אשר (יעבדו) יעבדו דן אנכי ואחרי כן יצאו
ברכש גדול.

והיא שעמדה לאבותינו ולנו שלא אחד בלבד
עמד עלינו לכלותנו אלא שבכל דור ודור
עומדים עלינו לכלותנו והקדוש ברוך הוא מצילנו
מידם.

צא ולמד מה ביקש לבן הארמי לעשות לאבינו
שפרעה לא גזר אלא על הזכרים ולבן ביקש
לעקור את הכל כמה שנאמר ארמי אבד אבי
וירד מצרימה ויגר שם במתי מעט ויהי שם לגוי
גדול ורב.
וירד מצרימה אנוס על פי הדבור, ויגר שם
מלמד שלא ירד יעקב להשתקע במצרים אלא

In a dark cellar, in the heart of Nazi Europe, the Ganz family lived, hiding from the Nazis. The festival of Pesach was coming close, but they did not have a haggadah. The father of the family, Dr. Menachem Mendl Ganz, sat down and wrote the haggadah from memory, with startling accuracy, with very few errors. This was a Jew who, even within a dark cellar, continued to be a free man! A Jew who, even within the darkness, produced light, and did not give in to the terrible and painful situation.

that I can tell it now, at the brit of my grandson, Aharon Chananel.

On the morning before Pesach eve in the year 5705 (1945) I set out for hard physical labor in the Bergen-Belsen concentration camp, as I had done every day for the previous two years. I came back at night, utterly and totally exhausted, as I did every night during those two years. I was 19 years old. My father was already dead, my older brother, Elchanan, was already dead, my younger brother, Shalom, was already dead, and my younger sister, Bayta, was also not among the living.

The Bergen-Belsen camp was not an extermination camp but a labor camp, and Jews died of the unbelievably hard labor, the terrible cold, starvation, and disease. During that time, hundreds of Jews died each day in Bergen-Belsen.

I went to the hut where my mother was. She was very ill. I sat next to her and began to recite the haggadah. We had no wine, we had no matzot, we did not even have any bread. We only had one thing – in the greatest abundance – maror! There was a very great amount of maror – bitterness – in our hearts! I whispered the haggadah, and I was not sure whether my mother heard

◂ me or

מניחים את הכוס, מגלים את המצות ואומרים:

צֵא וּלְמַד

מַה בִּקֵּשׁ לָבָן הָאֲרַמִּי לַעֲשׂוֹת לְיַעֲקֹב אָבִינוּ. שֶׁפַּרְעֹה לֹא גָזַר אֶלָּא עַל הַזְּכָרִים וְלָבָן בִּקֵּשׁ לַעֲקוֹר אֶת הַכֹּל. שֶׁנֶּאֱמַר:

---

me or did not hear me. When I came to the blessing of deliverance, and I said the words, "So too, Lord our God and God of our fathers, enable us to reach future holidays and festivals in peace, rejoicing in the rebuilding of Your city and ecstatic in Your service," I felt that for the first time I did not believe what I was saying. Would any of us there reach future holidays and festivals? Would anyone of us ever see Jerusalem? Would any of us ever rejoice again? I burst into tears, and in the middle of the blessing I stopped reciting the haggadah…

If only I had been able to describe to myself on that Pesach eve of 5705 a hint of what has taken place today, had I been able to imagine that I would be privileged to come to Eretz Yisrael with my sister and my two brothers, that I would be privileged to live in a Jewish country, that I would be able to establish a family, to raise seven children, to be a sandek at the brit of my grandson in Jerusalem forty years later… had I been able to image any of that – I might have been able to complete the reading of the haggadah… ▪

Riddles

35. "It sustained us" – what was it that sustained our fathers?
36. The photograph here is a page of a haggadah that was written from memory. Prove this!
37. Can we prove if the writer was Ashkenazic or Sefardic? (Hint: In Ashkenazic pronunciation, what letters sound alike that do not sound alike in Sefaradic pronunciation?)

Topic for discussion

j. How can a person feel free on Pesach, even though our history of exile has shown that we are in some ways still enslaved?

The cup is put down, the matzot are uncovered, and the following is said:

GO AND LEARN WHAT LAVAN THE ARAMEAN wanted to do to our father Jacob. For Pharaoh had issued a decree only against the male children, but Lavan wanted to uproot everyone, as it says:

The Source of the Haggadah

In Parashat Ki Tavo, the Torah provides a short account of the Exodus from Egypt (Deuteronomy 26:5–8). The editor of the haggadah expounds and expands on these four verses. A similar interpretation is found in Sifri (Deuteronomy 301 and other places), but in a different, abridged form. The Mishnah (116a) writes about the obligation to interpret these verses on the Seder night: "He expounds from 'An Aramean sought to destroy my father' until he completes the whole section."

The editor of the haggadah takes each verse, and interprets it in two ways: a) interpretations and inferences from the words: the editor of the haggadah explains the content of the verses and what should be inferred from them. For example, "'and with signs' – this refers to the staff"; "'and with wonders' – this refers to the blood." b) expansions on a topic. Generally, the expansions are from other verses in Tanach and explain a particular point only briefly referred to in the original verse in Deuteronomy. For example, "'Few in number' as it says: 'Your fathers went down to Egypt with seventy persons, and now, the Lord, your God, has made you as numerous as the stars of heaven.'" These interpretations continue until "at the sea they were struck by 250 plagues" (that being the end of the interpretations of the fourth verse).

The fifth verse: The editor of the haggadah stopped before the fifth verse (Deuteronomy 26:9), "And He brought us to this place, and He gave us this land, a land flowing with milk and honey," and did not expound on it. He may have stopped before this verse because, unfortunately, it simply was not true when the Jews were in exile. However, this verse does not even appear in the haggadot of Eretz Yisrael. It is likely that as most Jews lived outside of Israel at that time, the verse was deemed irrelevant even for those who did live in the country. If that is indeed the case, there is a valid reason to add that verse into the haggadah in our times. Even though, in general, people do not add the verse, we must at least remember the obligation to thank God for giving us Eretz Yisrael – the beginning of the blossoming of our redemption! ▪

Food For Thought

Why do we expound on verses from Deuteronomy and not from Exodus?

At first, it would appear that the book of Exodus would be the best way to tell the story of the Exodus from Egypt. The editor of the haggadah, however, chose four verses in Parashat Ki Tavo in Deuteronomy, which tell the story of the Exodus from Egypt in brief. Had we wanted to use the verses in the book of Exodus, it would have made the haggadah much longer and we might have been obliged to skip certain verses. When we use the verses that were chosen, dealing with the first fruits, we can cover the complete story with a relatively short passage. One can fulfill the exposition, in the words of the Mishnah, that "He expounds… *until he completes the whole section.*"

Another reason for choosing these verses is that the verses in Deuteronomy are part of the mitzvah of bringing in one's first fruits, whereby each person is required to bring his first fruits and to tell others about the Exodus from Egypt. This is a description of the past and a demonstration of how to properly tell over the Exodus from Egypt as more than just a description of events that took place.

Moreover, the mitzvah of bringing in first fruits expresses *gratitude*. The person goes down to his field, looks at his crop, and knows that everything is from God: "You shall rejoice with all the good that the Lord, your God, has granted you and your household" (Deuteronomy 26:11). The operative verb root in this passage, which is appears a symbolic seven times, is נתן, *to give*. By being grateful, being able to identify with God's abundant generosity, a person learns to thank God for all that He has done for Am Yisrael, for its deliverance, and for its redemption.

We can offer yet another reason why the haggadah uses the verses in Deuteronomy rather than those in Exodus. While it is true that the text regarding the first fruits is much shorter than that in Exodus, the former text, unlike the latter, presents the Exodus in historical perspective – beginning with the description of the redemption from the time of Jacob, and ending with *Am Yisrael*'s return to their own land. One thanks God by examining the course of history of Am Yisrael. This way, we understand that there is a Divine plan that leads our nation, from the beginning of our forefathers to the present day. Our thanks are not only for the Exodus from Egypt. *The Exodus is but an example of how God has helped Israel over the generations,* and we thank Him on the Seder night for all of His help.

Lavan wanted to uproot *everyone?*

Was Lavan really worse than Pharaoh? How do we learn that he wanted to

◂ destroy

destroy *everyone*? It appears that one can discern Lavan's deep-seated motivation from his last words before he left Jacob (Genesis 31:43):

> And Lavan answered and said to Jacob, "The daughters are my daughters, and the sons are my sons, and the animals are my animals, and all that you see is mine..."

Lavan wanted to *take complete control of Jacob's family.* Lavan felt that he was *the father of the family! All belonged to him – "the daughters are my daughters, and the sons are my sons, and the animals are my animals."* Lavan wanted Jacob's family to become Aramean and to be part of his family. This desire to indicate his control over Jacob was the reason he switched Leah for Rachel, the reason he wanted Jacob's family to live with him. He even controlled Jacob's wives, and he was the one to decide whom Jacob was to marry!

In this, Lavan's decree was worse than that of Pharaoh, for Pharaoh decreed against the males – in a direct physical confrontation with Am Yisrael. Lavan, on the other hand, wanted to control everything – to destroy the very essence of Am Yisrael's identity. That is the greatest danger to Am Yisrael. A physical confrontation is easily recognized for what it is, and, thank God, despite numerous such struggles in our history, we have always survived. However, the times when another nation has imposed an alien culture upon us have proven far more dangerous. Many times, people are not aware of the danger until it is too late.

On the Seder night, the night of freedom, we proclaim: Jews, watch out! Lavan wishes to destroy all! Be wary of being swallowed up by foreign culture (although, if approached properly, it is permissible and even desirable to accept ideas from the rest of the world in order to sanctify them). *Be mindful of assimilation among other nations, and know that it is very difficult to struggle against the "Lavan" of each generation. Always remember: the struggle to maintain the identity of Am Yisrael is a struggle for the very existence of the nation, because "Lavan wished to destroy all!"* ▪

A model of Rachel's tomb, brass
The Wolfson Museum, Hechal Shlomo, Golnitzki Collection

אֲרַמִּי אֹבֵד אָבִי, וַיֵּרֶד מִצְרַיְמָה וַיָּגָר שָׁם בִּמְתֵי מְעָט, וַיְהִי שָׁם לְגוֹי גָּדוֹל עָצוּם וָרָב (דברים כ"ו, ה).

וַיֵּרֶד מִצְרַיְמָה - אָנוּס עַל פִּי הַדִּבּוּר.

וַיָּגָר שָׁם - מְלַמֵּד שֶׁלֹּא יָרַד יַעֲקֹב אָבִינוּ לְהִשְׁתַּקֵּעַ בְּמִצְרַיִם אֶלָּא לָגוּר שָׁם, שֶׁנֶּאֱמַר: וַיֹּאמְרוּ אֶל פַּרְעֹה לָגוּר בָּאָרֶץ בָּאנוּ כִּי אֵין מִרְעֶה לַצֹּאן אֲשֶׁר לַעֲבָדֶיךָ כִּי כָבֵד הָרָעָב בְּאֶרֶץ כְּנָעַן, וְעַתָּה יֵשְׁבוּ נָא עֲבָדֶיךָ בְּאֶרֶץ גֹּשֶׁן (בראשית מ"ז, ד).

בִּמְתֵי מְעָט - כְּמָה שֶׁנֶּאֱמַר: בְּשִׁבְעִים נֶפֶשׁ יָרְדוּ אֲבֹתֶיךָ מִצְרָיְמָה, וְעַתָּה שָׂמְךָ יְהוָֹה אֱלֹהֶיךָ כְּכוֹכְבֵי הַשָּׁמַיִם לָרֹב (דברים י', כב).

Food For Thought

The significance of the first verse – Going down to Egypt

The first verse describes the descent to Egypt. Let us briefly mention the main points of the verse and the interpretations of the editor of the haggadah:

"And sojourned there, few in number" – seventy souls (Genesis 46:27; the editor of the haggadah specifically quotes Deuteronomy 10:22 because this verse explains the expression "few in number"). *One must be careful about living among other nations, even for a limited time.* Am Yisrael arrived in Egypt as a small family, intending to stay temporarily ("Our father Jacob did not go down to Egypt to settle, but only to live there temporarily"), but in the end they remained there for 400 years!

"Great and mighty" – Am Yisrael increased at a supernatural rate. The Sages also describe this increase in order to acknowledge the dedication of the women: "It was due to the merit of the righteous women of that generation that Israel was redeemed from Egypt" ◄ (Sotah

The first verse of the first fruits declaration:

"An Aramean sought to destroy my father; AND HE WENT DOWN TO EGYPT AND SOJOURNED THERE, FEW IN NUMBER; AND HE BECAME THERE A NATION – GREAT AND MIGHTY AND NUMEROUS" (Deuteronomy 26:5).

"AND HE WENT DOWN TO EGYPT" – forced by Divine decree.

"AND SOJOURNED THERE" – this teaches that our father Jacob did not go down to Egypt to settle, but only to live there temporarily. As it says: "They said to Pharaoh: 'We have come to sojourn in the land, for there is no pasture for your servants' flocks because the famine is severe in the land of Canaan; and now, please, let your servants dwell in the land of Goshen'" (Genesis 47:4).

"FEW IN NUMBER" – as it says: "Your fathers went down to Egypt with seventy persons, and now, the Lord, your God, has made you as numerous as the stars of heaven" (Deuteronomy 10:22).

(Sotah 11b, and elsewhere). The women of Israel, despite the slavery and Pharaoh's decrees, became pregnant (and even enticed their husbands to do so) and gave birth, risking their lives. The Sages tell us (Exodus Rabbah 1:8) that "each of them gave birth to six at one time." The simple meaning of the midrash is that each woman gave birth to six children at once. However, it is possible that the midrash means that each woman gave birth to six children, but one at a time. If that is the case, what is the miracle? The miracle is that despite the harsh conditions of slavery, the women managed to bear and raise six children! While their births were entirely normal ones, *it was still miraculous how they persevered under such circumstances, due to their tremendous dedication.* Despite all the dangers, they were still willing to give birth and raise children (I heard this from Rav Yaakov Medan). ▪

וַיְהִי שָׁם לְגוֹי - מְלַמֵּד שֶׁהָיוּ יִשְׂרָאֵל מְצֻיָּנִים שָׁם.

גָּדוֹל עָצוּם - כְּמָה שֶׁנֶּאֱמַר: וּבְנֵי יִשְׂרָאֵל פָּרוּ וַיִּשְׁרְצוּ וַיִּרְבּוּ וַיַּעַצְמוּ בִּמְאֹד מְאֹד וַתִּמָּלֵא הָאָרֶץ אֹתָם (שמות א׳, ז).

וָרָב - כְּמָה שֶׁנֶּאֱמַר: רְבָבָה כְּצֶמַח הַשָּׂדֶה נְתַתִּיךְ וַתִּרְבִּי וַתִּגְדְּלִי וַתָּבֹאִי בַּעֲדִי עֲדָיִים, שָׁדַיִם נָכֹנוּ וּשְׂעָרֵךְ צִמֵּחַ וְאַתְּ עֵרֹם וְעֶרְיָה (יחזקאל ט״ז, ז).

יש מוסיפים:

וָאֶעֱבֹר עָלַיִךְ וָאֶרְאֵךְ מִתְבּוֹסֶסֶת בְּדָמָיִךְ וָאֹמַר לָךְ בְּדָמַיִךְ חֲיִי וָאֹמַר לָךְ בְּדָמַיִךְ חֲיִי (שם, ו).

Riddles

38. What is the source of the verses in the section of "Go and learn?"
39. What is the meaning of "*metzuyanim sham*" – "distinctive there?"
40. Where else in the Torah do we find the term, "*atzum ve'rav*" – "mighty and great?" Where does it say "*rav ve'atzum*" – "great and mighty?"
41. The editor of the haggadah interprets "few in number" as meaning 70 people. From where did he learn this? Would you have learned it from a different place?

Topic for discussion

k. Had you needed to tell the story of the Exodus from Egypt, which book of the Torah would you have used? Why, in your opinion, did the editor of the haggadah specifically choose the verses in Deuteronomy?

"**AND HE BECAME THERE A NATION**" – this teaches that Israel was distinctive there.

"**GREAT AND MIGHTY**" – as it says: "And Bnei Yisrael were fruitful and increased and multiplied and became very mighty, and the land became filled with them" (Exodus 1:7).

"**AND NUMEROUS**" – as it says: "I caused you to thrive like the plants of the field, and you increased and grew and became very beautiful. Your breasts were formed and your hair had grown, but you remained naked and bare" (Ezekial 16:7).

Some add:

"And I passed over you and saw you downtrodden in your blood, and I said to you, 'By your blood you shall live.' And I said to you, 'By your blood you shall live'" (Ezekial 16:6).

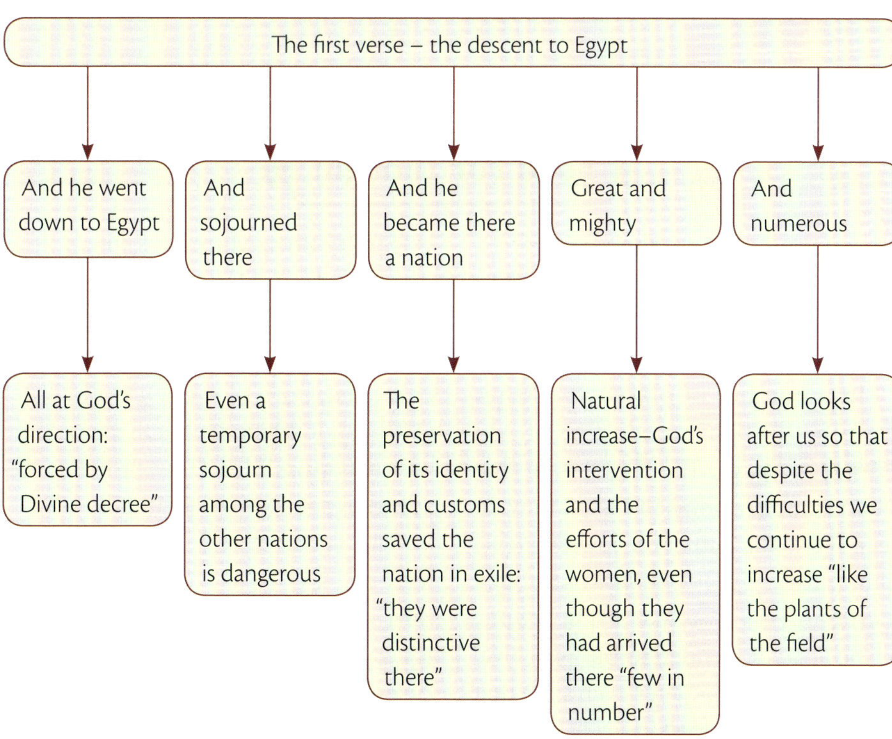

פסוק שני ממקרא ביכורים:

וַיָּרֵעוּ אֹתָנוּ הַמִּצְרִים וַיְעַנּוּנוּ, וַיִּתְּנוּ עָלֵינוּ עֲבֹדָה קָשָׁה (דברים כ"ו, ו).

וַיָּרֵעוּ אֹתָנוּ הַמִּצְרִים - כְּמָה שֶׁנֶּאֱמַר: הָבָה נִתְחַכְּמָה לוֹ, פֶּן יִרְבֶּה וְהָיָה כִּי תִקְרֶאנָה מִלְחָמָה וְנוֹסַף גַּם הוּא עַל שֹׂנְאֵינוּ, וְנִלְחַם בָּנוּ וְעָלָה מִן הָאָרֶץ (שמות א', י).

וַיְעַנּוּנוּ - כְּמָה שֶׁנֶּאֱמַר: וַיָּשִׂימוּ עָלָיו שָׂרֵי מִסִּים לְמַעַן עַנֹּתוֹ בְּסִבְלֹתָם וַיִּבֶן עָרֵי מִסְכְּנוֹת לְפַרְעֹה אֶת פִּתֹם וְאֶת רַעַמְסֵס (שמות א', יא).

וַיִּתְּנוּ עָלֵינוּ עֲבֹדָה קָשָׁה - כְּמָה שֶׁנֶּאֱמַר: וַיַּעֲבִדוּ מִצְרַיִם אֶת בְּנֵי יִשְׂרָאֵל בְּפָרֶךְ (שמות א', יג).

Food For Thought

The second verse – the slavery

The Egyptians were evil (*vayarei'u*) toward us – they made us into evil ones (*ra'im*).

In a number of places, the Sages describe the spiritual decline of Am Yisrael in Egypt. The Sages state that when Am Yisrael was in Egypt, they descended to the 49th – the lowest – level of impurity (*Zohar Chadash Yitro*, 39:1: "Certainly Israel was like this in Egypt… as they had descended to the 49th level of impurity"). The Sages even state that Am Yisrael worshiped idolatry in Egypt (Mechilta Bo 5; Midrash Rabbah, Exodus 16:2; also see Ezekial 20). The Sages state that Am Yisrael acted just like the Egyptians: "both of them were uncircumcised, both of them grew locks…" (Midrash Rabbah, Leviticus 23:2). How was this possible? How did they descend to such a low spiritual level?

The verse states, "The Egyptians were evil toward us" (in Hebrew, "*vayarei'u otanu hamitzrim*"). This statement is very difficult to understand. In most cases, the verse states "*vayarei'u lanu Mitzrayim*" (Numbers 20:16). What is

◂ meant

The second verse of the first fruits declaration:

"THE EGYPTIANS WERE EVIL TOWARD US AND THEY OPPRESSED US, AND THEY IMPOSED HARD LABOR UPON US" (Deuteronomy 26:6).

"THE EGYPTIANS WERE EVIL TOWARD US" – as it says: "Come, let us deal cunningly with them lest they multiply and, if a war breaks out, they will join our enemies and fight against us, and escape from the land" (Exodus 1:10).

"AND THEY OPPRESSED US" – as it says: "They placed taskmasters over them in order to oppress them with their burdens, and they built store cities for Pharaoh, Pitom and Ramses" (Exodus 1:11).

"AND THEY IMPOSED HARD LABOR UPON US" – as it says: "The Egyptians made Bnei Yisrael work with rigor" (Exodus 1:13).

---

meant by "*vayarei'u otanu?*" (This construction appears only two other times in all of Tanach – in Numbers 16:15; and in 1 Shmuel 25:34 – see the book *Me'ir Ayin*).

Rav Avraham Yitzchak Kook (in his *Olat Re'iyah* on the haggadah, notes, p. 38) explains this in an astounding way:

> "*Vayarei'u otanu*" means that the Egyptians *made us into wicked people!* That was the absolute worst and most destructive part of the slavery in Egypt. That indicated the tremendous decline in our spiritual values, to which we were dragged down by the Egyptians.

However, even when Am Yisrael was at its low point spiritually, it preserved its humanity and its personal identity, as it says, "and the people were not suspected of sexual immorality or of slander, and did not change their names or their language" (Mechilta, Bo, 5). Thus, it states in the haggadah, "this teaches that Israel was distinctive there" – that they maintained their identity.

In its essence, Am Yisrael is honest and pure; the chosen nation. The Egyptians made Am Yisrael into wicked people, and caused them to act in ways that were unbecoming of the Jewish humanity contained within them.

◂ Thus,

פסוק שלישי ממקרא ביכורים:

וַנִּצְעַק אֶל יְהֹוָה אֱלֹהֵי אֲבֹתֵינוּ, וַיִּשְׁמַע יְהֹוָה אֶת קֹלֵנוּ, וַיַּרְא אֶת עָנְיֵנוּ וְאֶת עֲמָלֵנוּ וְאֶת לַחֲצֵנוּ (דברים כו ז).

וַנִּצְעַק אֶל יְהֹוָה אֱלֹהֵי אֲבֹתֵינוּ - כְּמָה שֶׁנֶּאֱמַר: וַיְהִי בַיָּמִים הָרַבִּים הָהֵם, וַיָּמָת מֶלֶךְ מִצְרַיִם, וַיֵּאָנְחוּ בְנֵי יִשְׂרָאֵל מִן הָעֲבֹדָה וַיִּזְעָקוּ, וַתַּעַל שַׁוְעָתָם אֶל הָאֱלֹהִים מִן הָעֲבֹדָה (שמות ב׳, כג).

וַיִּשְׁמַע יְהֹוָה אֶת קֹלֵנוּ - כְּמָה שֶׁנֶּאֱמַר: וַיִּשְׁמַע אֱלֹהִים אֶת נַאֲקָתָם, וַיִּזְכֹּר אֱלֹהִים אֶת בְּרִיתוֹ אֶת אַבְרָהָם אֶת יִצְחָק וְאֶת יַעֲקֹב (שמות ב׳, כד).

Thus, upon being set free, Am Yisrael reverted to its natural purity, its morality, and its perfect humanity, which are the true characteristics of Am Yisrael.

The Sefat Emet (Exodus 5640, midrash) explains that the Exodus revealed the innate goodness of Am Yisrael:

Immediately after they left the oppression of Egypt, the goodness of their hearts came to the fore, and they immediately were transformed from showing concern only for bricks and mortar to being ready to receive the Torah. *That is clear evidence that, in the depths of their hearts, Bnei Yisrael were good!* ▪

Food For Thought

The third verse – the nation prays and God hears – did they cry out to God or cry out in pain?

To explain the words, "And we cried out to the Lord, the God of our fathers," the verse cited is, "And it came to pass during that long period that the king of Egypt died; and Bnei Yisrael groaned because of the servitude, *and they cried out.* And their cry for help from their servitude rose up to God." (Exodus 2:23)

What is meant by "and they cried out?" *Did they cry out to God as a prayer,*

◂ *or was*

The third verse of the first fruits declaration:

"AND WE CRIED OUT TO THE LORD, THE GOD OF OUR FATHERS, AND THE LORD HEARD OUR VOICE AND SAW OUR SUFFERING, OUR LABOR AND OUR OPPRESSION" (Deuteronomy 26:7).

"AND WE CRIED OUT TO THE LORD, THE GOD OF OUR FATHERS" – as it says: "And it came to pass during that long period that the king of Egypt died; and Bnei Yisrael groaned because of the servitude, and they cried out. And their cry for help from their servitude rose up to God" (Exodus 2:23).

"AND THE LORD HEARD OUR VOICE" – as it says: "And God heard their moaning, and God remembered His covenant with Abraham, Isaac, and Jacob" (Exodus 2:24).

---

or was it because of the anguish of slavery?

Seforno explains that they cried out in pain:

> And they cried out (*vayizaku*) – they cried out in pain from their labor, as in (Isaiah 14:31), "Wail, O city gate! Cry out (*za'aki*), O city."

This is also the explanation of Or HaChaim: they cried out like a person cries out when he is in pain. However, if that is the case, then the rest of the verse is not clear: "And their cry for help from their servitude rose up to God." After all, according to this interpretation, they did not pray.

Nevertheless, *the editor of the haggadah has a different explanation.* He quotes the verse from Exodus, "Bnei Yisrael groaned because of the servitude, and they cried out," as an explanation of that which the Torah states in Deuteronomy, "And we cried out to the Lord, the God of our fathers." In Deuteronomy, it is clearly a prayer to God; therefore, in Exodus it must also be a reference to prayer to God. It is possible that the editor of the haggadah learns this from the verse in Deuteronomy, as well as from the continuation of the verse in Exodus, "And their cry for help from their servitude rose up to God," which one would more logically be interpreted as a prayer to God (that is the way Ramban explains Exodus 2:25).

A third opinion may reconcile these two interpretations of the verse. Their

◂ cry

וַיַּרְא אֶת עָנְיֵנוּ - זוֹ פְּרִישׁוּת דֶּרֶךְ אֶרֶץ. כְּמָה שֶׁנֶּאֱמַר: וַיַּרְא אֱלֹהִים אֶת בְּנֵי יִשְׂרָאֵל, וַיֵּדַע אֱלֹהִים (שמות ב׳, כה).

וְאֶת עֲמָלֵנוּ - אֵלּוּ הַבָּנִים. כְּמָה שֶׁנֶּאֱמַר: כָּל הַבֵּן הַיִּלּוֹד הַיְאֹרָה תַּשְׁלִיכֻהוּ וְכָל הַבַּת תְּחַיּוּן (שמות א׳, כב).

וְאֶת לַחֲצֵנוּ - זֶה הַדְּחַק. כְּמָה שֶׁנֶּאֱמַר: וְגַם רָאִיתִי אֶת הַלַּחַץ אֲשֶׁר מִצְרַיִם לֹחֲצִים אֹתָם (שמות ג׳, ט).

---

cry was because of their pain, but *when a child cries out, he does so for his father to hear him!* The son does not always approach his father directly, and he does not always know how to do so. That is why *he cries out next to his father – he knows that his father will hear his cry and help him! Am Yisrael cried out in pain, but it was a cry to God!* It is possible that the very awareness of God's presence, the very ability to cry out with faith that God hears one's cries, is of great merit in itself. It might even be that the merit of this faith led to Israel being redeemed, even without any formal prayer: "And their cry for help from their servitude rose up to God, and God heard their moaning." ▪

Food For Thought

Why did they not listen to Moshe?

> Moshe spoke thus to Bnei Yisrael, but they did not hearken to Moshe because of shortness of breath and because of hard labor (Exodus 6:9).

Why did Bnei Yisrael not listen to Moshe? After all, did he not give them a message of encouragement, consolation, and redemption? Did Moshe not speak in the name of God, and make them lofty promises?

My teacher, Rav Aharon Lichtenstein, explained this matter.

The Torah seems to address this question, and describes the reason they didn't listen to Moshe: "because of shortness of breath and because of hard labor." However, this is still surprising. It is true that the nation found itself in very difficult straits, and therefore found it difficult to hear and understand a complicated message – but even so, wouldn't the promise of an

◂ end

"**AND SAW OUR SUFFERING**" – this refers to the separation of husband and wife, as it says: "God saw Bnei Yisrael and God took note" (Exodus 2:25).

"**OUR LABOR**" – these are the sons, as it says: "Every boy that is born, you shall throw into the river and every girl you shall keep alive" (Exodus 1:22).

"**AND OUR OPPRESSION**" – this refers to the pressure, as it says: "I have seen the oppression with which the Egyptians are oppressing them" (Exodus 3:9).

---

end to their suffering be eagerly welcomed?

There are two explanations:

a. The term "because of shortness of breath and because of hard labor" can be interpreted according to its simple meaning – weariness and mental distress because of the hard labor. However, it is possible to explain the words, "shortness of breath" in a different way. The nation was in a very depressed state, and it was therefore unable to hear promises such as "I will take you to Me as a people… I will bring you to the land." The nation would have been happy had it been told that it was to receive a week off from its hard work, or a certain lessening of its burdens. However, it was neither interested nor capable of comprehending the great promises made by Moshe.

b. It is possible that the nation was able to hear what Moshe had said, but not the timetable that he had set out. The people wanted immediate redemption, and were not interested in long-term solutions, in becoming a free nation, as long as they were still being whipped. Moshe' promise was for the future – "I will take you out… I will save you," and that was why the people found it so difficult to listen to him. Thousands of years have passed since that time, but there is still great significance to these words. It is important to recognize the difficulty in listening to ideological long-term messages when one is in a situation of "shortness of breath and hard labor." We strive to bring the message of redemption to the entire nation, and to live of spiritual significance, but for that we have to ensure that we do not reach a state of shortness of breath because of hard labor.

If a person is involved too deeply in material concerns, always concerned as to whether he can survive financially, and is enslaved to material things and money, he gradually loses his spiritual

◂ aspirations,

פסוק רביעי ממקרא ביכורים:

וַיּוֹצִאֵנוּ יְהֹוָה מִמִּצְרַיִם בְּיָד חֲזָקָה וּבִזְרֹעַ נְטוּיָה וּבְמֹרָא גָּדוֹל וּבְאֹתוֹת וּבְמֹפְתִים (דברים כ"ו, ח).

וַיּוֹצִאֵנוּ יְהֹוָה מִמִּצְרַיִם - לֹא עַל יְדֵי מַלְאָךְ וְלֹא עַל יְדֵי שָׂרָף וְלֹא עַל יְדֵי שָׁלִיחַ, אֶלָּא הַקָּדוֹשׁ בָּרוּךְ הוּא בִּכְבוֹדוֹ וּבְעַצְמוֹ. שֶׁנֶּאֱמַר: וְעָבַרְתִּי בְאֶרֶץ מִצְרַיִם בַּלַּיְלָה הַזֶּה וְהִכֵּיתִי כָל בְּכוֹר בְּאֶרֶץ מִצְרַיִם מֵאָדָם וְעַד בְּהֵמָה וּבְכָל אֱלֹהֵי מִצְרַיִם אֶעֱשֶׂה שְׁפָטִים אֲנִי יְהֹוָה (שמות י"ב, יב).

"וְעָבַרְתִּי בְאֶרֶץ מִצְרַיִם בַּלַּיְלָה הַזֶּה" אֲנִי וְלֹא מַלְאָךְ. "וְהִכֵּיתִי כָל בְּכוֹר בְּאֶרֶץ מִצְרַיִם" אֲנִי וְלֹא שָׂרָף. "וּבְכָל אֱלֹהֵי מִצְרַיִם אֶעֱשֶׂה שְׁפָטִים" אֲנִי וְלֹא הַשָּׁלִיחַ. "אֲנִי יְהֹוָה" אֲנִי הוּא וְלֹא אַחֵר.

---

aspirations, and even when lofty events occur around him, he remains apathetic. Such a person cannot receive and hear lofty and spiritual messages, and cannot live by their light.

We must free ourselves and our nation of the condition of shortness of breath – only by doing so, we can be worthy of hearing the sound of redemption in our generation, and can act to bring about the redemption soon. ▪

Food For Thought

The fourth verse – Exodus to freedom! Why not through an angel?

The editor of the haggadah stresses the fact that the redemption was carried out by God Himself. Why? If an agent could carry out the mission satisfactorily, why not use him? Why did God Himself have to take Bnei Yisrael out from Egypt?

The continuation of the passage answers this question: "And with great awe – this refers to the revelation of the Divine Presence."

◂ The

The fourth verse of the first fruits declaration:

"And the Lord took us out of Egypt with a strong hand and an outstretched arm, and with great awe, and with signs and wonders" (Deuteronomy 26:8).

"**AND THE LORD TOOK US OUT OF EGYPT**" – not through an angel, not through a seraph and not through a messenger. The Holy One, Blessed be He, did it in His glory by Himself. As it says: "In that night I will pass through the land of Egypt, and I will smite every firstborn in the land of Egypt, from man to beast, and I will carry out judgments against all the gods of Egypt, I am the Lord" (Exodus 12:12).

"In that night I will pass through the land of Egypt" – I and not an angel – "And I will smite every firstborn in the land of Egypt" – I and not a seraph – "And I will carry out judgments against all the gods of Egypt" – I and not a messenger – "I am the Lord" – it is I and no other.

The revelation of the Divine Presence was the true aim of the Exodus from Egypt, and that is why this was carried out by God Himself. The Exodus was not only an ex post facto rectification of the injustice of the enslavement of Am Yisrael. Its aim was not merely technical – to punish the Egyptians, and to take Israel out of Egypt. The aim was *to reveal God's glory in the world, to reveal the Divine Presence.*

When God's glory is revealed, it creates a new reality, introducing new ideas and new meaning to the world. Ever since, Israel and God have been linked. That was not simply the result of the redemption, but rather its intention. These matters are clarified in the sections in the Torah dealing with the Tabernacle (Exodus 29:45–46):

> I will dwell in the midst of Bnei Yisrael and I will be their God. They will know that I, the Lord, am their God, Who brought them out of the land of Egypt in order that I may dwell in their midst; I am the Lord, their God.

The Exodus from Egypt and the revelation of the Divine Providence created a new reality among Am Yisrael: *from then on, the Holy One, Blessed be He, dwells among them!* ▪

בְּיָד חֲזָקָה - זוֹ הַדֶּבֶר. כְּמָה שֶׁנֶּאֱמַר: הִנֵּה יַד יְהֹוָה הוֹיָה בְּמִקְנְךָ אֲשֶׁר בַּשָּׂדֶה בַּסּוּסִים בַּחֲמֹרִים בַּגְּמַלִּים בַּבָּקָר וּבַצֹּאן דֶּבֶר כָּבֵד מְאֹד (שמות ט׳, ג).

וּבִזְרֹעַ נְטוּיָה - זוֹ הַחֶרֶב. כְּמָה שֶׁנֶּאֱמַר: וְחַרְבּוֹ שְׁלוּפָה בְּיָדוֹ נְטוּיָה עַל יְרוּשָׁלָיִם (דברי הימים א כ״א, טז).

וּבְמֹרָא גָּדֹל - זוֹ גִּלּוּי שְׁכִינָה. כְּמָה שֶׁנֶּאֱמַר: אוֹ הֲנִסָּה אֱלֹהִים לָבוֹא לָקַחַת לוֹ גוֹי מִקֶּרֶב גּוֹי, בְּמַסֹּת בְּאֹתֹת וּבְמוֹפְתִים וּבְמִלְחָמָה, וּבְיָד חֲזָקָה וּבִזְרוֹעַ נְטוּיָה וּבְמוֹרָאִים גְּדֹלִים, כְּכֹל אֲשֶׁר עָשָׂה לָכֶם יְהֹוָה אֱלֹהֵיכֶם בְּמִצְרַיִם לְעֵינֶיךָ (דברים ד׳, לד).

וּבְאֹתוֹת - זֶה הַמַּטֶּה. כְּמָה שֶׁנֶּאֱמַר: וְאֶת הַמַּטֶּה הַזֶּה תִּקַּח בְּיָדֶךָ אֲשֶׁר תַּעֲשֶׂה בּוֹ אֶת הָאֹתֹת (שמות ד׳, יז).

Food For Thought

What blood?

"And wonders – this refers to the blood." What blood is this referring to?

1. This may refer to the plague of Blood (Shibolei HaLeket in his commentary on the haggadah 218). If that is the case, why specifically this plague? Blood may have been singled out because it was the first plague, or because the plague caused a change in nature itself (Maharal on the haggadah, in *Devar Negidim*).

2. This may refer to the miracle of the blood used by Moshe (*Orchot Chaim* 32, and *Kolbo* on the haggadah, 51). This places the explanation of "And wonders" as a continuation of "And with signs – this refers to the staff" (*Seder HaAruch* – Part III, p. 214 – quoted in the name of Gra, that the reference here is to two things: both to the plague of blood and the sign of blood, and that is why it is written in the plural as "wonders").

3. This may refer to the blood *on the doorposts, the blood that saved Am Yisrael during the plague of the firstborn.*

Based on this, it is worth examining

◂ *the*

"**WITH A STRONG HAND**" – this refers to the *dever* [pestilence] as it says: "The hand of the Lord will strike your livestock that are in the field – the horses, the donkeys, the camels, the oxen and the sheep – with a very severe pestilence" (Exodus 9:3).

"**AND AN OUTSTRETCHED ARM**" – this refers to the sword, as it says: "His sword was drawn in His hand, stretched out over Jerusalem" (1 Chronicles 21:16).

"**AND WITH GREAT AWE**" – this refers to the revelation of the Divine Presence, as it says: "Has God ever tried to take unto Himself a nation from the midst of another nation, with trials, signs and wonders, with war, with a mighty hand and an outstretched arm, and with awesome revelations, like all that the Lord your God did for you in Egypt before your eyes?" (Deuteronomy 4:34).

"**AND WITH SIGNS**" – this refers to the staff, as it says: "Take into your hand this staff with which you shall perform the signs" (Exodus 4:17).

---

the significance of the sign of the blood – does God really need a sign to know where Jews are? Similarly, why was the blood placed on the **inside** of the doorposts, where it could not be seen from the outside?

Mechilta (*d'Rabi Yishmael, Bo, Parashah* 7), states, "'The blood will be a sign for you' – it shall be a sign for you, but not for Me." In other words, this was not an external sign for others, but something needed by Am Yisrael. Why?

Mechilta continues:

Rabbi Yishmael would say: "Isn't everything revealed to Him?... Rather, it is a reward for performing this mitzvah that I am revealing Myself to you and having mercy on you.

The mitzvah of painting the blood and thus fulfilling God's word was meant to add to Am Yisrael's merits so that they would be worthy of being redeemed.

Placing the blood on the doorposts may also have been part of the offering

◂ *of the*

נוהגים להטיף מעט יין בשעה שאומרים דם ואש ותימרות עשן (סך הכל שלוש פעמים).
נוהגים להטיף באצבע (על פי הרמ"א דווקא באצבע. ויש הנוהגים בזרת, ויש הנוהגים בקמיצה),
ויש הנוהגים שלא להטיף באצבע אלא בהטיית הכוס (על פי האר"י).

וּבְמֹפְתִים - זֶה הַדָּם. כְּמָה שֶׁנֶּאֱמַר: וְנָתַתִּי מוֹפְתִים בַּשָּׁמַיִם וּבָאָרֶץ

דָּם וָאֵשׁ וְתִימְרוֹת עָשָׁן (יואל ג', ג).

דָּבָר אַחֵר: "בְּיָד חֲזָקָה" - שְׁתַּיִם. "וּבִזְרֹעַ נְטוּיָה" - שְׁתַּיִם. "וּבְמֹרָא גָּדֹל" - שְׁתַּיִם. "וּבְאֹתוֹת" - שְׁתַּיִם. "וּבְמֹפְתִים" - שְׁתַּיִם.

The verse begins by mentioning the plagues that were inflicted upon Egypt – "with a strong hand and an outstretched arm" (pestilence and sword); follows with the special revelation of the Divine Presence in Egypt ("and with great awe") and the signs that Moshe showed to Am Yisrael and to Pharaoh; and finally, it speaks of the sprinkling of blood on the doorposts as a sign and symbol for rescuing Israel, which created a very special bond between Am Yisrael and God.

Why couldn't they have had only a single plague – blood?

At first glance, it appears that Moshe could have limited the number of plagues to just one. Had Moshe said to Pharaoh: "Until Bnei Yisrael are freed, I

◂ will

of the sacrifice. The Pesach sacrifice was eaten by Am Yisrael, while the blood on the doorpost expressed the actual offering, the act of serving God.

Offering the Pesach sacrifice involved a great deal of danger, because they were slaughtering a lamb, one of the Egyptian gods. The offering of the Pesach sacrifice was an expression of *complete severance from Egypt and its gods, while simultaneously declaring their loyalty to God, who saved them. Placing the blood on the doorposts was a way for Am Yisrael to perform an act that expressed their desire to be liberated from their idolatrous Egyptian society.*

Am Yisrael was not saved because *God saw the blood and knew whom not to harm. It was saved because God saw that Israel was now serving Him and had abandoned idolatry.*

It is customary to spill a small amount of wine when saying "Blood, fire and columns of smoke" (a total of three times). It is customary to use a finger (according to Rama, specifically the forefinger. Others use the little finger or the ring finger), and some have the custom of not using any finger but by tipping the cup (according to Ari).

"AND WONDERS" – this refers to the blood, as it says: "And I shall show wonders in the heavens and on the earth

BLOOD, FIRE AND
COLUMNS OF SMOKE" (Joel 3:3).

Another interpretation: "WITH A STRONG HAND" – two plagues. "AND AN OUTSTRETCHED ARM" – two. "AND WITH GREAT AWE" – two. "AND WITH SIGNS" – two. "AND WONDERS" – two.

---

will not take away this plague," there is no doubt that, in the end, Pharaoh would have broken down and let them go. Why, then, did they need all ten plagues?

According to the text, even when the water had been turned to blood, the Egyptians still had access to water, even though it was not from the river (Exodus 7:24, and see Ibn Ezra): "All the Egyptians dug around the Nile for water to drink because they could not drink from the water of the Nile." However, this could not have lasted for long, as the Nile is the primary source of water for Egypt. Furthermore, according to an interpretation of the Sages (also based on the simple meaning of the verse in Exodus 7:19), whatever water there was turned into blood, even water within the houses: "Throughout the land of Egypt – even in the bathhouses and baths in the homes" (Rashi 7:19). Why, then, did they need more than a single plague?

The answer is that *the plagues had symbolic significance in themselves,* beyond their use as a tool to coerce Pharaoh to free Am Yisrael. If we study the verses, we will see that the Torah repeats time and time again the idea

◂ of "in

Spice box, silver, filigree
The Wolfson Museum, Hechal Shlomo, Max Grundt Collection

אֵלּוּ עֶשֶׂר מַכּוֹת שֶׁהֵבִיא הַקָּדוֹשׁ בָּרוּךְ הוּא עַל הַמִּצְרִים בְּמִצְרַיִם, וְאֵלּוּ הֵן:

נוהגים להטיף מעט יין בכל אחת מעשר המכות.

דָּם. צְפַרְדֵּעַ. כִּנִּים. עָרוֹב. דֶּבֶר. שְׁחִין. בָּרָד. אַרְבֶּה. חֹשֶׁךְ. מַכַּת בְּכוֹרוֹת.

---

of "in order that you shall know that I am the Lord in the midst of the earth" (Exodus 8:18). The aim of the plagues was to show that God rules the world. The plagues were meant not only for Pharaoh's punishment, and not only in order to free Am Yisrael, *but in order to reveal God's presence to the world.*

It is possible that there is further significance to the plagues of Egypt, which we will see when dealing with another question. The Torah describes how God hardened Pharaoh's heart. If Pharaoh's heart was hardened, why was he punished when he could not stop himself from sinning? (We will address this at length on p. 97.)

These questions may be connected. It is possible that God did not actively harden Pharaoh's heart, but gave him the *feeling that he would be able to oppose God.* This feeling of Pharaoh's was tested in the ten plagues that were inflicted on Egypt. God brought the plague of blood. As a result, Pharaoh promised to free Am Yisrael, and the plague came to an end. Pharaoh then reneged on his promise, feeling that he was able to act against God and to mock Him. This may be what it means when we are told his heart was hardened: He gave Pharaoh *the feeling that he was in control of the situation.* That is why ten plagues were needed. Morally, there was no problem of punishing Pharaoh, because God had not prevented Pharaoh from repenting, but had only created a situation that enabled him to feel as if he could mock God (for more on this topic, see Abarbanel Exodus 7:3; *Sefer HaIkarim*, fourth *ma'amar*, 25; also heard from Rav Yaakov Medan).

In our lives, we often fail to see God's control of the world. If we had the ability to see how God punishes every sin or rewards every good deed, we would not have free will – we would be forced to obey God's will. God gives us the possibility of acting according to our own desires, but we must be wary not to harden our own hearts. We must always remember that God is always in control of every situation, no matter how much power we may feel. We are

◂ given

THESE ARE THE TEN PLAGUES THAT the Holy One, Blessed be He, brought upon the Egyptians in Egypt, and they are as follows:

As each of the plagues is mentioned, it is customary to remove a drop of wine from the cup.

BLOOD. FROGS. LICE. WILD BEASTS. PESTILENCE. BOILS. HAIL. LOCUSTS. DARKNESS. SLAYING OF THE FIRSTBORN.

A lock and key from an ark in which a Torah scroll was kept, Slovakia, 18th century, iron
The Wolfson Museum, Hechal Shlomo

given freedom of choice for us to recognize that our freedom is to do what God wants in the world.

The significance of the ten plagues

As we saw, the significance of the ten plagues was *to reveal God's presence in the world.* Ramban (Exodus 13:16), discusses this at length, and *determines important principles regarding faith,* and it is therefore advisable for everyone to learn it from time to time. (The passage may be too long for the Seder night, but is most appropriate for the family to learn it the next day.) in brief, the main points of his words:

Ramban says that there are *many types of heretics:* there are those who think that God did not create the world; and those who believe that He did create it, but do not believe in Divine Providence, namely that He still intervenes in the world. In addition, there is a third type – people who do not believe that God has absolute power, that He is able to change nature. The miracles of Egypt were meant to teach all these types of heretics that God is in the world, and that He observes, knows, and acts as He wishes. Beyond that, the plagues of Egypt were also meant to teach heretics of future generations, because God will not perform new miracles for each individual heretic. That is

◂ why

נוהגים להטיף מעט יין כשאומרים דצ"ך, עד"ש באח"ב (סך הכל שלוש פעמים).

רַבִּי יְהוּדָה הָיָה נוֹתֵן בָּהֶם סִימָנִים:

דְּצַ"ךְ: עֲדַ"שׁ בְּאַחַ"ב.

why the memory of the Exodus from Egypt is emphasized, with so many mitzvot that serve as "a remembrance of the Exodus from Egypt."

From these open miracles, we can learn about the hidden miracles that God performs for us every hour of every day, and learn to recognize God's control of every single detail of our lives.

In order to understand the division of the plagues, and how they contradict all the beliefs of the different types of heretics, see the next section: DeTzaCh, ADaSh, BeAChaV. ▪

Halachic Summary

Rama writes (473:7) in the name of Maharil that it is customary to spill wine from the cup with one's finger sixteen times: for the words, "Blood, fire and columns of smoke" (three spills), for each of the ten plagues (another ten spills), and for "*DeTzach, ADaSh, BeAChaV*" (the last three spills).

> It is customary to spill a little from the cup when one reaches "Blood, fire and columns of smoke," and so too when one mentions the ten plagues, and with "*DeTzaCh, ADaSh, BeAChaV*" – a total of 16 times.

Why is the wine spilled?

Maharil (on the haggadah, in the name of Ra'avyah) writes:

> This was what Ra'avyah did. It appears to him that the reason [for doing so] is that we ask to be saved from all of these [plagues] and that they should befall our enemies, for the cups are for the welfare of Israel.

In other words, spilling the wine represents a hope that *these plagues will strike our enemies and not Am Yisrael.* How does spilling the wine symbolize this? Many explanations, all logical and acceptable, have been given for this, but it seems that the simple meaning is that as we spill each drop, representing another plague, we are removing the plagues from the cup and drinking the wine without them.

◂ How

It is customary to spill a small amount of wine when saying *DeTzaCh, ADaSh, BeAChaV* (a total of three times).

Rabbi Yehudah abbreviated them by their initials:

DETZACH, ADASH, BE'ACHAV.

How does one spill the wine? A number of the rabbinic decisors write that one removes the wine *with a finger.* That is what Maharil writes (without specifying which finger). Ra'avyah (quoted in Hagahot HaMinhagim Rav E. Tirna, 98), writes that one uses the little finger. Rama (*ibid.*, and in *Darkei Moshe*), writes that one uses the forefinger and not the little finger, because the Torah states, "it is the forefinger of God." Magen Avraham (473:28) writes that one uses the ring finger. Mishnah Berurah (in *Sha'ar Tziyon ibid.*, subsection 81) writes that one who is fastidious about hygiene, and cannot drink wine if a finger was dipped in it, can spill the wine out of the cup.

Seder plate, United States, 1979, porcelain
The Wolfson Museum, Hechal Shlomo

According to Ari there are those who do not use their finger to spill the wine, but *tilt the cup* (*Kaf HaChaim* 473; one opinion in *Shulchan Aruch HaRav,* subsection 51; *Likutei Maha-ri'ach* III, on the haggadah, in the name of Gra). The reason, evidently, is so the wine on the finger does not mix with the wine in the cup.

Wine of the Shemitah year – If one has Israeli wine of the shemitah (sabbatical) year, it has special sanctity, and one may not spill any of it (Rav Avraham Yitzchak Kook in *Olat Re'iyah,* II, p. 40 – see the discussion in my book, Halachah MiMekorah – Shemitah). ▪

חוזרים וממלאים את הכוסות.

רַבִּי יוֹסֵי הַגְּלִילִי אוֹמֵר: מִנַּיִן אַתָּה אוֹמֵר שֶׁלָּקוּ הַמִּצְרִים בְּמִצְרַיִם עֶשֶׂר מַכּוֹת וְעַל הַיָּם לָקוּ חֲמִשִּׁים מַכּוֹת, בְּמִצְרַיִם מַה הוּא אוֹמֵר: וַיֹּאמְרוּ הַחַרְטֻמִּם אֶל פַּרְעֹה אֶצְבַּע אֱלֹהִים הִיא (שמות ח׳, טו), **וְעַל הַיָּם מַה הוּא אוֹמֵר: וַיַּרְא יִשְׂרָאֵל אֶת הַיָּד הַגְּדֹלָה אֲשֶׁר עָשָׂה יְהֹוָה בְּמִצְרַיִם, וַיִּירְאוּ הָעָם אֶת יְהֹוָה, וַיַּאֲמִינוּ בַּיהֹוָה וּבְמשֶׁה עַבְדּוֹ** (שמות י״ד, לא). **כַּמָּה לָקוּ בְּאֶצְבַּע - עֶשֶׂר מַכּוֹת. אֱמוֹר מֵעַתָּה: בְּמִצְרַיִם לָקוּ עֶשֶׂר מַכּוֹת, וְעַל הַיָּם לָקוּ חֲמִשִּׁים מַכּוֹת.**

Food For Thought

The plagues are divided into groups based on the different levels of God's supervision in the world:

1. *The first group: blood, frogs, lice – an assault on the source of power and the source of Egypt's god to cause recognition of the existence of God:*

An assault on the river (blood, frogs), which was not only affected, but became repulsive.

An assault on the necromancers, who were affected by the lice and were forced to admit that "it is the finger of God."

An assault on the gods, the gods of Egypt, which were also affected by the lice ("the lice were upon man and beast").

An assault on Pharaoh: According to the Sages, these plagues were also an assault specifically on *Pharaoh's* honor because he believed that he, himself, was a god – "My river is my own, and I made myself" (Ezekial 29:3). The Sages say that he would use the river very early each morning as his toilet, so that he would be able to claim that he, unlike mere mortals, had no bodily needs (*Rashi* 7:15). When Moshe came to him early in the morning, he showed Pharaoh that he knew that Pharaoh was not a god! (This was repeated in the first plague of each of the groups. The emphasis that Pharaoh was not a god was of the utmost importance).

The goal of the first three plagues was to show the heretics of the world *that God exists in the world and that*

◂ *their*

The wine cups are refilled.

RABBI YOSSI THE GALILEAN SAID: HOW do you know that the Egyptians were struck by ten plagues in Egypt and then were struck by fifty plagues at the sea? Concerning the plagues in Egypt, what does it say? "The sorcerers said to Pharaoh, 'It is the finger of the Lord'" (Exodus 8:15). But of the events at the sea, it says, "Israel saw the great hand that the Lord laid against Egypt; and the people feared the Lord, and they believed in the Lord and in His servant Moshe" (Exodus 14:31). How many plagues did the Egyptians receive from one finger? Ten. From here we can conclude that if they suffered ten plagues in Egypt, at the sea they suffered fifty plagues.

---

their gods were not God. This is consistent with the theme of the first group of plagues: "that I am the Lord" – the recognition of the sovereignty of God!

2. *The second group: wild beasts, pestilence, boils – a display of God's direct involvement in supervising the world:*

In this group, Pharaoh was told in advance (in the first two plagues of the group) *that God would set Israel apart from the Egyptians.* This shows the degree of *God's supervision of the world – not only that God exists, but that He intervenes in what is happening in the world and decides who will be harmed by plagues and who will not.*

This was expressed in the fact that Moshe declared that each of these two plagues would come the next day: "*tomorrow* there will be this sign" (8:19), "*tomorrow* the Lord will do this plague to the land" (9:5). The fact that Moshe set a date proved that it was an action by God and that He acts in and supervises what happens in the world.

It is true that in the case of the *boils* there was no prior warning, but on the other hand, this is the only plague that specifically states that the necromancers were afflicted, while Moshe stood by them and was not harmed: "And the necromancers could not stand before Moshe because of the boils, for the boils were upon the necromancers and upon all Egypt" (9:11). (We are also told that in the case of the hail and darkness, there was a differentiation between the Egyptians and Am Yisrael, but inboth cases it does not state that Pharaoh knew about this in advance).

This group of plagues was directed against the heretics who believed that God exists and that He created the world, but did not believe that

◂ He *actively*

רַבִּי אֱלִיעֶזֶר אוֹמֵר: מִנַּיִן שֶׁכָּל מַכָּה וּמַכָּה שֶׁהֵבִיא הַקָּדוֹשׁ בָּרוּךְ הוּא עַל הַמִּצְרִים בְּמִצְרַיִם הָיְתָה שֶׁל אַרְבַּע מַכּוֹת, שֶׁנֶּאֱמַר: יְשַׁלַּח בָּם חֲרוֹן אַפּוֹ עֶבְרָה וָזַעַם וְצָרָה מִשְׁלַחַת מַלְאֲכֵי רָעִים (תהלים ע"ח, מט). "עֶבְרָה" - אַחַת, "וָזַעַם" - שְׁתַּיִם, "וְצָרָה" - שָׁלֹשׁ, "מִשְׁלַחַת מַלְאֲכֵי רָעִים" - אַרְבַּע. אֱמוֹר מֵעַתָּה: בְּמִצְרַיִם לָקוּ אַרְבָּעִים מַכּוֹת, וְעַל הַיָּם לָקוּ מָאתַיִם מַכּוֹת.

He *actively intervenes.* This is in accordancc with *the theme of these three plagues* – "that I am the Lord *in the midst of the earth!*"

3. *The third group: hail, locusts, darkness – a proof that God's power is unlimited:*

Regarding the first two plagues of this group (hail and locusts), it is emphasized that plagues such as these *had never been seen in Egypt since its founding and would never again recur.* Beyond that, the hail totally defied nature – fire and water mixed together: "There was hail, and fire flaming within the hail" (9:24). Similarly, the plague of darkness, according to the Sages (and this appears to be the simple meaning of the text), was not simply an absence of light, but a darkness that was tangible: "There was *thick* darkness" (10:22), and that was why "no one rose from his place for three days" (10:23). These plagues were not merely extreme examples of known phenomena, like the other plagues, *but there was a substantive change in the rules of nature, conditions that had never occurred before and have never occurred since!*

That is why Pharaoh's servants and the nation of Egypt recognized God's power: in the plague of hail only some of them recognized it – "He who feared the word of the Lord of Pharaoh's servants" – while with the locusts everyone already said, "Don't you yet know that Egypt is lost?" After the plague of darkness, all knew that "the man Moshe was highly esteemed in the eyes of Pharaoh's servants and in the eyes of the people." The entire country was in panic because of the supernatural plagues they had suffered (everyone, that is, except for Pharaoh, who would acknowledge this only at the end).

This group of plagues was aimed at those heretics who felt that even though God does supervise the world, He is not all-powerful. These plagues showed that God is capable of acting without any constraints, even in ways that are against nature. This is consistent with

◄ "in

RABBI ELIEZER SAID: HOW DO WE KNOW that each individual plague that the Holy One, Blessed be He, brought upon the Egyptians in Egypt consisted of four plagues? For it says: "He sent upon them His fierce anger: wrath, fury, trouble, and a team of hostile angels" (Psalms 78:49). "Wrath" is one, "fury" is two, "trouble" is three, and "a team of hostile angels" is four. From here we can conclude that in Egypt they were struck by forty plagues, and at the sea they were struck by 200 plagues.

"in order that you know that *there is none like Me* in the entire earth."

This is the aim of the Seder night. The Seder night is the time when we testify to these miracles, a night of strengthening our faith in God, a night in which we all must internalize the great power of God in the world, His supervision of the world and His special love for Am Yisrael. This is a night of faith, which leads to and transforms the night into one of thanks.

Why did God harden Pharaoh's heart?

The Torah tells us that God hardened Pharaoh's heart and did not enable him to repent. How could that be? If Pharaoh had wanted to repent, why would God not have allowed him to do so?

1. Rambam (*Hilchot Teshuvah* 6:3) answers as follows:

> A person might commit a terrible sin or many sins until he is finally punished… by being prevented from repenting and not being given permission to return from his wickedness, so that when he dies he will die with that sin which he committed… Therefore, it states in the Torah that "I will harden Pharaoh's heart," as he at first sinned himself by harming Israel who lived in his land, as it states, "let us deal shrewdly with them." God's justice thus prevented him from repenting.

In other words, according to Rambam, Pharaoh was so evil a person that the punishment that God gave him was that he would be unable to repent.

We can still ask about what Rambam said – why, then, did God send Moshe to Pharaoh, for in any event He would not allow Pharaoh to repent and rectify his actions?

Rambam (*ibid.*) asks this same question himself and answers it:

> Why did [God] send him Moshe and tell him, "send [them] and repent?"… This was to tell everyone that when God prevents a person

◂ from

רַבִּי עֲקִיבָא אוֹמֵר: מִנַּיִן שֶׁכָּל מַכָּה וּמַכָּה שֶׁהֵבִיא הַקָּדוֹשׁ בָּרוּךְ הוּא עַל הַמִּצְרִים בְּמִצְרַיִם הָיְתָה שֶׁל חָמֵשׁ מַכּוֹת, שֶׁנֶּאֱמַר: יְשַׁלַּח בָּם חֲרוֹן אַפּוֹ עֶבְרָה וָזַעַם וְצָרָה מִשְׁלַחַת מַלְאֲכֵי רָעִים (תהלים ע"ח, מט). "חֲרוֹן אַפּוֹ" - אַחַת, "עֶבְרָה" - שְׁתַּיִם, "וָזַעַם" - שָׁלֹשׁ, "וְצָרָה" - אַרְבַּע, "מִשְׁלַחַת מַלְאֲכֵי רָעִים" - חָמֵשׁ. אֱמוֹר מֵעַתָּה: בְּמִצְרַיִם לָקוּ חֲמִשִּׁים מַכּוֹת, וְעַל הַיָּם לָקוּ חֲמִשִּׁים וּמָאתַיִם מַכּוֹת.

from repenting, he cannot repent and will die a sinner.

In other words, Moshe was sent to Pharaoh so that the entire world would learn that if a person is a great sinner, God will not enable him to repent.

This approach of Rambam was not unequivocally accepted. Akeidah, Rabbi Isaac Aramah, was not willing to accept Rambam's statement. According to him, every person can repent, and God does not prevent anyone from doing so. He bases himself on a verse in Ezekial (18:32):

> For I do not desire the death of one who dies, says the Lord, God, so turn away and live!

In other words, God wants every person to repent!

2. Ramban (Exodus 7:3) explains that in the first five plagues, Pharaoh himself hardened his heart. Consequently, as he had chosen this evil path, God hardened his heart in the other plagues (see the table: at first, God did not harden his heart, and only did so for the plagues of boils, locusts, darkness, and the slaying of the firstborn). Again, according to this approach, God did not allow him to repent, as Rambam writes.

3. *Meshech Chochmah* (Exodus 3:19) explains that every normal person has an internal good side, even when he sins. There are situations where the Talmud states that "one forces him until he says, 'I assent'" (*Kiddushin* 50a), and Rambam explains (*Hilchot Gerushin* 2:20) that this is valid because his heart is presumably intent on doing what is proper. However, Pharaoh had proven in the first five plagues that his heart was evil, for in spite of the plagues he did not rectify himself. Thus he proved that there was no hope for him to repent, and that was why God hardened his heart in the other plagues

◂ to withstand

RABBI AKIVA SAID: HOW DO WE KNOW that each individual plague that the Holy One, Blessed be He, brought upon the Egyptians in Egypt consisted of five plagues? For it says: "He sent upon them His fierce anger: wrath, fury, trouble, and a team of hostile angels" (Psalms 78:49). "Fierce anger" is one, "wrath" is two, "fury" is three, "trouble" is four and "a team of hostile angels" is five. From here we can conclude that in Egypt they were struck by 50 plagues, and at the sea they were struck by 250 plagues.

to withstand them, thereby to cause a sanctification of God's name. In other words, the hardening of his heart was not so that he would not be able to repent, but so that he could withstand the pain of the other plagues (as his heart was evil, he would not repent regardless. This is evidently one of the interpretations of Akeidah).

4. Maharal of Prague (*Gevurot Hashem*, 31) explains the hardening of the heart differently. Pharaoh denied the existence of God and, therefore, refused to listen to Him (Exodus 5:2):

> And Pharaoh said, "Who is the Lord that I should heed His voice to let Israel out? I do not know the Lord, neither will I let Israel out."

Pharaoh's punishment for his great audacity and for his claim that he didn't recognize the existence of God was that he would be smitten with many plagues, until the entire world would know that there is God in the world! Pharaoh

◄ caused

Riddles

42. Where does the interpretation of the fourth verse, "he took us out," end?
43. One man had a body part that was hard. Which person and which part?

Topics for Discussion

l. Why did God Himself punish the Egyptians and take Am Yisrael out of Egypt? Why was it so important as to be done by "I, and not an angel?"

m. Why was there a need for ten plagues? Why could one not have been enough, provided that it remained in place until Pharaoh conceded and freed Am Yisrael? There is no doubt that Pharaoh would eventually have given in.

n. Why did God harden Pharaoh's heart? Was it fair to harden his heart and then to punish him for this?

Riddles

The riddles below relate to the plagues in Egypt. The solutions to some of these riddles can be found in the parashiyot of Va'era and Bo, which are at the end of the haggadah, p. 270. There you will find the text divided according to the plagues.

44. What were the plagues in Egypt? Explain exactly what happened during each plague.

45. "They gathered them into many heaps" – which plague is referred to? What exactly does the verse mean?

46. Which plagues are mentioned in Parashat Va'era and which ones in Parashat Bo? How can one remember this?

47. What plague, besides the ninth one, had darkness?

48. Why didn't Pharaoh die in any of the plagues in Egypt? (Hint: see Exodus 9:14–16).

49. Which plague is still around today, mainly affecting children (though not as badly, we hope!)?

50. Which plagues were given directly by God?

51. About which plagues does it say that there had never been any like it or would be thereafter?

52. Where else does the Torah mention "heaps?"

53. Which plagues came without any warning? What do these plagues have in common?

54. Which plague is referred to as "death?"

55. What plague mentions that it was "thick?" How do the Sages explain this?

56. In which plague were the hearts of Pharaoh's servants also hardened?

57. There were three miracles that Pharaoh's necromancers were able to duplicate (to a certain extent). Name them. (Hint: two are in Chapter 7 and one is in Chapter 8).

58. In three cases, the necromancers of Pharaoh saw that they were unable to do what Moshe and Aaron had done. Name them. (Hint: Exodus 7:12; 8:14; 9:11).

59. Four times Pharaoh asked Moshe to pray on his behalf. About which plagues were these prayers? Hint: "entreat" means to pray in this context. In two of these cases Pharaoh said, "I have sinned." In which?

60. What did Am Yisrael smear on the doorposts and on the lintels (the wood on the top of the doorposts)?

61. Which nation was affected by Pharaoh's hardening of his heart? (Hint: this appears in Samuel 1).

62. Who was affected by the plague of the firstborn, besides the firstborns themselves?

63. In two places, the Torah states that they "obscured the view of the earth?" Where and about whom is this statement? (Hint: once in regard to Egypt, and once in Numbers).

64. Which plague affected only animals and not people? Why? (Hint: Exodus 9:15–16).

65. When did Pharaoh say to Moshe that if Moshe would come one more time to see him, he would kill Moshe? Did Moshe see Pharaoh after that time?

66. There are two miracles related to the miracles in Egypt about which we are told that a very strong wind blew. Which are they?

67. The Torah states specifically that there were five plagues that did not affect Am Yisrael. Which were they?

68. What was affected by the plague of hail that had not been affected until then? What was not affected by the plague of hail but was affected by the plague of locusts?

69. The Torah says about the locusts, "They alighted within all the border[s] of Egypt, very severe; before them, there was never such a locust [plague], and after it, there will never be one like it." Look at Joel 2:2, and find what appears to be a contradiction to this. In order to attempt to answer this, see Rashi on Exodus 10:14; he answers the seeming contradiction based on Joel 1:4.

Activity

One can make a family game about the ten plagues as we did with the people in the haggadah – see above, p. 61. Before the festival, prepare as many crowns as you need and attach paper clips to them. Write the names of the plagues on pieces of paper. Place crowns on everyone's heads and attach one of the slips of paper with the name of a plague, so that everyone can see that name except the person whose crown it is.

Each participant, in turn, can ask a single yes/no question. The winner is the first person to guess what plague is on his crown.

One can also use different concepts related to the haggadah, such as the names of foods related to the festival, etc.

כַּמָּה מַעֲלוֹת טוֹבוֹת לַמָּקוֹם עָלֵינוּ.

אִלּוּ הוֹצִיאָנוּ מִמִּצְרַיִם וְלֹא עָשָׂה בָהֶם שְׁפָטִים דַּיֵּנוּ.
אִלּוּ עָשָׂה בָהֶם שְׁפָטִים וְלֹא עָשָׂה בֵאלֹהֵיהֶם דַּיֵּנוּ.
אִלּוּ עָשָׂה בֵאלֹהֵיהֶם וְלֹא הָרַג אֶת בְּכוֹרֵיהֶם דַּיֵּנוּ.
אִלּוּ הָרַג אֶת בְּכוֹרֵיהֶם וְלֹא נָתַן לָנוּ אֶת מָמוֹנָם דַּיֵּנוּ.

---

caused a desecration of God's name in the world, and God therefore hardened his heart, so as to make a great sanctification of His name in the world.

Fifty, two hundred, two hundred and fifty – why is this important?

Why is it important for us to know how many plagues there were in Egypt? What is the purpose of increasing the number of plagues that there were in Egypt?

Gra (*Kol Eliyahu* p. 91) explains that the Torah states, "all the sicknesses that I have visited upon Egypt I will not visit upon you" (Exodus 15:26) – it is important for us to multiply the number of plagues in Egypt because we know that these will not strike Am Yisrael.

One can explain that the plagues in Egypt teach us *about the struggle of God with the evil in the world.* The more plagues the Egyptians received, the greater God sanctified Himself in the world through the Exodus. *The greater number of plagues indicates a greater rectification in the world*, as the verse states, "and all evil will disappear as smoke."

I heard another explanation from my father-in-law and teacher, Rav Blumenzweig, which requires a brief introduction in order to be fully understood:

In some of the plagues, it states clearly that Am Yisrael would not be affected, but it is not clear that this was the case with all the plagues. Ibn Ezra holds that if it does not say specifically that Am Yisrael was not affected, they too were afflicted by that plague (because these were not dangerous plagues, and when they left Egypt they were cured). Ramban, though, holds that none of the plagues affected Am Yisrael. The reason the Torah mentioned specifically in the case of the plagues of wild beasts and pestilence that Am Yisrael was not affected was that these were plagues that were not restricted to a specific area. Therefore, the Torah needed to stress that Am Yisrael was not harmed by them (one can, though, question whether the plague of frogs was such a plague, and there the Torah does not mention that Am Yisrael

◄ was

SO MANY levels of favors has God bestowed upon us:

Had He brought us out from Egypt,
and not executed judgment against the Egyptians,
IT WOULD HAVE BEEN ENOUGH FOR US!

Had He executed judgment against them,
and not against their gods,
IT WOULD HAVE BEEN ENOUGH FOR US!

Had He executed judgment against their gods,
and not slain their firstborn,
IT WOULD HAVE BEEN ENOUGH FOR US!

Had He slain their firstborn, and not given us their wealth,
IT WOULD HAVE BEEN ENOUGH FOR US!

---

was not harmed. On the other hand, in the case of the hail, which was not a "mobile" plague, the Torah nevertheless stresses that Am Yisrael was not harmed).

If we look at it simply, and certainly from the haggadah, *Am Yisrael was not harmed at all*, and all the plagues affected only the Egyptians. This can be seen in the verse that states, "in order that you shall know that the Lord will separate between the Egyptians and between Israel" (Exodus 11:7 – in regard to the plague of the firstborn), and "I will make a redemption between My people and your people" (Exodus 8:19 – the plague of wild beasts), which refers to all the plagues.

The plagues clarified the difference between Am Yisrael and Egypt. Every plague that God inflicted on Egypt helped to uproot evil from the world and also showed *God's love of Am Yisrael. The more we stress the larger number of plagues that were inflicted on Egypt, the more we emphasize how much God preserves us, looks after us, and loves us.*

If that is the case, multiplying the number of plagues was not to add plagues to Egypt, but to heighten awareness of *the special love between God and Am Yisrael, who were not harmed by the plagues: "Blessed are You, Our Lord, who loves His nation, Israel!"*

Why doesn't Moshe appear in the haggadah?

An important point, which sometimes goes unnoticed, is the fact that *Moshe does not appear in the haggadah* (except for one time, incidentally: "Rabbi Yossi the Galilean said… they believed in the Lord and in His servant Moshe")! Why is this?

◂

אִלּוּ נָתַן לָנוּ אֶת מָמוֹנָם וְלֹא קָרַע לָנוּ אֶת הַיָּם דַּיֵּנוּ.

אִלּוּ קָרַע לָנוּ אֶת הַיָּם וְלֹא הֶעֱבִירָנוּ בְתוֹכוֹ בֶּחָרָבָה דַּיֵּנוּ.

אִלּוּ הֶעֱבִירָנוּ בְתוֹכוֹ בֶּחָרָבָה וְלֹא שִׁקַּע צָרֵינוּ בְּתוֹכוֹ דַּיֵּנוּ.

אִלּוּ שִׁקַּע צָרֵינוּ בְּתוֹכוֹ

וְלֹא סִפֵּק צָרְכֵּנוּ בַּמִּדְבָּר אַרְבָּעִים שָׁנָה דַּיֵּנוּ.

---

is this? After all, Moshe was the one who led the entire redemption process in Egypt!

Many commentators deal with this question. Some explain that the editor of the haggadah wanted to stress that the redemption came entirely through God – "I and not a messenger." That was why the last plague, death of the firstborns, was executed by God alone (Gra).

Rav Yosef Dov Soloveitchik (in An Exalted Evening: The Seder night by Rabbi Genack) explains beautifully that even Moshe was not included in the haggadah to show that all are equal this night before God:

> *On that night, which is surrounded by mystery, God appeared, garbed in majesty and splendor, before the entire community. All, the greatest scholar and the weak-minded individual, king and slave, rich man and poor man, noble and common man – all saw God and all stood in His presence.*

The emphasis on the equality of the entire Nation of Israel expresses the might of God's revelation during the Exodus from Egypt. Life creates differences and different classes among people. However, when God reveals Himself and appears, all such differences are erased – all are equal before Him. We have to learn how to maintain this feeling throughout the rest of the year, to remember that all differences between us pale when we stand before our Creator.

"Had He given us their wealth" – extracting the sparks of holiness

"Each woman shall borrow from her neighbor and from the dweller in her house silver and gold objects and garments" (Exodus 3:22). I heard from Rav Yehuda Amital, of blessed memory, in the name of Ari, that the inner significance of taking these silver and gold objects from Egypt was to take the sparks of holiness out of Egypt.

Egypt's culture was corrupt and oppressive. However, even in Egypt there were good things. Nothing that God created in His world was created in vain. Each has a spark of holiness. It is the mission of Am Yisrael to search

◄ for

Had He given us their wealth, and not split the sea for us,
IT WOULD HAVE BEEN ENOUGH FOR US!
Had He split the sea for us, and not led us through it on dry land,
IT WOULD HAVE BEEN ENOUGH FOR US!
Had He led us through it on dry land,
and not drowned our tormentors in it,
IT WOULD HAVE BEEN ENOUGH FOR US!
Had He drowned our tormentors in it,
and not provided for our needs in the desert for forty years,
IT WOULD HAVE BEEN ENOUGH FOR US!

---

for the good in every place in the world, and *to find the sparks of holiness from every place.*

This explains why the Egyptians chased Bnei Yisrael to the sea. When the Egyptians were in Egypt, even though there was a tremendous amount of spiritual impurity and corruption there, there were still some good points in the country, and it was these that enabled the country to survive.

When Am Yisrael took out these sparks of holiness from Egypt, they took out all the good in the country, leaving Egypt totally empty of the inner goodness that had sustained their empire. There was no vitality left in the country, and the Egyptians died at the seashore.

One must find the sparks of holiness in every place where they are to be found. One must believe that in every object, in every person, and in every situation – however lowly it may seem – there is inner good, holiness a person must search for and find. One must be careful not to remove sparks of holiness along with the sparks of impurity. One must learn to find the balance between keeping one's distance, being careful to keep away from the impure, and the belief that good exists in everything.

Had He split the sea for us, and not led us through it on dry land, would it have been enough for us?

What is the meaning of this entire passage? Would it really have been enough for us if we left Egypt and did not receive the Torah? Would it have been enough for us if we did not receive the Shabbat? Would it have been enough for us if we did not receive Eretz Yisrael?

One explanation is that we recognize that at every stage we were not worthy of receiving the next one, and yet God, in His infinite mercy, nevertheless granted it to us (based on Rashba and Ritva on the haggadah).

◂ One

אִלּוּ סִפֵּק צָרְכֵּנוּ בַּמִּדְבָּר אַרְבָּעִים שָׁנָה
וְלֹא הֶאֱכִילָנוּ אֶת הַמָּן דַּיֵּנוּ.
אִלּוּ הֶאֱכִילָנוּ אֶת הַמָּן וְלֹא נָתַן לָנוּ אֶת הַשַּׁבָּת דַּיֵּנוּ.
אִלּוּ נָתַן לָנוּ אֶת הַשַּׁבָּת וְלֹא קֵרְבָנוּ לִפְנֵי הַר סִינַי דַּיֵּנוּ.
אִלּוּ קֵרְבָנוּ לִפְנֵי הַר סִינַי וְלֹא נָתַן לָנוּ אֶת הַתּוֹרָה דַּיֵּנוּ.
אִלּוּ נָתַן לָנוּ אֶת הַתּוֹרָה וְלֹא הִכְנִיסָנוּ לְאֶרֶץ יִשְׂרָאֵל דַּיֵּנוּ.
אִלּוּ הִכְנִיסָנוּ לְאֶרֶץ יִשְׂרָאֵל
וְלֹא בָנָה לָנוּ אֶת בֵּית הַבְּחִירָה דַּיֵּנוּ.

Riddles

70. How are the praises arranged in "would it have been enough for us?" Are they arranged chronologically?
71. How many favors are mentioned in the piyyut? Why? (Hint: Psalms 120–134 – it will be enough to check the first two words of each psalm. Another hint: *Mishnah Sukkah* 5:4).

Topic for discussion

o. How can we say that "Had He split the sea for us, and not led us through it on dry land, would it have been enough for us?" How can we say that "Had He brought us before Har Sinai, and not given us the Torah, it would have been enough for us?"

One can possibly explain this in a different way. The simple meaning of "it would have been enough for us" is that at each stage we needed to thank God (Malbim on the haggadah). We obviously want Shabbat, Eretz Yisrael, and the Bet HaMikdash, but at each stage there was an obligation to thank God.

However, there are sentences where this explanation does not fit. For example, "Had He split the sea for us, and not led us through it on dry land, it would have been enough for us!" What would have been the purpose of this? How are we to thank God for that? Or another example, which is even more problematic: "Had He brought us before Har Sinai, and not given us the Torah,

◂ Torah,

Had He provided for our needs in the desert for forty years,
and not fed us the manna,

IT WOULD HAVE BEEN ENOUGH FOR US!

Had He fed us the manna, and not given us Shabbat,

IT WOULD HAVE BEEN ENOUGH FOR US!

Had He given us Shabbat,
and not brought us before Mount Sinai,

IT WOULD HAVE BEEN ENOUGH FOR US!

Had He brought us before Har Sinai, and not given us the Torah,

IT WOULD HAVE BEEN ENOUGH FOR US!

Had He given us the Torah,
and not brought us into the Land of Israel,

IT WOULD HAVE BEEN ENOUGH FOR US!

Had He brought us into Eretz Yisrael,
and not built the Holy Bet HaMikdash,

IT WOULD HAVE BEEN ENOUGH FOR US!

Torah, it would have been enough for us!" What is the significance of standing before Har Sinai if we would not have received the Torah?

This piyyut comes to teach us that *every step is important, and every stage in the process of redemption of the Jewish People is significant*, advancing the progress of the redemption.

The splitting of the sea was an unprecedented miracle, and the very fact that it happened taught Am Yisrael about the power and might of God. This miracle has remained engraved on the minds of future generations as a sign of God's Providence over us. However, even moments after the miracle took place, Bnei Yisrael weren't sure what purpose it would solve in itself. Could they cross the sea? And even if they could cross it, how would that help, when the Egyptians were hot on their heels?

Clearly, in the end we needed the next stage as well – the stage of crossing the sea – but from this we can learn an important message for future generations: we do not always understand what we are going through. Sometimes we see open miracles, but along with them there may be problems – sometimes we find ourselves in a condition of uncertainty. We must always remember that each stage in our redemption

◄ is of

עַל אַחַת כַּמָּה וְכַמָּה טוֹבָה כְפוּלָה וּמְכֻפֶּלֶת לַמָּקוֹם עָלֵינוּ - שֶׁהוֹצִיאָנוּ מִמִּצְרַיִם, וְעָשָׂה בָהֶם שְׁפָטִים, וְעָשָׂה בֵאלֹהֵיהֶם, וְהָרַג אֶת בְּכוֹרֵיהֶם, וְנָתַן לָנוּ אֶת מָמוֹנָם, וְקָרַע לָנוּ אֶת הַיָּם, וְהֶעֱבִירָנוּ בְתוֹכוֹ בֶּחָרָבָה, וְשִׁקַּע צָרֵינוּ בְּתוֹכוֹ, וְסִפֵּק צָרְכֵּנוּ בַּמִּדְבָּר אַרְבָּעִים שָׁנָה, וְהֶאֱכִילָנוּ אֶת הַמָּן, וְנָתַן לָנוּ אֶת הַשַּׁבָּת, וְקֵרְבָנוּ לִפְנֵי הַר סִינַי, וְנָתַן לָנוּ אֶת הַתּוֹרָה, וְהִכְנִיסָנוּ לְאֶרֶץ יִשְׂרָאֵל, וּבָנָה לָנוּ אֶת בֵּית הַבְּחִירָה לְכַפֵּר עַל כָּל עֲוֹנוֹתֵינוּ.

רַבָּן גַּמְלִיאֵל הָיָה אוֹמֵר: כָּל שֶׁלֹּא אָמַר שְׁלשָׁה דְּבָרִים אֵלּוּ בַּפֶּסַח לֹא יָצָא יְדֵי חוֹבָתוֹ, וְאֵלּוּ הֵן:

פֶּסַח. מַצָּה. וּמָרוֹר.

---

is of importance, even if right now we are in the middle of the process, and cannot understand how our redemption will come from that miracle. *It is not only the final result, the redemption of Israel, that is important; the process, too, is significant,* and not only because it leads to our goal. The process is meaningful in itself, in building the faith of Israel, and in transforming us into a nation.

In our generation, we have the privilege of bearing witness to the great miracle of the return of the nation to its land and the ingathering of the exiles. At the same time, there are still major difficulties that we face, and times

Shabbat candlesticks,
Persia, 19th century, silver
The Wolfson Museum, Hechal Shlomo

◂ of trouble

THUS, HOW MUCH MORE SO SHOULD WE BE grateful to God for the manifold goodness that He has showered upon us; for He brought us out of Egypt, and executed judgment against them and against their gods, and slew their firstborn, and gave us their wealth, and split the sea for us, and led us through it on dry land, and drowned our tormentors in it, and provided for our needs in the desert for forty years, and fed us the manna, and gave us Shabbat, and brought us before Har Sinai, and gave us the Torah, and brought us into Eretz Yisrael, and built for us the Holy Bet HaMikdash to atone for all our sins.

RABBAN GAMLIEL USED TO SAY: WHOEVER does not discuss the following three things on Pesach has not fulfilled his obligation, and these are:

PESACH, MATZAH and **MAROR**.

---

of trouble and confusion. We cannot, Heaven forbid, deny the good that God has done for us just because we cannot understand how the present situation will bring us to the final redemption. We must remember that we have to thank God for each stage, and believe that we will be privileged to have the complete redemption soon in our days, Amen!

In summary: One can explain *Dayenu* in three ways: a) At each stage we can say that we were not worthy of receiving anything more (Rashba, Ritva); b) We need to thank God for each stage (Malbim); c) Each stage has significance in itself, even though we would not be content with stopping at intermediate stages, such as witnessing the splitting of the sea, or standing at Har Sinai before receiving the Torah.

Pesach, Matzah and Maror – the importance of visualization

What is the source for Rabban Gamliel's words – that one who does not discuss these three things has not fulfilled his obligation? According to Tosafot (116a, *Va'amartem*), the source for this is the verse, "You shall say, 'It is a Pesach sacrifice'" (Exodus 12:27), which teaches us that one must say: "This Pesach sacrifice that we are eating." Rabban Gamliel extended the obligation to include the other major mitzvot.

However, Shibolei HaLeket (on the haggadah, 218), said that this obligation

◄ stems

כשאומרים "פסח" מביטים בזרוע (ב"ח, סימן תע"ג, בשם מהר"י וייל),
אבל לא אוחזים אותה ביד, כדי שלא ייראו כאילו מקדישים ואוכלים קודשים בחוץ לשם פסח
(גמרא קטז: ורשב"ם שם; משנה ברורה, תע"ג, ס"ק עב).

פֶּסַח

שֶׁהָיוּ אֲבוֹתֵינוּ אוֹכְלִים בִּזְמַן שֶׁבֵּית הַמִּקְדָּשׁ הָיָה קַיָּם עַל שׁוּם מָה? עַל שׁוּם שֶׁפָּסַח הַקָּדוֹשׁ בָּרוּךְ הוּא עַל בָּתֵּי אֲבוֹתֵינוּ בְּמִצְרַיִם. שֶׁנֶּאֱמַר: וַאֲמַרְתֶּם זֶבַח פֶּסַח הוּא לַיהוָה אֲשֶׁר פָּסַח עַל בָּתֵּי בְנֵי יִשְׂרָאֵל בְּמִצְרַיִם, בְּנָגְפּוֹ אֶת מִצְרַיִם וְאֶת בָּתֵּינוּ הִצִּיל, וַיִּקֹּד הָעָם וַיִּשְׁתַּחֲווּ (שמות י"ב, כז).

Case for matzot, 1900, blue velvet
The Wolfson Museum, Hechal Shlomo, Golnitzki Collection

stems from the verse, "It is because of this that the Lord did [all these miracles] for me when I left Egypt" (Exodus 13:8):

The explanation [of the above is that] he now returns to the answer of Mah Nishtanah… and because of these three things, *the mitzvah of the haggadah is based* on saying "It is because of this," *at the time that they are in front of you…*

In other words, this law is based on the verse, "It is because of this," that the items must be before us when we tell the story of the Exodus from Egypt. Rabban Gamliel learned from this that the statement, "It is because of this" teaches us the obligation to say these words when the items are in front of us. (See above, the section on "Matzah and maror – the unity of opposites," p. 60. There, we explained that there is a dispute whether the items must be physically before us, or that the verse only describes the time for the telling of the story of the Exodus from Egypt – the time that these mitzvot are performed).

The Talmud in Pesachim 116b states that one must *lift the matzah and maror*

◂ (but

When one says "*Pesach*" he looks at the zero'a (Bach 473, in the name of Mahari Weil), but does not pick it up, so that it should not appear as though we are consecrating and eating the meat of the Pesach sacrifice (Talmud 116b; and Rashbam ibid.; Mishnah Berurah, 473:72).

THE PESACH SACRIFICE THAT OUR FATHERS ate during the period of the Holy Bet HaMikdash – what is its meaning? It is because the Holy One, Blessed be He, passed over our fathers' houses in Egypt, as it says: "You shall say, 'It is a Pesach sacrifice to the Lord who passed over the houses of Bnei Yisrael in Egypt when He smote the Egyptians and saved our houses.' And the people bowed down and prostrated themselves" (Exodus 12:27).

(but not the zero'a, so that it should not appear as if one is eating a sacrifice outside the Bet HaMikdash). The Talmud also says a blind person might be exempt from telling the story of the Exodus, because he cannot see these items, point to them, and say "It is because of this" (both Rav Yosef and Rav Sheshet hold that a blind person is also obligated).

Based on this, it appears that Rabban Gamliel emphasizes *that one must visualize the story of the Exodus from Egypt*. It is not enough to tell the story – one must integrate the visual aids, must point to them, and say them aloud. Otherwise, one has not fulfilled his obligation!

With this section, we have concluded the *four ways to retell the story of the Exodus*. These four sections are four possible approaches to retelling the Exodus:

a. "*We were slaves*" – the story of the Exodus according to Samuel, who explains it by means of a *story*, and emphasizes our *physical redemption.*

b. "*In the beginning, our ancestors were idol worshipers*" – *the story* of the Exodus according to Rav, who explains it by means of a story, and emphasizes the our *spiritual redemption.*

c. "*Go and learn*" – The story of the Exodus in a *scholarly* way, using the verses of the bringing of the first fruits.

d. "*Pesach, Matzah and Maror*" – the story of the Exodus from Egypt through *visualization* of the major mitzvot, which expresses the primary themes of the Seder night.

We should learn from the haggadah, and attempt to have our children reenact the story of the Exodus through visualization in order to experience this special night as fully as possible.

◂ "This

מגביה את המצה ומראה למסובים (גמרא קטז; שולחן ערוך, תע"ג, ז).

מַצָּה **זוֹ שֶׁאָנוּ אוֹכְלִים עַל שׁוּם מָה? עַל שׁוּם שֶׁלֹּא הִסְפִּיק בְּצֵקָם שֶׁל אֲבוֹתֵינוּ לְהַחְמִיץ עַד שֶׁנִּגְלָה עֲלֵיהֶם מֶלֶךְ מַלְכֵי הַמְּלָכִים הַקָּדוֹשׁ בָּרוּךְ הוּא וּגְאָלָם. שֶׁנֶּאֱמַר: וַיֹּאפוּ אֶת הַבָּצֵק אֲשֶׁר הוֹצִיאוּ מִמִּצְרַיִם עֻגֹת מַצּוֹת כִּי לֹא חָמֵץ כִּי גֹרְשׁוּ מִמִּצְרַיִם וְלֹא יָכְלוּ לְהִתְמַהְמֵהַּ וְגַם צֵדָה לֹא עָשׂוּ לָהֶם** (שמות י"ב, לט).

"This matzah" – Why do we eat matzot on Pesach?

The mitzvah most associated with the Festival of Pesach is that of eating matzah. Why, indeed, do we eat matzah on Pesach?

The haggadah's answer is "because our fathers' dough did not have time to rise." That is a familiar answer, but it presents several difficulties:

a. The mitzvah to eat matzah preceded the Exodus from Egypt (Exodus 12:15).

b. Matzah is mentioned in the Torah as a symbol of freedom (Exodus 12:7), and not as fleeing from slavery.

c. Matzah was used in the *Bet HaMikdash* as the ideal bread (Leviticus 6:10; 2:11) – how is this consistent with its representation of unrisen, "unfinished" dough?

d. The Mishnah (116b) writes that one eats matzah "because our forefathers were redeemed."

In order to address these issues, let us consider the significance of matzah.

It is generally accepted that matzah is a symbol of humility. Although this interpretation may be true, it is only a partial answer. Through this interpretation, one can see the aspect of freedom in matzah, but there is another aspect. The Torah (Deuteronomy 16:30) refers to matzah as "bread of affliction," which implies that it has an aspect of poverty. However, these characteristics can be explained in a different light.

In general, one can note the characteristics of matzah:

a. Matzah does not rise. b. Matzah is made only of basic ingredients.

Another characteristic that was pointed out by Maharal (*Gevurot Hashem* 51, 60, as pointed out by my father-in-law and mentor, Rav Blumenzweig) is the fact that matzah is never identified positively, but only by negation – dough that has *not* risen, something baked that is *not* chametz).

These characteristics teach us that matzah symbolizes symbolizes *our pure and wholesome internal identity,*

◂ which

One raises the matzah and shows it to the participants (Talmud 116b; Shulchan Aruch 473:7).

THIS MATZAH THAT WE EAT – WHAT IS ITS meaning? It is because our fathers' dough did not have time to rise before the King of kings: the Holy One, Blessed be He, revealed Himself to them and redeemed them. As it says: "They baked the dough that they had brought out of Egypt into cakes of matzah, for it had not leavened; because they were driven out of Egypt and could not delay, nor had they prepared provisions for themselves" (Exodus 12:39).

---

which one cannot define or characterize. which one cannot define or characterize. Matzah teaches us about modesty and humility – without any external and inflated facets, an expression of simplicity and naivetè, without any technology, sophistication, or human distortion. That is why matzah is able to be the perfect bread, the one offered in the Bet HaMikdash.

That is why matzah is, on the one hand, the "bread of affliction" – simple, humble, pure – and on the other hand it is "the bread of freedom," as it symbolizes the true internal nature of the person. Matzah as the "bread of affliction" does not contradict its symbolizing of freedom and redemption – on the contrary, it is what enables this. When Am Yisrael left Egypt, it returned to its internal independence, and, through that, it was able to free itself and be redeemed.

The dough of Israel was indeed not able to rise, not because of weakness or fleeing, but because Am Yisrael revealed its true interior, bared its soul. While the haste of their departure technically resulted in this shape, this outer form is significant on a spiritual level, for matzah – which does not rise and has no added ingredients – appropriately reflected Israel's inner state. God commanded them to eat matzah in order to be worthy of being redeemed, and it is because of this spiritual level that Israel became worthy of redemption.

The moment this independence was revealed, the essence of the bond between God and Am Yisrael was exposed: God's command to eat matzah reflected the inner essence of His people, pure and unfermented as matzah. From this we learn that our inner essence is pure and Divine, and here we are most deeply connected to God. We must remove the external barriers, remove our external enslavements, and from the freedom of our souls we will merit God's revelation.

Therefore, the haggadah is correct

◂ in explaining

מגביה את המרור ומראה למסובים (גמרא קטז; שולחן ערוך, תע"ג, ז).

מָרוֹר

זֶה שֶׁאָנוּ אוֹכְלִים עַל שׁוּם מָה? עַל שׁוּם שֶׁמֵּרְרוּ הַמִּצְרִים אֶת חַיֵּי אֲבוֹתֵינוּ בְּמִצְרָיִם. שֶׁנֶּאֱמַר: וַיְמָרְרוּ אֶת חַיֵּיהֶם בַּעֲבֹדָה קָשָׁה בְּחֹמֶר וּבִלְבֵנִים וּבְכָל עֲבֹדָה בַּשָּׂדֶה, אֵת כָּל עֲבֹדָתָם אֲשֶׁר עָבְדוּ בָהֶם בְּפָרֶךְ (שמות א׳, יד).

---

in explaining that the obligation to eat matzah stems from Bnei Yisrael's dough not having time to ferment. Moreover, the *Mishnah expresses how this is inherently connected to* Bnei Yisrael's redemption: "This matzah that we eat … It is because our fathers' dough did not have time to rise *before the King of kings: the Holy One, Blessed be He, revealed Himself to them and redeemed them.*" The dough that did not ferment was an expression of Am Yisrael's internal state, which brought about *God's revelation and the redemption of Israel.*

Eating matzah on Pesach teaches us how to return to our inner selves, how to live according to our true nature. The symbolic power of this eating will reverberate for the rest of the year; we will go back to eating chametz, but we will be sure to do so with a sense of obligation towards our inner nature. We will learn from the world around us and all that happens in it, but we will do so in a way that is true to ourselves, harnessing the external to serve the internal, and not the other way around.

This maror

We emphasize the eating of maror for two main reasons: a) Maror teaches us to feel the significance and importance of redemption. b) Maror teaches us to consider and understand that *bitterness is also part of the process of redemption.* The redemption process includes various stages – some are good, and the end result is good, but some stages may be difficult and bitter. It is important to remember that God looks after Am Yisrael throughout the process of redemption, especially in the most difficult of times, and He is constantly bringing us closer to the ultimate redemption.*

Why in haste?

One of the definitive characteristics of the redemption from Egypt is its marked *haste*, *chipazon* (Exodus 12:11):

> And this is how you shall eat it: your loins girded, your shoes on your feet,

◂

*See the discussion about yachatz, whether matzah is a symbol of slavery or of freedom, and the section "This night we are going free," p. 43.

One raises the maror and shows it to the participants (Talmud 116b; Shulchan Aruch, 473:7).

THIS BITTER HERB THAT WE EAT – WHAT is its meaning? It is because the Egyptians embittered our fathers' lives in Egypt, as it says: "They made their lives bitter with hard labor, with mortar and with bricks, and with all manner of labor in the field; whatever they made them do was with rigor" (Exodus 1:14).

---

feet, and your staff in your hand; and you shall eat it in haste; it is a Pesach sacrifice to the Lord.

The midrash (Mechilta Bo, 7:44) notes that the *haste* of the Exodus was evident in every aspect of the redemptive process: The Egyptians hastened to drive away Israel, Am Yisrael hastened to leave, and God hastened to take them out:

> Rabbi Joshua said: "'You shall eat it in haste.' This refers to the haste of Israel. Perhaps it refers to the haste of the Egyptians? When it states, 'Because they were chased out of Egypt' this refers to the haste of the Egyptians…"
>
> Abba Chanan says in the name of Rabbi Elazar: "That is the haste of the Divine Presence, and though there is no proof of this, there is a hint for this: 'The sound of my beloved! Behold, he is coming, skipping over the mountains, jumping over the hills'" (Shir HaShirim 2:8).

What is meant by "in haste?" Why is this emphasized as a major characteristic of the Exodus from Egypt?

What is most surprising is a verse in Deuteronomy (16:3):

> For seven days you shall eat with it matzot, the bread of affliction, for in haste you went out of the land of Egypt, so that you shall remember the day when you went out of the land of Egypt all the days of your life.

Even in this short verse, the Torah chooses to emphasize haste as a characteristic of the festival of Pesach and the obligation to eat matzah. Maharal (Or Chadash in the introduction "*ki hadavar shehu bazman*"; Maharal on the haggadah, p. 53, "*ki mah shehayu yotzim bechipazon*") and following in his footsteps, Rav Avraham Yitzchak Kook (*Ma'amarei Re'iyah*, p. 165; *Olat Re'iyah*, Part II, p. 287) writes that haste expresses a basic principle in the redemption of Israel:

> For seven days you shall eat with it matzot, the bread of affliction, for in haste you went out of the land of Egypt, because when they left in

◂ haste,

haste, without any time frame, that teaches us that they went out in a supernatural way. And the action that came from this was without a fixed time, unlike natural events whose actions are in a definite time frame. This is not the case when redemption is by natural means, which takes a certain amount of time. Here, though, the redemption was by supernatural means, and that is why it was in haste without time.

Haste expresses something that does not progress in a slow and gradual process. A slow process symbolizes nature, but haste symbolizes what is beyond nature. The Exodus from Egypt, therefore, which was a Divine and supernatural process, took place in haste. That was why God skipped and passed over the houses, and that is why the matzah was prepared in haste. Rambam (Guide for the Perplexed III:46) explains that the laws relating to the Pesach sacrifice – to eat it roasted and not to break any bones – were meant to enable Am Yisrael to eat it in haste.

Haste teaches us that the Exodus of Am Yisrael from Egypt was so sublime that it was not suitable to the natural processes of the world. The transition from slavery to freedom had to take place in haste; it had to take place through supernatural means.Through the Exodus and the splitting of the sea, it became clear that the Exodus of Am Yisrael not only influenced Egypt, but the entire world. The plagues of Egypt exercised their might over all the forces of Nature, thus rectifying them; and the splitting of the sea expressed the culmination of Divine revelation within a natural reality, because of God's care for Am Yisrael. All of these showed the panoramic significance of the Exodus beyond the particular redemption of Am Yisrael, which was the beginning of the rectification of the world. The Exodus began the repair of all the forces of evil in the world. The haste of the Exodus and the special Divine might that was unleashed delivered a new message to the world.

Therefore, immediately after the splitting of the sea, Amalek came to wage war against Am Yisrael. The significance of Am Yisrael's redemption, the call for morality, the active intervention of God in the world – greatly disturbed the other nations of the world, and in reaction Amalek came and tried to rebel and wage war against this call.

The haste of the Exodus teaches us that the redemption of Israel is something unnatural, something revolutionary that transcends the laws of nature. The revelation of the Exodus should be a beacon of light and hope during darker times during the process of redemption, inspiring us to pray that we be granted the privilege to see our nation's full redemption speedily, with haste, in our time.

The redemption that is in process in our generation is without haste

The redemption from Egypt was a supernatural redemption, characterized

◂ by haste

Case for matzot, silk embroidered with gold threads
The Wolfson Museum, Hechal Shlomo, Golnitzki Collection

by haste – a catalyzed process rather than a gradual one, transcending the laws of nature. However, this understanding of the significance of the redemption of Israel evokes a question, based on the words of the prophet Isaiah (52:12):

> For *not with haste* shall you go forth and *not in a flurry of flight* shall you go, for the Lord goes before you.

Our Sages in Mechilta (Bo, Parashah 7:44) attributed these verses to the future redemption. The difference between this redemption and the redemption from Egypt was discussed by the Maharal* and by Rav Avraham Yitzchak Kook,** who explain that *the future redemption, a redemption where the process will not be in haste, is greater.* Why?

Haste signifies that the redemption transcends the natural processes of this world. That is why the world cannot comprehend its power and the Divine message of the redemption. Therefore, its influence on the world is only partial, for such supernatural intervention cannot be fully understood.

The future redemption will take place gradually, through human action, step by step. Thus, the world can fully internalize and comprehend its light. The redemption in Egypt had

* Introduction to *Or Chadash*; *Netzach Yisrael* 47; *Gevurot Hashem*, p. 265

** *Orot*, p. 44; *Olat Re'iyah*, I:26; *Ma'amarei HaRe'iyah* p. 165; *Olat Re'iyah* II:270, 287, 279

◂ be supernatural,

to be supernatural, in order to convey the might of God, which would have been impossible to express through merely natural processes. Now, our task is to gradually realize the redemption *within* the parameters of nature, to instill the Divine *within* the natural, to sanctify and elevate our reality.

Redemption through natural processes is accompanied by difficulties and obstacles. However, these problems are not an indication of the limitations of the redemption process – on the contrary, they indicate how the redemption process is relevant and fully pertinent to the real world; how there is a real need to struggle in order to achieve true redemption, in order to illuminate the natural world with Divine light.

Therefore, when the Sages described the future redemption, they did not seek miraculous or non-natural descriptions, but described it in natural terms. In Tractate Sanhedrin (98a) our Sages stated that *there is no more revealing sign of the end of our exile than if the trees of Israel bear fruit.* It is not the supernatural which signifies the coming of the final redemption, but the fact that millions of Jews are leading normal lives in Eretz Yisrael, building homes, planting trees, raising their families. This normality, this natural, wonderful blossoming of Eretz Yisrael – that is the clearest sign of the redemption we are living through. Natural progress and development, painstakingly, gradually achieved.

The stories of what Eretz Yisrael was like before the chalutzim, the pioneers, came are well-known, Eretz Yisrael was a land of deserts and swamps until the Jews came and succeeded, with God's help, to make the wasteland bloom.

I spoke to farmers who lived in Gush Katif, whom we are helping to find employment through JobKatif (an organization that helps former residents of Gush Katif return to the ◂ workforce).

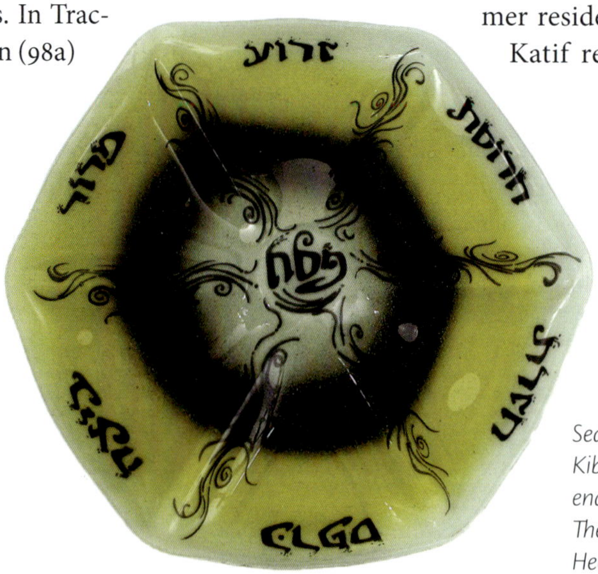

Seder plate, Kibbutz Nachshon, end of 20th century The Wolfson Museum, Hechal Shlomo

Riddles

72. "This matzah" – what is matzah shemurah?
73. What is matzah ashirah? May one eat it on Pesach?
74. What is "mayim shelanu?"
75. What item on the seder plate is meant to symbolize the Pesach sacrifice?
76. Which Rabban Gamliel said this? There was a Rabban Gamliel who lived at the time of the Bet HaMikdash, who was the grandson of Hillel the Elder, and there was a Rabban Gamliel who was the Nasi in Yavneh after the destruction of the Second Bet HaMikdash. Which of the two made this statement? Prove it.
77. If a person was unable to bring the Pesach sacrifice, what did he do?

For the next questions, one must look in Exodus ch. 12.

78. What did the Torah mandate us to eat along with the Pesach sacrifice? (See again the words of Rabban Gamliel in the haggadah. Hint: look at Exodus ch. 12, verse 8).
79. What is the Pesach of Egypt and what is the Pesach of future generations thereafter?
80. What special Jewish Laws were observed in Pesach in Egypt? (Use Exodus 12:7, 11, 22. Similarly, look at Exodus 12:3 and look at Rashi there, or Mishnah 9:5 in Pesachim.)
81. What laws do Pesach in Egypt and Pesach in future generations thereafter have in common? (See Exodus 12: 5, 6, 8, 9, 10, 46).

workforce). I asked them what happened to the hothouses they left behind. They told me: the Arab workers who took over the greenhouses have been calling us every so often, complaining that haven't managed to growing anything. That is a clear sign of what the Sages told us about the future redemption – Eretz Yisrael only blossoms for Am Yisrael.

We must rejoice and be grateful that, with God's help, we are able to be partners in this awe-inspiring and remarkable process, and see the redemption unfold before our very eyes. We must also remember that the difficulties we face are an expression of the greatness of our redemption, and pray that we should witness its completion very soon. ▪

צריכים להתכוון באמירה זו ולחוש בה שגם אנחנו יצאנו ממצרים!

בְּכָל דּוֹר וָדוֹר חַיָּב אָדָם לִרְאוֹת אֶת עַצְמוֹ כְּאִלּוּ הוּא יָצָא מִמִּצְרָיִם, שֶׁנֶּאֱמַר: וְהִגַּדְתָּ לְבִנְךָ בַּיּוֹם הַהוּא לֵאמֹר בַּעֲבוּר זֶה עָשָׂה יְהֹוָה לִי בְּצֵאתִי מִמִּצְרָיִם (שמות י"ג, ח). **לֹא אֶת אֲבוֹתֵינוּ בִּלְבַד גָּאַל הַקָּדוֹשׁ בָּרוּךְ הוּא, אֶלָּא אַף אוֹתָנוּ גָּאַל עִמָּהֶם, שֶׁנֶּאֱמַר: וְאוֹתָנוּ הוֹצִיא מִשָּׁם, לְמַעַן הָבִיא אֹתָנוּ לָתֶת לָנוּ אֶת הָאָרֶץ אֲשֶׁר נִשְׁבַּע לַאֲבֹתֵינוּ** (דברים ו', כג).

Food For Thought

In every generation, it is one's duty to see himself

In the Rambam's version of the haggadah, as well as Sefardic haggadot, the text reads (*Hilchot Chametz U'Matzah* 7:5): "it is one's duty to show himself as though he had just come out from the slavery of Egypt."

The Exodus from Egypt is not just history – its effects are still felt today, affecting each and every one of us. On this night, we must feel and even act as if we had just left Egypt. We do not merely need "to see ourselves," in this light theoretically. We are required to actually "show ourselves" – to live this fact, to feel it, and to have this affect the way we live.

On Pesach, we must strive to tune into our inner feelings. We should reach in and connect internally, and express these feeling externally. The soul is stirred, the heart beats, we are overwhelmed by our emotions – we are being set free! Our inner feelings burst out. It is impossible to cage the feeling of freedom, and we must allow ourselves to express it, to lets its power illuminate the our lives. All those around us should also know and feel the same thing: we are all experiencing the freedom of the Exodus from Egypt together – we are all being released from slavery into freedom!

(For further discussion, see *Halachah MiMekorah – Kinor David, Maggid* p. 103, as well as in the passage on leaning, and the summary table on the topic of freedom on p. 285). ▪

When saying the following, one must have the intention of feeling as if we had just left Egypt!

IN EVERY GENERATION, IT IS ONE'S DUTY to see himself as though he had personally come out from Egypt, as it says: "You shall tell your son on that day: 'It is because of this that the Lord did [all these miracles] for me when I left Egypt'" (Exodus 13:8). Not only our fathers did the Holy One, Blessed be He, redeem from Egypt, but He redeemed us with them as well, as it says: "It was us that He brought out from there, so that He might bring us to give us the land that He promised to our fathers" (Deuteronomy 6:23).

Halachic Summary

The Rishonim (*Sefer HaPardes LeRashi*, p. 51; Avudraham on the haggadah; Hagahot Maimoniot on the haggadah and others, as well as Tur and Shulchan Aruch 473:7) write that the cup is raised when reciting the paragraph on the next page ("Therefore, it is our duty…"). Until when does one hold up the cup? Most Rishonim write that one keeps it up *until the end of the blessing of "ga'al yisrael" – "He who has redeemed Israel"* (Rashi *ibid.*; *Hagahot Maimoniot* in the name of Maharam, and others. That is the ruling of Shulchan Aruch *ibid.*). There are others who only raise the cup until, "Let us recite before Him a new song: Halleluyah!" That is what Hagahot Maimoniot writes, and he adds that this is the custom. In Sefer HaManhig (*Hilchot Pesach*, 75), the author writes that there are those whose custom it is to raise the cup until the end of hallel.

What is the reason for raising the cup? The Talmud in Berachot (35a) states that "one only recites a song of praise over wine." As we are beginning the recital of a song of praise at this point, we raise our cup of wine in order to link the praise and the drinking of wine (Rashi and Tur *ibid.*, and others).

We already explained at the beginning of the haggadah that whenever the cup is raised, one must first cover the matzot in order not to "shame" the matzah, for one is normally required to recite the blessing on bread before the blessing on wine (as we cover the challah for kiddush each week). ▪

מכסים את המצות ומגביהים את הכוס, עד לחתימה של "גאל ישראל", ויש המגביהים רק עד "שירה חדשה, הללויה".

באמירה זו, בפרקי ההלל ובברכת הגאולה, אנו מודים לקב"ה מתוך שמחה עצומה על כל הטובה שגמל עמנו. זוהי התכלית של ליל הסדר – להודות על היציאה לחירות, להודות על כך שזכינו להיות עבדי ה'! (עיינו ביסוד ושורש העבודה, שער הצאן, פרק ו').

לְפִיכָךְ: **אֲנַחְנוּ חַיָּבִים לְהוֹדוֹת, לְהַלֵּל, לְשַׁבֵּחַ, לְפָאֵר, לְרוֹמֵם, לְהַדֵּר, לְבָרֵךְ, לְעַלֵּה וּלְקַלֵּס לְמִי שֶׁעָשָׂה לַאֲבוֹתֵינוּ וְלָנוּ אֶת כָּל הַנִּסִּים הָאֵלּוּ, הוֹצִיאָנוּ מֵעַבְדוּת לְחֵרוּת, מִיָּגוֹן לְשִׂמְחָה, וּמֵאֵבֶל לְיוֹם טוֹב, וּמֵאֲפֵלָה לְאוֹר גָּדוֹל, וּמִשִּׁעְבּוּד לִגְאֻלָּה, וְנֹאמַר לְפָנָיו שִׁירָה חֲדָשָׁה הַלְלוּיָהּ.**

Food For Thought

Therefore, it is our duty to thank, praise, hail, glorify…
As we explained, this section is mentioned in the Mishnah as a continuation of the words of Rabban Gamliel. The main purpose of relating the story of the Exodus is to move us to thank and praise God. Therefore, after having told the story of the Exodus using the fourth method, "we are obligated *to thank and praise*" God.

Saying this passage at the end of the fourth account is significant beyond just thanking God for the Exodus.

Before this passage, we said, "In every generation, it is one's duty to see himself as though he had personally come out from Egypt." The word "therefore," which opens this passage, joins the two passages: because we, too, left Egypt, *because the Exodus from Egypt has tremendous influence on every generation, we must also offer thanks* (see Maharal, *Gevurot Hashem*, beginning of ch. 61)!

This is not an expression of our duty to thank and praise God for the miracles of the past that He did for our

◂ forefathers.

The matzot are covered and the cup is raised until the conclusion of the blessing of "*ga'al yisrael*" – "He who has redeemed Israel," and there are those who only raise the cup until "*shirah chadashah, Halleluyah*" – "a new song: Halleluyah."

When saying these sections of hallel and the blessing on our redemption, we joyfully thank God for all that He has given us. That is the purpose of the Seder night – to thank God for taking us out from slavery to freedom, and to thank Him for having granted us the great privilege of being servants of God! (See *Yesod VeShoresh HaAvodah, Sha'ar HaTzon*, ch. 6).

THEREFORE, IT IS OUR DUTY TO THANK, praise, hail, glorify, exalt, honor, bless, extol and celebrate Him, He who did all these miracles for our fathers and us. He brought us forth from slavery to freedom, from sorrow to joy, and from mourning to festivity, and from darkness to great light, and from servitude to redemption. Let us recite before Him a new song: Halleluyah!

Charity box, Ein HaBesor, 1992, ceramic, artist: Ella Weizman
The Wolfson Museum, Hechal Shlomo

forefathers. We have must internalize the significance of the Exodus from Egypt within *our own generation.*

That is the main point of the Seder night: through understanding the bitterness of the slavery in Egypt, we must internalize that the concepts of enslavement and redemption are not only part of our history, but a real, ongoing, internal conflict. We too must liberate ourselves from our own external enslavements, be they cultural, psychological, or physical. When we work on ourselves and achieve true inner freedom, *we are inspired to offer thanks to God for the daily miracles He provides for us.* ▪

רבים ממשיכים להגביה את הכוס עד סוף ברכת הגאולה, אולם יש המניחים את הכוס ומגלים את המצות לפני ההלל, וחוזרים להגביהה קודם ברכת הגאולה (לאחר "חלמיש למעינו מים").

הַלְלוּיָהּ, הַלְלוּ עַבְדֵי יְהֹוָה, הַלְלוּ אֶת שֵׁם יְהֹוָה. יְהִי שֵׁם יְהֹוָה מְבֹרָךְ, מֵעַתָּה וְעַד עוֹלָם. מִמִּזְרַח שֶׁמֶשׁ עַד מְבוֹאוֹ, מְהֻלָּל שֵׁם יְהֹוָה. רָם עַל כָּל גּוֹיִם יְהֹוָה, עַל הַשָּׁמַיִם כְּבוֹדוֹ. מִי כַּיהֹוָה אֱלֹהֵינוּ, הַמַּגְבִּיהִי לָשָׁבֶת. הַמַּשְׁפִּילִי לִרְאוֹת, בַּשָּׁמַיִם וּבָאָרֶץ. מְקִימִי מֵעָפָר דָּל, מֵאַשְׁפֹּת יָרִים אֶבְיוֹן. לְהוֹשִׁיבִי עִם נְדִיבִים, עִם נְדִיבֵי עַמּוֹ. מוֹשִׁיבִי עֲקֶרֶת הַבַּיִת אֵם הַבָּנִים שְׂמֵחָה, הַלְלוּיָהּ. (תהלים קי"ג)

The Source of the Haggadah

The source for the obligation to recite hallel is in the Mishnah (116a). It is true that there is a dispute in the Mishnah between Hillel and Shammai regarding how much of hallel is said before the meal. Shammai holds that one only says the first psalm of hallel – while according to Hillel, one says the first two psalms.

In the Jerusalem Talmud (10:5) this dispute is explained (see also Babylonian Talmud 117b; and also *Halachah MiMekorah – Kinor David*, Hallel p. 268). From there we see that Shammai holds that one is not able to say the second psalm of hallel before midnight, because the death of the firstborns only took place at midnight, and Am Yisrael had not yet begun to leave. However, one is still able to say the first psalm before midnight as the people's servitude had already been abolished before midnight. According to Hillel, one also says the second psalm, which deals with the Exodus from Egypt, because if we were to wait until the actual time they left Egypt, we would have to wait until the morning, as the actual Exodus took place during the day, as it says, "it came to pass on that very day" (Exodus 12:41. The time of the actual Exodus is also relevant to the piyyut, "And it came to pass at midnight!" p. 213 and p. 219. We can recite hallel at night and mention the Exodus from Egypt even before midnight because that is when the process of the Exodus began.

◂ We can

Many continue to hold the cup up until the blessing of the redemption, but there are those who put it down and uncover the matzot before hallel, and pick it up again before the blessing of the redemption (after "the flint into a fountain of water").

PRAISE THE LORD. PRAISE, YOU SERVANTS of the Lord. Praise the name of the Lord. Blessed be the name of the Lord from now and forevermore. From the rising of the sun to its setting, the Lord's name is praised. The Lord is high above all nations. His glory is above the heavens. Who is like the Lord, our God, who dwells on high? Who looks down low upon the heavens and upon the earth? He raises the poor from the dust, and the mendicant from the dunghill. He lifts the needy to seat him with princes, with the princes of His people. He seats the barren woman in her house as the joyful mother of children. Praise the Lord (Psalms 113).

We can explain Hillel's view in a different way. This hallel is referred to as Hallel HaMitzri – the "Egyptian Hallel" – as its first two psalms deal with *the Exodus from Egypt* (*Berachot* 56a – as opposed to *Hallel HaGadol* – the "Great Hallel" – Psalms 136, "Praise the Lord," which is said after the meal).

Just like all of our discussions of the Exodus, these psalms are said before midnight as part of maggid, which is said before the meal. The rest of hallel deals with the *future redemption,* and that is why it is separated from the beginning of hallel and is said after the meal. It is possible that the meal in the middle is a se'udat hodayah – a thanksgiving meal – which links the past to the future, and the miracles of Egypt to our future miracles (see *Halachah Mi-Mekorah – Kinor David*, Hallel p. 268). ▪

Food For Thought

Praise, you servants of the Lord

Servants of the Lord! The essence of the Exodus from Egypt was our transformation into the servants of God. We became people who are faithful to their inner beings, who are able to cut themselves off from external servitudes (both physical and spiritual) in order to be fully connected to God. Finally, we became free men who perform God's

◂ will

בְּצֵאת יִשְׂרָאֵל מִמִּצְרָיִם, בֵּית יַעֲקֹב מֵעַם לֹעֵז. הָיְתָה יְהוּדָה לְקָדְשׁוֹ, יִשְׂרָאֵל מַמְשְׁלוֹתָיו. הַיָּם רָאָה וַיָּנֹס, הַיַּרְדֵּן יִסֹּב לְאָחוֹר. הֶהָרִים רָקְדוּ כְאֵילִים, גְּבָעוֹת כִּבְנֵי צֹאן. מַה לְּךָ הַיָּם כִּי תָנוּס, הַיַּרְדֵּן תִּסֹּב לְאָחוֹר. הֶהָרִים תִּרְקְדוּ כְאֵילִים, גְּבָעוֹת כִּבְנֵי צֹאן. מִלִּפְנֵי אָדוֹן חוּלִי אָרֶץ, מִלִּפְנֵי אֱלוֹהַּ יַעֲקֹב. הַהֹפְכִי הַצּוּר אֲגַם מָיִם, חַלָּמִישׁ לְמַעְיְנוֹ מָיִם. (תהלים קי״ד)

Medallion of "Moses and the Ark," bronze
The Wolfson Museum, Hechal Shlomo

will in the world. God's servants, particularly on the night of the Exodus from Egypt, must thank and praise Him! It is not only an obligation, but a special privilege to be a servant of God, a special privilege to appear before the Creator and praise Him.

Therefore, even though this psalm does not deal directly with the Exodus from Egypt, it does speak of our eternal servitude to God that resulted from this revelation.

The psalm is divided into three parts that describe the God's existence and control of the world:

a. 1–3: God's servants praise Him at all times ("from now and forevermore") and in every place ("from the rising of the sun to its setting").

b. 4–6: God is in the highest of places ("The Lord is high above all nations… above the heavens… dwells on high"). He nevertheless descends and is connected to the lowest of places ("Who looks down low upon the heavens and upon the earth"). *In all His exalted Divinity, God still connects to the smallest and lowliest, and exalts them and raises them up.*

c. 7–9: God does not only take care of the nation as a whole (as can be seen in the next psalm), but also each

◂ individual

WHEN ISRAEL WENT OUT OF EGYPT, the house of Jacob from a people of a foreign language, Judah became His sanctuary, Israel His dominion. The sea saw and fled; the Jordan turned backward. The mountains skipped like rams, the hills like lambs. What has happened to you, O sea, that you flee? O Jordan, that you turn backward? You mountains, that you skip like rams? You hills, like lambs? Tremble, O earth, at the presence of the Lord, at the presence of the God of Jacob. Who turned the rock into a pool of water, the flint into a fountain of water (*Psalms* 114).

---

individual ("He raises the poor… He seats the barren woman…" The latter suggests Hannah, I Samuel 1).

The psalm begins with "Halleluyah! Praise…" and ends with "Halleluyah." This teaches us that the servants of God never cease to praise and thank Him. They praise Him for His greatness, and for the fact that God, who is *the highest of the high, nevertheless cares for the smallest of the small!*

Can the inanimate speak?

"What has happened to you, O sea, that you flee?" The author of the psalm poses a question to the sea, and later to the Jordan River, the mountains and the hills. They answer, "before the Lord, before the God of Jacob." They acted this way because of the appearance of God and His Divine Presence.

What is the significance of this dialogue with inanimate objects?

This dialogue is not just a metaphorical exchange between the poet and how he imagines nature answering him – it has deeper meaning.

After a craftsman has finished making a vessel or work of art, he is no longer involved with it – his work is done. However, when God created the world, He did not depart. God continues to keep the world alive: "He constantly renews, in his goodness, the act of creation" (from Shacharit).

When we examine the world, we understand *that God is constantly involved with His world.* There is no reality without His presence. *Nature proclaims: "God created me!"* Meditation upon nature reveals that the earth חולי before God. The word חולי has several possible meanings: One meaning is derived from the word מחולל, "fashioned, shapes"; another meaning, the plain meaning of the text, to *tremble* – the land *trembles* before God; a third meaning can be derived from the word machol, which means "to *dance*." The third interpretation is strengthened by

◂ the

מכסים את המצות ומגביהים את הכוס (לנוהגים שלא להגביה את הכוס עד כה). ואומרים:

בָּרוּךְ אַתָּה יְהוָה אֱלֹהֵינוּ מֶלֶךְ הָעוֹלָם, אֲשֶׁר גְּאָלָנוּ וְגָאַל אֶת אֲבוֹתֵינוּ מִמִּצְרַיִם, וְהִגִּיעָנוּ הַלַּיְלָה הַזֶּה לֶאֱכָל בּוֹ מַצָּה וּמָרוֹר. כֵּן, יְהוָה אֱלֹהֵינוּ וֵאלֹהֵי אֲבוֹתֵינוּ, יַגִּיעֵנוּ לְמוֹעֲדִים וְלִרְגָלִים אֲחֵרִים הַבָּאִים לִקְרָאתֵנוּ לְשָׁלוֹם, שְׂמֵחִים בְּבִנְיַן עִירֶךָ, וְשָׂשִׂים בַּעֲבוֹדָתֶךָ, וְנֹאכַל שָׁם מִן הַזְּבָחִים וּמִן הַפְּסָחִים (במוצאי שבת אומרים: מִן הַפְּסָחִים וּמִן הַזְּבָחִים) אֲשֶׁר יַגִּיעַ דָּמָם עַל קִיר מִזְבַּחֲךָ לְרָצוֹן, וְנוֹדֶה לְּךָ שִׁיר חָדָשׁ עַל גְּאֻלָּתֵנוּ וְעַל פְּדוּת נַפְשֵׁנוּ. בָּרוּךְ אַתָּה יְהוָה גָּאַל יִשְׂרָאֵל.

---

the parallel noted earlier: "The mountains skipped like rams." At first glance, these two meanings appear to be opposites: did the earth tremble before God or did it come in joy and dance? Which is the correct interpretation?

In such a poem of awe and ecstasy, all three meanings can be embraced. Indeed, there is trembling, but not trembling due to fear. This is trembling and dancing resulting from the recognition of the glory of God that is revealed in the world: "rejoice with quaking" (Psalms 2:11). This is the trembling of the forces of nature, who acknowledge the greatness of God and His sovereignty over them, and through this they express their love and joy to the Master of all and to Am Yisrael that has just left Egypt.

Meditating upon the might and majesty of nature moves one to feel the might of God who created all, moves one to sing to the Creator of all. In the beautiful words of my late grandfather, the poet Rabbi Y. Rimon:

How can I sing about day and night –
When God created them?
How can I sing about heaven and earth –
When God founded them?
How can I sing about mountains and hills –
When God mounted them?
How can I sing about seas and deserts –
When God made them?
How can I sing about the entire earth –
When God commanded them?
I will sing to the Creator of all, the exalted above all –
To God I will sing! ▪

One covers the matzot and lifts up the cup (for those who were not already holding the cup), and says:

BLESSED ARE YOU, LORD OUR GOD, King of the universe, who has redeemed us and redeemed our fathersfrom Egypt, and enabled us to reach this night that we may eat matzah and maror on it. So too, Lord our God and God of our fathers, enable us to reach future holidays and festivals in peace, rejoicing in the rebuilding of Your city and ecstatic in Your service. And there we will partake of the sacrifices and Pesach offerings (on Saturday night substitute: of the Pesach offerings and of the sacrifices) whose blood will be sprinkled on the wall of Your altar for gracious acceptance. We will then thank You with a new song for our redemption and for the deliverance of our souls. Blessed are You, God, who has redeemed Israel.

The Source of the Haggadah

The Mishnah (116b) brings a dispute between Rabbi Akiva and Rabbi Tarfon regarding the text of this blessing:

> And he concludes with [a formula of] redemption. Rabbi Tarfon used to say "who has redeemed us and redeemed our fathers from Egypt," but he did not conclude [with a blessing]. Rabbi Akiva said: 'So too, Lord our God and God of our fathers, enable us to reach future holidays and festivals in peace, rejoicing in the rebuilding of Your city and ecstatic in Your service. And there we will partake of the sacrifices and the Pesach offerings… [up to] Blessed are You, God, who has redeemed Israel."

According to Rabbi Tarfon the text is a short one, and that is why one does not conclude with "Blessed are You." On the other hand, according to Rabbi Akiva the text is a long, and therefore has a concluding blessing: "Blessed are You" (See Tosafot *ibid.*, *VeChoteim*).

From the words of Rashbam (*ibid.*, *VeChoteim*, and it seems to be Tosafot's opinion as well) we see that the difference in how one concludes the blessing stems from one's definition of the blessing's nature. According to Rabbi Tarfon, *this is a blessing of thanks*, and, therefore, there is no concluding blessing, as with all blessings of thanks. According to Rabbi Akiva, though, this is

◂ also

מברכים "בורא פרי הגפן", ושותים כוס שנייה בהסבה ואין מברכים ברכה אחרונה.

יש נוהגים לומר לפני ברכת "בורא פרי הגפן":

הִנְנִי מוּכָן וּמְזֻמָּן לְקַיֵּם מִצְוַת כּוֹס שֵׁנִי שֶׁל אַרְבַּע כּוֹסוֹת. לְשֵׁם יִחוּד קוּדְשָׁא בְּרִיךְ הוּא וּשְׁכִינְתֵּיהּ עַל יְדֵי הַהוּא טָמִיר וְנֶעְלָם בְּשֵׁם כָּל יִשְׂרָאֵל. וִיהִי נֹעַם אֲדֹנָי אֱלֹהֵינוּ עָלֵינוּ וּמַעֲשֵׂה יָדֵינוּ כּוֹנְנָה עָלֵינוּ וּמַעֲשֵׂה יָדֵינוּ כּוֹנְנֵהוּ.

בָּרוּךְ אַתָּה יְהֹוָה אֱלֹהֵינוּ מֶלֶךְ הָעוֹלָם, בּוֹרֵא פְּרִי הַגָּפֶן.

A goblet for kiddush, Jerusalem, 19th century, bitumen stone
The Wolfson Museum, Hechal Shlomo

also a *request*, which is associated with a concluding blessing.

Today we act in accordance with Rabbi Akiva (Tosafot *ibid.*) and conclude with a blessing (in the text of our blessing we also include the words that appear in Rabbi Tarfon's version, which were evidently accepted by all).

Rashba gives an interesting opinion here, based on the Jerusalem Talmud (Berachot 1:5). The Jerusalem Talmud says that there are "two here – one for the past and one for the future," which Rashba explains is a combination of two blessings: the first, "Blessed are You… who has redeemed us and redeemed our fathers from Egypt," and the second, "So too, Lord our God and God of our fathers, enable us to reach future holidays and festivals… Blessed are You, God, who has redeemed Israel." The first blessing thanks God for the past, while the second refers to the future (there are Rishonim who explain the Jerusalem Talmud in different ways. Ramban at the end of Tractate *Pesachim* explains that this is the blessing

◂ on hallel

One recites the blessing over wine and drinks the second cup while leaning, and does not recite the concluding blessing afterwards.

There are those who say the following before reciting the blessing over wine:

I am prepared and ready to fulfill the mitzvah of the second cup of four cups. For the sake of the unification of the Holy One, Blessed be He, and His Presence, in the name of all Israel. And may the pleasantness of the Lord our God be upon us, and the work of our hands establish for us, and may the work of our hands establish it.

BLESSED ARE YOU, LORD OUR GOD, King of the universe, who creates the fruit of the vine.

---

on hallel – according to his view, that one recites a blessing on reciting hallel – and on the blessing of the redemption. See also Tosafot Berachot 14a, *Yamim*).

Rashbam (116b, *VeChoteim*) writes that the blessing of redemption *concludes* the haggadah. On the other hand, Ritva (in his commentary on the haggadah) writes that after one concludes the haggadah one recites the blessing of redemption – that is, the blessing of redemption is not part of the haggadah. ▪

Food For Thought

Of the sacrifices and Pesach sacrifices "Who has redeemed" or "who redeems?"

The Talmud (117b) states that one concludes the blessing with "who has redeemed Israel" and not with "who redeems Israel," as our main focus is on the redemption that already took place (Rashbam *ibid.*, *VeHallel*. Even if there are two blessings in the blessing of the redemption, the first on the past and the second on the future, the main thanks is for the past, and that is the way the blessing is concluded – Rashba *ibid.*).

For one of the most fundamental principles of the Seder night is the understanding and the internalization that we also left Egypt – for each person has "to see himself as though he had personally come out from Egypt." The fact that the blessing uses the past tense teaches us that *the redemption from Egypt also had our redemption embedded within it.* The use of past tense implies that the basis for our redemption, and the redemption of every generation, was concealed within the Exodus from Egypt. *It is our task to realize this redemption in every generation and to carry it out until the final redemption.*

◂ This

This is our profound connection to the Exodus from Egypt. We perpetuate the spirit of the first great redemption by actively striving to achieve redemption in our own generation. The awareness that everything we do, every decision that we make, and every mitzvah we have the privilege of fulfilling stems from the tremendous force of the Exodus from Egypt, enables us to joyously recite the blessing of "Blessed are You, God, who has redeemed Israel," with a panoramic perspective of the past, present and future, which we hope and pray will bring the final redemption speedily, in our time. ▪

Etrog container, 19th century, silver
The Wolfson Museum, Hechal Shlomo, Max Grundt Collection

Rochtzah

At the beginning of the seder we must purify ourselves – *urchatz*. Now, after we have purified ourselves, ascended spiritually, and have even been involved in the spiritual mitzvot of the night – telling the story of the Exodus from Egypt – we wash ourselves to *become more holy* as we observe the mitzvah of *eating*. Now, with God's help, not only will our thoughts and words be sanctified, but we will also *sanctify our physical actions and eat matzah in holiness!*

נוטלים ידים לסעודה ומברכים: "על נטילת ידים".

בָּרוּךְ אַתָּה יְהֹוָה אֱלֹהֵינוּ מֶלֶךְ הָעוֹלָם, אֲשֶׁר קִדְּשָׁנוּ בְּמִצְוֹתָיו, וְצִוָּנוּ עַל נְטִילַת יָדָיִם.

One washes one's hands for the meal, and recites the blessing:

BLESSED ARE YOU, LORD OUR GOD, King of the universe, who has sanctified us with His mitzvot and commanded us concerning the washing of the hands.

Halachic Summary

One washes one's hands and recites the blessing. Many have the custom of having another person pour the water on the hands of the head of the household as an expression of freedom. ▪

Vessel for hand washing, Jerusalem, 1979, ceramic,
Bezalel Academy of Arts and Design
The Wolfson Museum, Hechal Shlomo

Motzi Matzah

We are privileged to fulfill the Torah-mandated mitzvah of eating matzah! Matzah, made of flour and water alone, will bring us to humility, but will also bring us to our personal freedom; to purity and simplicity of soul; to freedom from all external enslavements; and to deep, pure yearning to cleave to our Creator.

מגביהים את שתי המצות השלמות והפרוסה שביניהן ומברכים ברכת "המוציא".

בָּרוּךְ **אַתָּה יְהֹוָה אֱלֹהֵינוּ מֶלֶךְ הָעוֹלָם, הַמּוֹצִיא לֶחֶם מִן הָאָרֶץ.**

מניחים את המצה התחתונה, ומברכים "על אכילת מצה" ומכוונים לפטור גם את המצה שב"כורך" ואת ה"אפיקומן".

בָּרוּךְ **אַתָּה יְהֹוָה אֱלֹהֵינוּ מֶלֶךְ הָעוֹלָם, אֲשֶׁר קִדְּשָׁנוּ בְּמִצְוֹתָיו, וְצִוָּנוּ עַל אֲכִילַת מַצָּה.**

לוקחים כזית בשיעור גדול (בדיוק בגודל שבתמונה) מהמצה הפרוסה, משלימים מעט מן השלמה ואוכלים את שניהם בהסבה.

One lifts up the two whole matzot and the broken one between them and makes the *hamotzi* blessing.

BLESSED ARE YOU, LORD OUR GOD, King of the universe, who brings forth bread from the earth.

One puts down the bottom matzah and recites the blessing for matzah, keeping in mind that this blessing is also to include the *korech* – "the Hillel sandwich" – and the afikoman.

BLESSED ARE YOU, LORD OUR GOD, King of the universe, who has sanctified us with His mitzvot and commanded us concerning the eating of matzah.

One takes a large piece of matzah (at least as large as in the photograph on the opposite page) of the broken matzah, adds a little of the complete matzah, and eats both while leaning.

Food For Thought

Eating matzah – to feel internal freedom

The act of eating matzah is a multi-symbolical act: it is an expression of annulling one's pride and privileging one's innermost, simple nature over the superficial, external layers that we build around ourselves. Moreover, eating matzah expresses the return to our internal and fundamentally holy state, where we can truly be ourselves, unenslaved to any external, material influences. The matzah as a food of the "poor," as *lechem oni*, is also an expression of

◂ the

One eats a portion of handmade shemurah matzah as big as this (and there are those who hold that one can also fulfill the mitzvah by using machine-made shemurah matzah). This is the actual size of the matzah to be used. One who has difficulty eating this amount can eat the intermediate amount (p. 153), and one who is ill can eat a small amount (the size of the matzah on the page dealing with korech – p. 154).

the freedom it symbolizes: the ability to free ourselves from all external, false and showy wealth, to be faithful to ourselves, to our true natures. This freedom enables us to truly connect to our Creator, without any barriers or partitions (see also the section "'This matzah' – Why do we eat matzot on Pesach?" – p. 112).

Halachic Summary

How to break the matzah – One holds all three matzot and recites the *hamotzi* blessing. He puts down the bottom matzah and then recites the *al achilat matzah* blessing on the top two matzot, *keeping in mind that this blessing will also cover the matzah in korech and the afikoman.* One takes *kezayit* of the top whole matzah and *kezayit* of the middle broken matzah, and eats both while leaning. Each person is given that amount of matzah. If there is not enough matzah in these two matzot, the person conducting the seder augments these with other matzot.

The mitzvah to eat matzah is a Torah mitzvah, even nowadays. One should eat matzah while leaning and in joy, and should think that he is fulfilling the positive Torah mitzvah of eating matzah.

To fulfill the mitzvah of eating matzah, one should eat the equivalent of *three quarters of a machine made matzah.* (If that is difficult, one can eat half a matzah. A sick person need eat only a third). See the photographs for the size of the matzah.

One should use matzah shemurah for this, and ideally, it should be handmade.

Ideally, one should consume this amount within four minutes. One need not look at one's watch, but should eat at a normal, yet brisk pace, without talking or being involved in any other activity until the full amount has been eaten.

Ideally, one should not talk except for the needs of the meal (matzah, maror, and korech), from the reciting of the blessing until after korech has been eaten.

Torah pointer, Poland, 19th century, silver
The Wolfson Museum, Hechal Shlomo

MOTZI MATZAH

The Torah-mandated mitzvah:	Eating matzah is a Torah-mandated mitzvah today, even though there is no Pesach sacrifice. In fact, this is the only Torah mitzvah that mandates the eating of a specific food in our time, and that is why one must be very careful in its observance. One is to eat matzah in joy, and with full intention to fulfill the words, "on the evening you shall eat matzot."
How much matzah must one eat?	According to Rosh, one must eat a portion the size of two *kezaitim*, one from the whole matzah and one from the broken matzah. That is also the ruling of Shulchan Aruch. This ruling might have have evolved from doubt whether one must eat the *kezayit* from the whole matzah or from the broken matzah. Mishnah Berurah questions this ruling, and Chazon Ish disagrees with it and writes that one *kezayit* is enough. Therefore, even though it is preferable to eat two *kezaitim*, one can be lenient regarding *the second kezayit,* as below.
How much is a *kezayit?*	There are three major views: THE LARGE QUANTITY (Chazon Ish according to Tosafot): 47.5 cc. (1.61 fluid ounces). THE MEDIUM QUANTITY (Rav Chaim Naeh according to Tosafot): 27 cc. (0.91 fluid ounces). THE SMALL QUANTITY (Rav Chaim Naeh according to Rambam): about 19 cc. (0.64 fluid ounces), and some say 17 cc. (0.57 fluid ounces).
Calculating based on volume	There are those who calculate the size based on weight, and that is the ruling of a number of Sefardic rabbis (Kaf HaChaim, Yechaveh Da'at), but from the Mishnah, the Rishonim, and the Ashkenazic authorities it appears that the calculation should be by volume, and that is the way the Ashkenazic rabbis and some Sefardic rabbis rule. The differences between the two can be considerable, as matzah weighs about half the same volume of water. Thus one who bases himself on weight will eat twice as much as one who bases himself on volume.

How much must one eat in practice?	The calculation below is based on volume (if one wishes to rule according to weight, he will need to double all these figures), and is based on machine matzot as they are uniform in size (if using hand matzah, one must take an equivalent piece). The volume of a machine matzah is about 60 cc. (2.03 fluid ounces). THE FIRST *KEZAYIT*: As this is a Torah-mandated mitzvah, one should ideally eat slightly more than ¾ of a machine matzah, the largest *kezayit* volume, or at least half a matzah, the medium ruling . One who is ill can eat the small quantity – 19 cc. (0.64 fluid ounces) about ⅓ of a matzah. THE SECOND *KEZAYIT*: As the second *kezayit* is only a stringency, one can regard the amount we took for the first *kezayit*, or ¾ of a matzah, as being equivalent to the size of two small *kezaitim*. Thus, one can eat just a little more than ¾ of a matzah (for both *kezaitim* together), and fulfill the Torah mitzvah in the most ideal way, while simultaneously fulfilling the requirement for two *kezaitim* in a minimal way.
Summary of total matzah eaten during Seder night	EATING MATZAH: ¾ of a matzah (or at least a half – a sick person can eat a third). KORECH: Half a matzah (and if that is too difficult – a third of a matzah) AFIKOMAN: If it is not difficult – ⅔ of a matzah. If that is difficult – half a matzah, or even a third.
Within how much time must one eat it?	Ideally, one should eat the above quantity within four minutes (and children within nine minutes). One does not have to time this exactly, but should eat at a normal, yet brisk pace, without speaking or doing anything else.

How are the matzot divided among the participants?	The best way is for the one who conducts the Seder night to give each person present a large kezayit of the top matzah and of the middle matzah in front of him. If that is not enough for all participants, there are two possible ways to deal with this: a. Only the person conducting the seder will have three matzot. He will give a little of both matzot to each person, and will add other matzah for each person. b. Each person, or at least every few people, will have their own three matzot.
What is the process for making the blessings and eating matzah?	One holds all three matzot and recites the hamotzi blessing. He puts down the bottom matzah and then recites al achilat matzah on the top two matzot, keeping in mind that this blessing should also cover the matzah in korech and the afikoman. One takes a large *kezayit* of matzah (preferable the majority from the broken matzah, and added matzah from the top matzah), and eats it while leaning, at a normal pace yet without interruption, and with the intent of fulfilling the mitzvah of "on the evening you shall eat matzot."
The type of matzah	For the matzah of the Torah-mandated mitzvah, one must eat matzah shemurah (if it is machine made, he has on whom to rely – and some even prefer it).
The type of matzah during the other days of Pesach	Throughout the rest of the festival, one may eat matzah that is not shemurah, but it is proper to use only matzah baked under good rabbinic supervision, as kosher – for-Pesach matzah is difficult to make. Some people eat matzah shemurah throughout the whole of Pesach, but they need not eat only hand-made matzah (beyond the requirement to use matzah shemurah to fulfill the mitzvah on the first night, though there are those who eat only hand-made matzah on the *Seder* night).

For greater detail, see *Halachah MiMekorah – Kinor David, Motzi Matzah* p. 127.

MOTZI MATZAH

Hamotzi and *Al achilat matzah*

The top matzah is for *hamotzi* and one eats a *kezayit* of it (the small quantity).

The middle, broken matzah, is for the mitzvah of eating matzah and one eats *kezayit* of it (the large quantity).

The third matzah, the bottom one, is made for *lechem mishneh* – the second loaf one needs at Shabbat and festival meals, and that is why it is held for the *hamotzi* blessing. One eats *kezayit* of it for *korech*.

THE AMOUNT TO EAT

How much is a *kezayit*?
(according to the accepted custom of working by volume)

- The large quantity (Noda BiYehudah and Chazon Ish according to Tosafot): 47.5 cc. (1.61 fluid ounces).
- The medium quantity (Rav Chaim Naeh based on Tosafot): 27 cc. (0.91 fluid ounces)
- The small quantity (Rav Chaim Naeh based on Rambam): 19 cc. (0.64 fluid ounces)

The quantity of a *kezayit* of matzah (machine-made matzah, with a volume of 60 cc. (2.03 fluid ounces). For hand-made matzah, one should take an equivalent piece).

- The large quantity – about ¾ of a matzah.
- The medium quantity – about half a matzah.
- The small quantity – about ⅓ of a matzah.

THE AMOUNT TO BE EATEN AT THE SEDER

EATING MATZAH: (the size of two kezaitim): about ¾ of a matzah (if it is too difficult, a half. One who is sick, a third).

KORECH: Half a matzah (for one for whom this is difficult – a third)

AFIKOMAN: Ideally, ⅔ of a matzah (as it is preferable to eat the size of two *kezaitim*), but one can settle for half a matzah (and if that is difficult – a third)

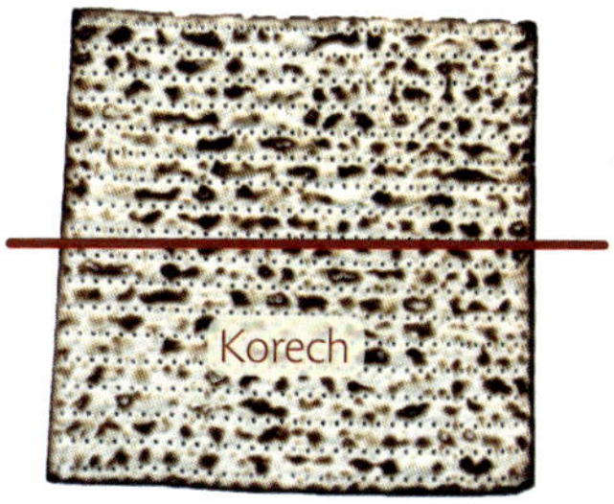

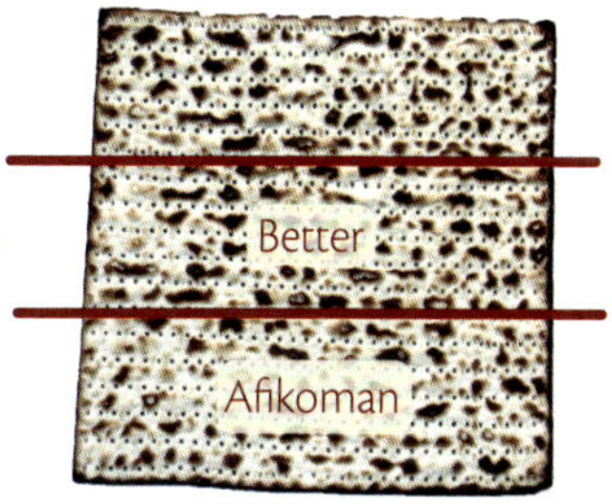

Maror

By eating maror, we are reminded that *God's supervision of the world* drives everything – both the good and the bad. Even the bitter was known to Him in advance, and bitterness also has a role to play. We eat maror and internalize the great thanks we owe to God for His great rescue. We eat maror and pray in our hearts for Am Yisrael, who has already gone through so much bitterness – in Egypt, in the exile to Babylon, in the Inquisition, in the Crusades, in the expulsion from Spain, in the Holocaust, and so on. As we eat the maror, we pray that the future will bring not bitterness, but sweetness, light and redemption.

יש נוהגים לומר לפני הברכה:

הִנְנִי מוּכָן וּמְזוּמָּן לְקַיֵּם מִצְוַת אֲכִילַת מָרוֹר. לְשֵׁם יִחוּד קוּדְשָׁא בְּרִיךְ הוּא וּשְׁכִינְתֵּיהּ עַל יְדֵי הַהוּא טָמִיר וְנֶעְלָם בְּשֵׁם כָּל יִשְׂרָאֵל. וִיהִי נֹעַם אֲדֹנָי אֱלֹהֵינוּ עָלֵינוּ וּמַעֲשֵׂה יָדֵינוּ כּוֹנְנָה עָלֵינוּ וּמַעֲשֵׂה יָדֵינוּ כּוֹנְנֵהוּ.

לוקחים כזית מרור, טובלים בחרוסת, ומברכים: "על אכילת מרור", ומכוונים לפטור גם את המרור שב"כורך".

בָּרוּךְ: אַתָּה יְהֹוָה אֱלֹהֵינוּ מֶלֶךְ הָעוֹלָם, אֲשֶׁר קִדְּשָׁנוּ בְּמִצְוֹתָיו, וְצִוָּנוּ עַל אֲכִילַת מָרוֹר.

Halachic Summary

The mitzvah of maror was a Torah-mandated mitzvah at the time that the Pesach sacrifice was brought. Today it is only a rabbinic mitzvah. The best maror is lettuce, and one must ensure that it is insect-free. One must take a *kezayit* of maror. It is best to take 27 cc. (0.91 fluid ounces), which is about the size of an average lettuce leaf, but by the technical requirements of the law 19 cc. (0.64 fluid ounces) are enough. When reciting the blessing on maror, one must keep in mind that the blessing should also include the maror that will be used in korech. Then, dip charoset, shake off some of the charoset, and eat it without leaning, eating at a normal pace, but without stopping. ▪

Food For Thought

Maror – the importance of the enslavement

Rambam (8:8) writes that one should dip matzah into charoset: "and he dips matzah into charoset and eats." Ra'avad (*ibid.*) disagrees, and Maggid Mishneh (*ibid.*) cites other opinions that disagree and states that one eats matzah by itself, without charoset.

Sefer HaManhig (*Hilchot Pesach* 79) is surprised by Rambam's opinion:

> I was amazed that he wrote to dip matzah in charoset and I have never seen or heard this custom anywhere. One can one even ask how such a combination is logical. If matzah requires leaning because it is a remembrance of freedom, and charoset is a

◂ remembrance

There are those who have the custom to say the following before the blessing:

I am prepared and ready to fulfill the mitzvah of eating maror. For the sake of the unification of the Holy One, Blessed be He, and His Presence, in the name of all Israel. And may the pleasantness of the Lord our God be upon us, and the work of our hands establish for us, and may the work of our hands establish it.

One takes a *kezayit* of the maror, dips it into charoset, and recites the blessing for maror, keeping in mind that this blessing is also to include the maror in "korech."

BLESSED ARE YOU, LORD OUR GOD, King of the universe, who has sanctified us with His mitzvot and commanded us concerning the eating of maror.

---

remembrance of the clay of slavery, how can the contradictory values of freedom and slavery be combined? It is possible that *Rambam* is teaching us that very point – on this night it is important to *combine servitude and redemption.* Although it is not our custom to dip matzah into charoset, we do express this connection in other ways. When we eat maror directly after matzah, as well as by eating korech, we demonstrate that *slavery and redemption are intertwined.*

When we eat maror we think about the bitterness of slavery in order to instill in ourselves a greater appreciation of the miracle of the Exodus from Egypt. Simply put, in the wake of our thoughts about the difficulty and suffering during slavery, we can better appreciate the greatness of our salvation. Beyond this, eating maror teaches us that everything was planned by God – both the slavery and the redemption. Slavery also has a role to play in the process of redemption, and without it we would not have been redeemed. Sadly, on occasion, history has proven that bitterness and anti-Semitism have even prevented assimilation.

On the Seder night we do not ignore the bitterness and distress, nor do we repress the difficulties of the past. *On the contrary,* we eat maror and recite a blessing on it. By doing so, we acknowledge that the bitterness that we endured was also part of "He has sanctified us with His mitzvot." The mitzvah of eating maror teaches us to look directly at the difficulties of life, without fear and without evasion. We acknowledge that with every difficulty one grows, and every struggle reveals the powers within ourselves to continue focusing with joy and abundant good.

(See what I wrote on this topic at the end of this haggadah in the answers to the riddles concering the discussion about *yachatz*, as to whether matzah is a symbol of slavery or of freedom, p. 279, in the section of "This night we are going free," p. 43, as well as in the section of "Matzah and maror – the unity of opposites" p. 60). ▪

מרור – חסה – 19 סמ"ק – ניתן לקחת שיעור זה (חזון איש), וטוב להדר בשיעור 27 סמ"ק (משנה ברורה) – במידה ולוקחים חתיכה מעט יותר גדולה מהקלח מגיעים בקלות לשיעור זה.

Maror – lettuce – 19 cc. (0.64 fluid ounces) – one should take this quantity (Chazon Ish), and it is better to take 27 cc. (0.91 fluid ounces) (Mishnah Berurah) – if one takes a little of the stalk along with the leaf, this amount is easily reached.

Korech

The matzah is wrapped with maror. Even at our time of matzah (of joy), we must remember the problems we had during times of bitterness. Even when we are free, we must remember our slavery. We must acknowledge the role of slavery in our redemption, remember our heritage of slavery, which now enables us to be in servitude to God. We must remember the difficulties of those who are not free, and even when we are free we must know to treat other people with respect and with sympathy.

לוקחים כזית מהמצה השלישית וכזית מרור טובלים בחרוסת (יש המנערים ויש שאינם מנערים), כורכים אותם יחד, ואומרים "זכר למקדש כהלל וכו'" (ויש פוסקים לאכול תחילה ואחרי כן לומר):

זֵכֶר לַמִּקְדָּשׁ כְּהִלֵּל. כֵּן עָשָׂה הִלֵּל בִּזְמַן שֶׁבֵּית הַמִּקְדָּשׁ הָיָה קַיָּם: הָיָה כּוֹרֵךְ פֶּסַח מַצָּה וּמָרוֹר וְאוֹכֵל בְּיַחַד, לְקַיֵּם מַה שֶּׁנֶּאֱמַר: עַל מַצּוֹת וּמְרֹרִים יֹאכְלֻהוּ (במדבר ט', יא).

רצוי לאכול בהסבת שמאל.

One takes a *kezayit* of the third matzah and a *kezayit* of maror, dipped in charoset (some shake off the excess charoset and some do not). One wraps them together and says the following passage (some authorities rule that we eat first and then say the passage):

A REMEMBRANCE OF BET HAMIKDASH practice according to Hillel. We do as Hillel did at the time when Bet HaMikdash was standing. He would combine matzah and maror in a sandwich and eat them together, to fulfill what is written in the Torah, "with matzot and bitter herbs shall they eat it" (Numbers 9:11).

It is proper to eat korech while leaning to the left.

Halachic Summary

After we have eaten matzah and maror separately (and thereby have fulfilled the mitzvot according to the Sages), *we now eat matzah and maror together,* in remembrance of the practice of Hillel, who did this during the time of the Bet HaMikdash.One takes a *kezayit* of matzah (about half a machine-made matzah, and if that is difficult, one takes a third of a matzah) from the bottom matzah (that has not yet been used for any mitzvah), breaks it into two pieces, and places a lettuce leaf (27 cc., or 0.91 fluid ounces, and if that is too much – one can use only 19 cc., or 0.64 fluid ounces, or even 17 cc., 0.57 fluid ounces) between the matzah pieces. Before placing the leaf between the matzah pieces, one dips it into charoset. Some shake some of the charoset off, while others do not.

Before eating it, it is customary to

◂ say

אוכלים גודל זה ממצת יד שמורה (ויש הסבורים שניתן לצאת במצת מכונה שמורה). בתמונה זו מצה בשיעור בינוני, בגודל ממשי.

The picture shows a medium-sized portion of matzah, in actual size. One should eat this much in order to fulfill the mitzvah of *korech*. Ideally, the matzah should be handmade shemurah matzah, although some authorities hold that one can fulfill the requirement with machine-made shemurah matzah.

say "A remembrance of the Bet HaMikdash practice according to Hillel." There is an opinion that this phrase should be recited after eating it, but our custom nowadays is to say it beforehand.

Korech should be eaten without interruption and while leaning (if one did not lean, he has still fulfilled the requirement). ▪

מי שקשה לו יכול להסתפק בגודל זה ממצת יד שמורה (ויש הסבורים שניתן לצאת במצת מכונה שמורה). בתמונה זו מצה בשיעור קטן, בגודל ממשי (וחולה יכול לאכול לכורך ולאפיקומן אפילו חצי מכמות זו).

If one finds it difficult to eat the medium-sized portion of matzah, shown on the previous page, one may eat a smaller portion, shown here in actual size. A person who is ill can eat even half this amount for korech and afikoman.

Food For Thought

"Hillel… would combine matzah and maror in a sandwich and eat them together."

Before acting as Hillel did, wrapping matzah and maror together, we first ate them separately. Why? Matzah symbolizes freedom while maror symbolizes slavery. We reflect separately on the greatness of freedom and the troubles of slavery, and only then can we try to combine the two ideas, wrapping matzah and maror together.

Freedom and slavery together brought us to our redemption. We gained certain characteristics because we had been slaves. Slavery in itself is of course something terrible. However, through our slavery, we received the capacity *to accept authority, to be obedient.* This is an important quality to aid in our struggle against our passions and our lowliest urges. A person must know how to accept the authority

◂ of wisdom

of wisdom and knowledge, and how to suppress his animalistic urges. The power of slavery and the acceptance of authority is only useful to a person if he combines them with the feeling of freedom and liberty, as symbolized in the sandwiching of matzah and *maror* together.

This principle was clarified by Rav Avraham Yitzchak Kook (*Olat Re'iyah* on the haggadah, *Korech*, p. 49):

> The highest form of freedom, whose glory and beauty is only revealed by wearing the *crown of uplifitng slavery...* Therefore, the fullest manifestation of freedom comes when it is *sandwiched with slavery,* for this will enable the person to elicit the self-control befitting a truly free person – *controlling the greatest of forces, freedom.*

Seder plate, Jerusalem, 20th century, olive wood, artist: Tzion Drori
The Wolfson Museum, Hechal Shlomo

Freedom is important, but it can be a gift or a curse. *One must know how to live as a free person.* A person who is free of all constraints, and who can do whatever he wants, is not a truly free person. A free person is one *who can do whatever he wants to, but does only that which his pure soul instructs him to do.* A free person is one who *knows how to control his freedom.*

There is terrible slavery, but there is also "uplifting slavery." The latter refers to *using the strengths of one's body to advance the development of one's soul* (see pages 278 and 285). The aim of uplifting slavery is to enable the person to control all his powers and to channel them into the proper path, and primarily to control the greatest of forces – the force of freedom itself! One who is unable to control these powers, who gives free rein to every desire and every feeling, is not a free person but is enslaved by his desires and passions.

Slavery by itself is terrible, and that is why we do not lean when we eat maror. However, when slavery is united with the characteristics of freedom, when it complements a person's freedom, it is elevated, and that is why we lean for korech. This is the path of true freedom – freedom governed by self-control is uplifting servitude.

Slavery – A free person's obligation!

We have explained, based on the words of *Rav Avraham Yitzchak Kook,* that slavery was a necessary step on the

◂ path

path towards becoming servants of God.

Rav Yosef Dov Soloveitchik (*Festival of Freedom,* pp. 133–134) explains the meaning of slavery in a different way:

> The experience of Egyptian servitude underlies the very morality of the Jew... The fact that in Egypt the Jews were exposed to all kinds of chicanery and humiliation... engendered in the Jewish people sensitivity and tenderness toward their fellow man... Without the experience of slavery, we would have remained unexposed to suffering, emotionally vulgar and insensitive... Thus, only in Egypt could the Jews become an am [nation] and a goy gadol [great people]... This was necessary not only in order to develop rahmanut [merciful compassion]. The Jews had to see and experience evil, tyranny, ruthlessness – for one cannot hate Satan unless one knows him well and has dealt with him... In pain and despair, we have attained greatness and nationhood. "Like the rose among thorns, so is my beloved among the maidens" (Song of Songs 2:2).

Only when a person is confronted by slavery, when he feels what evil truly is, is he able to understand and truly hate evil. Joseph had to be sold to Potiphar in order to recognize human cruelty. Had Jacob and his sons stayed in Canaan, they and their descendants would not have developed their sensitivity to honesty and fairness. Had we not felt the yoke of slavery, we would not have understood the demand not to afflict the stranger (Rav Soloveitchik, *ibid.*).

"He became there a nation" (Deuteronomy 26:5). In Egypt, Israel became a nation, a people. The ability to be transformed from a family into a nation, and to bear all the complexities and struggles of being a nation, requires the ability to recognize the bad and difficult parts of life. One who has never left his protected and safe home and has not seen suffering and pain around him, cannot be a leader. In order for Am Yisrael to become "a kingdom of princes and a holy nation" (Exodus 19:6) and to serve as a light to the nations (Isaiah 42:6), it was necessary for them to experience the slavery of Egypt, to see and to feel what suffering is and what evil is.

It was this slavery that enabled Am Yisrael to be a truly free nation: a nation that is able to feel the problems of others, that is merciful, that detests evil and desires to connect with the good. We can all learn from the slavery of our forefathers, though we have been blessed by God with comfortable and safe lives, to strive towards live a meaningful life, a life conscious of the suffering of others. ▪

Shulchan Orech

Now we are privileged to eat a *thanksgiving meal*. This meal is eaten in the middle of hallel, showing that the meal itself is a form of praise and thanks to God. During the meal we should eat joyfully and focus on spiritually uplifting subjects.

One eats the festive meal.

אוכלים סעודת חג.

Pesach plate, Jerusalem, 19th century, glazed clay
The Wolfson Museum, Hechal Shlomo

Halachic Summary

One should eat joyfully and with great gratitude. This meal is eaten in the middle of hallel. Therefore, it is considered to be part of the praise and thanks to God. One should try to ensure that this meal serves as a religious experience to discuss Torah thoughts and talk about the Exodus from Egypt.

At this meal one does not eat roasted meat, but one may eat meat that was roasted in an oven with gravy.

Many begin the meal by eating eggs (and many dip the egg in salt water), as a reminder of the destruction of the Bet HaMikdash and a reminder of the *chagigah* – festival – sacrifice.

One should take care not to eat too much at the meal, in order to be able to enjoy eating the afikoman and not view it as purely an obligation. ▪

Tzafun

We have now reached the matzah of freedom. We eat it not because we are hungry, not because we need to eat. We eat it as free people.

בסיום הסעודה אוכלים בהסבת שמאל כזית מהמצה שהצפינו לאפיקומן [שיעור של חצי מצה. וטוב להדר בשיעור של שני שלישי מצת מכונה, ואם קשה – ניתן להסתפק אפילו בשליש].

יש נוהגים לומר לפני אכילת האפיקומן:

הִנְנִי מוּכָן וּמְזוּמָּן לְקַיֵּם מִצְוַת אֲכִילַת אֲפִיקוֹמָן. לְשֵׁם יִחוּד קוּדְשָׁא בְּרִיךְ הוּא וּשְׁכִינְתֵּיהּ עַל יְדֵי הַהוּא טָמִיר וְנֶעְלָם בְּשֵׁם כָּל יִשְׂרָאֵל. וִיהִי נֹעַם אֲדֹנָי אֱלֹהֵינוּ עָלֵינוּ וּמַעֲשֵׂה יָדֵינוּ כּוֹנְנָה עָלֵינוּ וּמַעֲשֵׂה יָדֵינוּ כּוֹנְנֵהוּ.

Food For Thought

Returning to the inner self – Afikoman

Rav Avraham Yitzchak Kook (in *Olat Re'iyah* on the haggadah, p. 50) explains that afikoman expresses the tzafun – the *hidden aspect of man and life.* The higher the spiritual level, the deeper and more concealed is its spirituality. The internal significance of afikoman is learned from the fact that one eats it when he is full, as emerges from Rav Kook's words:

> Afikoman is eaten when one is full, as an *end in itself,* and not as a necessity for maintaining one's worldly existence. From that perspective, it is appropriate for the deepest, most hidden (*tzafun*) feelings of the soul.

Generally, a person eats in order to be full, and food is only a means. Afikoman, on the other hand, is eaten when a person is already full, and from this it follows that afikoman is an aim in itself.

We learned about ("Why do we eat matzot on Pesach?" p. 112) the explanation of Maharal regarding the significance of eating matzah. Matzah, on the one hand, expresses servitude and difficulty – the "bread of affliction" – but, on the other hand, it also has characteristics that teach us about freedom and improvement.

Maharal explains that this is not a contradiction. Matzah is indeed the "bread of affliction," but only through this affliction, it is an expression of true freedom.

◂

Kiddush goblet, Nuremberg, 18th century, gold-plated silver
The Wolfson Museum, Hechal Shlomo, Max Grundt Collection

At the end of the meal, we lean to the left and eat matzah that has been put aside for afikoman [a quantity equal to half a matzah (the middle amount – see p. 153), and it is preferable to eat a quantity equal to ⅔ of a machine-made matzah. If that is difficult, one can eat only ⅓ of a matzah].

There are those who say the following before eating the afikoman:

I am prepared and ready to fulfill the mitzvah of eating afikoman. For the sake of the unification of the Holy One, Blessed be He, and His Presence, in the name of all Israel. And may the pleasantness of the Lord our God be upon us, and the work of our hands establish for us, and may the work of our hands establish it.

Halachic Summary

At the end of the meal we lean to the left and eat matzah that has been put aside for afikoman. Ideally, this too should be matzah shemurah. One should eat a *kezayit* of matzah, and some are careful to eat two such measures: one as a reminder of the Pesach sacrifice and one as a reminder of the matzah that was eaten with it. Therefore, if one is able, he should eat ⅔ of the size of a machine-made matzah (about 40 cc. – 1.35 fluid ounces), but if that is too hard, one can eat half a matzah (30 cc. or 1.01 fluid ounces) or even as little as ⅓ of a matzah (about 19 cc. or 0.64 fluid ounces).

One should try to finish eating afikoman by midnight (if one didn't manage it, one can make the condition of the Avnei Nezer – see the tables).

One may not eat after afikoman, but may drink water or weak liquids, such as tea or juice (but definitely not anything alcoholic), so as not to weaken the taste of the matzah. ▪

freedom. Matzah expresses the pure interior of the person, without any additions or external trappings.

We strive to live according to our true selves, based on our Divine nature and the pure soul that God placed inside us. When *Am Yisrael* reaches such a stage, and lives accordingly, our redemption will come.

Therefore, we were commanded to eat matzah before we left Egypt, for matzah was part of the redemption. According to this, eating matzah is not only a "reminder" of the historical event of the redemption from Egypt, but is the very reason for the redemption! Matzah expresses the level that Am Yisrael attained by casting off all external influences, and that brought about our redemption.

By eating matzah on the Seder night we are attempting to return to such a level, aspiring for our actions to reflect the truth of our internal self. The Seder

◂ night

night is a process of redemption for us as well: at the beginning of the seder we eat matza, symbolic of the state of our souls, but we eat it when we are hungry – our physical hunger mixed in with our spiritual aspirations. After we have gone through the entire process of the Seder night, with all its symbols and customs, we are now able to eat this matzah with pure intentions – without any real appetite and without any motives other than that of fulfilling the mitzvah. The eating of afikoman symbolizes our spiritual goals, what we hope to have accomplished on the Seder night, and what we strive for throughout the year. We hope to act in freedom, free of any physical influences, true to our inner selves.

Riddles

82. During which of the stage of the Seder night do we eat afikoman?

What is the significance of the word "afikoman?"

The word "afikoman" is used today in exactly the opposite way in which it was first used. The meaning of afikoman is the last course at the end of the meal. "*Afiko-man*" – "take out the dessert" (Rashi, 119b, *uvegozliya le'abba*). The Mishnah (119b) states that on the Seder night there is no last course, "one does not add an afikoman after the Pesach sacrifice." In other words, one does not eat a last course after the Pesach sacrifice. Nowadays we use this term as a loanword: as one is not to eat anything after the matzah at the end of the meal, that is considered to be the last course, and that is why the last matzah of the Seder night is now referred to as afikoman.

For further details see *Halachah Mi-Mekorah – Kinor David, Tzafun* p. 228.

Torah finial, Burma, Mandalay, 1896, silver
The Wolfson Museum, Hechal Shlomo

Barech

While reciting *birkat hamazon* on the Seder night, one should have special intent when saying "for having brought us out, Lord our God, from the land of Egypt and redeemed us from the house of slavery." We must also thank God for the wonderful land He has given us, the food we have, and the Torah. We would not have any of these if not for the Exodus from Egypt.

BARECH

The blessing over wine	During the year, most people do not recite birkat hamazon over a cup of wine (except when there is a minyan). However, on the Seder night, even a person by himself must recite birkat hamazon over a cup of wine (Tosafot). The one leading birkat hamazon should hold his cup in his right hand, above the table by at least 3.2 inches and look at it, so as not to be distracted. The other participants do not need to raise their cups, although some people do have this custom. Some also have the custom to hold the cup without raising it.
Who leads birkat hamazon?	Generally, a guest is asked to be the leader of birkat hamazon, so that he can also bless the head of the household. However, Rama writes, based on the verse: "He who has a generous eye will be blessed" (Proverbs 22:9), that since the head of the household invited all the guests he should be the leader (of course, it is permissible for him to ask someone else to lead).
It is proper to have a leader?	Throughout the year there is no requirement to seek out three people who ate together for birkat hamazon, but on the Seder night it is preferable to have three men recite birkat hamazon together, so that they will be partners in reciting hallel.
If a man forgot to say *Ya'aleh VeYavo*	If one forgot to recite *Ya'aleh VeYavo* and recalls only after reciting a full sentence of the subsequent blessing, he must begin birkat hamazon again. However, if he realized sooner, there is a special formulation that may be used instead (see chart).
If a woman forgot to say *Ya'aleh VeYavo*	Throughout the year, if a woman forgets the addition for Shabbat, *Retzei*, she must repeat birkat hamazon, but not if she forgot *Ya'aleh VeYavo*. However, if this happens on the Seder night, she must repeat birkat hamazon, as she is required to eat a *kezayit* of matzah.
Pouring wine for the head of the household	It is the custom to have someone else pour this cup of wine for the head of the household, as a symbol of freedom.
Leaning	One should not lean during birkat hamazon, as one must concentrate on the meaning of the words.

For further discussion, see *Halachah MiMekorah – Kinor David, Barech* p. 247.

BARECH – BIRKAT HAMAZON

If one forgot *Ya'aleh VeYavo* (or *Retzei* on Friday night),
If he remembers after he had said…

- ברוך אתה → He goes back to *Ya'aleh VeYavo.*
- ברוך אתה ה׳ → He continues with the words לַמְּדֵנִי חֻקֶּיךָ "teach me Your laws" and then goes back to *Ya'aleh VeYavo*.
- ברוך אתה ה׳ בונה ברחמיו ירושלים אמן → He says:
  ברוך אתה ה׳ אלהינו מלך העולם, אשר נתן ימים טובים לישראל לששון ולשמחה את יום חג המצות הזה, ברוך אתה ה׳ מקדש ישראל והזמנים
  "Blessed are You, Lord our God, King of the universe, who gave festival days to Israel for rejoicing and festivity, this day of the Festival of Matzot. Blessed are You, Lord, who sanctifies Israel and the seasons" and then continues with the fourth blessing of birkat hamazon.
- ברוך אתה ה׳ אלהינו מלך העולם (of the beginning of the next blessing) → He continues:
  אשר נתן ימים טובים לישראל לששון ולשמחה את יום חג המצות הזה, ברוך אתה ה׳ מקדש ישראל והזמנים
  "Blessed are You, Lord our God, King of the universe, who gave festival days to Israel for rejoicing and festivity, this day of the Festival of Matzot. Blessed are You, Lord, who sanctifies Israel and the seasons" and then starts the fourth blessing of birkat hamazon over again.
- ברוך... מלך העולם, האל → He repeats birkat hamazon.

If one only forgot to say *Retzei* on Friday night, he says:
ברוך אתה ה׳ אלהינו מלך העולם, שנתן שבתות למנוחה לעמו ישראל באהבה לאות ולברית, ברוך אתה ה׳ מקדש השבת
"Blessed are You, Lord our God, Who gave Shabbatot for rest to His nation Israel, in love as a sign and covenant. Blessed are You, Lord, who sanctifies Shabbat."

If one forgot both *Retzei* and *Ya'aleh Veyavo*, he says:
ברוך אתה ה׳ אלהינו מלך העולם, שנתן שבתות למנוחה לעמו ישראל באהבה לאות ולברית, וימים טובים לששון ולשמחה את יום חג המצות הזה, ברוך אתה ה׳ מקדש השבת וישראל והזמנים
"Blessed are You, Lord our God, who gave Shabbatot for rest to His nation Israel, in love as a sign and covenant, and festivals for rejoicing and festivity, this day of the Festival of Matzot. Blessed are You, Lord, who sanctifies Shabbat and the seasons."

If one does not remember this formulation, he must begin birkat hamazon again, but if he remembered at least the beginning and end of this formulation he does not have to begin again.

מוזגים כוס שלישית, נוטלים מים אחרונים ומברכים (ברכת המזון בנוסח ספרדים נמצא בעמ' 248)

ברכת המזון (בנוסח אשכנז)

שִׁיר הַמַּעֲלוֹת בְּשׁוּב יְהֹוָה אֶת שִׁיבַת צִיּוֹן הָיִינוּ כְּחֹלְמִים. אָז יִמָּלֵא שְׂחוֹק פִּינוּ וּלְשׁוֹנֵנוּ רִנָּה, אָז יֹאמְרוּ בַגּוֹיִם הִגְדִּיל יְהֹוָה לַעֲשׂוֹת עִם אֵלֶּה. הִגְדִּיל יְהֹוָה לַעֲשׂוֹת עִמָּנוּ, הָיִינוּ שְׂמֵחִים. שׁוּבָה יְהֹוָה אֶת שְׁבִיתֵנוּ כַּאֲפִיקִים בַּנֶּגֶב. הַזֹּרְעִים בְּדִמְעָה בְּרִנָּה יִקְצֹרוּ. הָלוֹךְ יֵלֵךְ וּבָכֹה נֹשֵׂא מֶשֶׁךְ הַזָּרַע, בֹּא יָבֹא בְרִנָּה נֹשֵׂא אֲלֻמֹּתָיו (תהלים קכ"ו).

יש נוהגים לומר לפני ברכת המזון

הִנְנִי מוּכָן וּמְזֻמָּן לְקַיֵּם מִצְוַת עֲשֵׂה שֶׁל בִּרְכַּת הַמָּזוֹן, שֶׁנֶּאֱמַר: וְאָכַלְתָּ וְשָׂבָעְתָּ וּבֵרַכְתָּ אֶת יְהֹוָה אֱלֹהֶיךָ עַל הָאָרֶץ הַטֹּבָה אֲשֶׁר נָתַן לָךְ. לְשֵׁם יִחוּד קוּדְשָׁא בְּרִיךְ הוּא וּשְׁכִינְתֵּיהּ עַל יְדֵי הַהוּא טָמִיר וְנֶעְלָם בְּשֵׁם כָּל יִשְׂרָאֵל. וִיהִי נֹעַם אֲדֹנָי אֱלֹהֵינוּ עָלֵינוּ וּמַעֲשֵׂה יָדֵינוּ כּוֹנְנָה עָלֵינוּ וּמַעֲשֵׂה יָדֵינוּ כּוֹנְנֵהוּ.

שלושה (או יותר) שאכלו כאחד – חייבים בזימון.

המזמן: **רַבּוֹתַי, נְבָרֵךְ.**

המסובים: **יְהִי שֵׁם יְהֹוָה מְבֹרָךְ מֵעַתָּה וְעַד עוֹלָם.**

המזמן: **בִּרְשׁוּת מָרָנָן וְרַבָּנָן וְרַבּוֹתַי נְבָרֵךְ** (במניין: אֱלֹהֵינוּ) **שֶׁאָכַלְנוּ מִשֶּׁלּוֹ:**

המסובים: **בָּרוּךְ** (במניין: אֱלֹהֵינוּ) **שֶׁאָכַלְנוּ מִשֶּׁלּוֹ וּבְטוּבוֹ חָיִינוּ:**

המזמן: **בָּרוּךְ** (במניין: אֱלֹהֵינוּ) **שֶׁאָכַלְנוּ מִשֶּׁלּוֹ וּבְטוּבוֹ חָיִינוּ:**

יש נוהגים שהמזמן אומר: **בָּרוּךְ הוּא וּבָרוּךְ שְׁמוֹ.**

Halachic Summary

All the participants recite birkat hamazon over a cup of wine, this being the third cup of the four. It is the custom for the head of the household to lead birkat hamazon (but he may ask someone else instead). It is the custom for someone

◄ else

The third cup of wine is poured. One washes his hands ("*mayim acharonim*") and then recites birkat hamazon. (The birkat hamazon according to the sepharadi rite is on page 249.

BIRKAT HAMAZON (ASHKENAZI RITE)

A SONG OF ASCENTS. WHEN THE LORD RETURNS the captives of Zion, we will be like dreamers. Then our mouth will be filled with laughter, and our tongue with joyous song. Then will they say among the nations, "The Lord has done great things for these." The Lord has done great things for us, we were joyful. Lord, return our captivity like water-springs in the southern desert. Those who sow with tears will reap with great joy. Though he goes on his way weeping as he carries the seeds through the field, he will return singing, bearing his sheaves (Psalms 126).

Some recite the following before birkat hamazon:
I am prepared and ready to fulfill the mitzvah of Grace after Meals, as it states, "And you will eat and be satisfied, and you shall bless the Lord, your God, for the good land He has given you." For the sake of the unification of the Holy One, Blessed be He, and His Presence, in the name of all Israel. And may the pleasantness of the Lord our God be upon us, and the work of our hands establish for us, and may the work of our hands establish it.

If three or more males above the age of thirteen ate together, they must recite the zimun (invitation) for birkat hamazon:

LEADER: Gentlemen, let us bless!

OTHERS: May the name of the Lord be blessed from now and forever.

LEADER: Blessed be the name of the Lord from now and forever. With the permission of the masters, teachers and gentlemen, let us bless (in a minyan, add: our God), from whose abundance we have eaten.

OTHERS: Blessed is (in a minyan, add: our God,) [the One] from whose abundance we have eaten and through whose goodness we live.

LEADER: Blessed is (in a minyan, add: our God,) [the One] from whose abundance we have eaten and through whose goodness we live.

According to some customs, the Leader continues: Blessed is He and blessed is His Name.

---

else to fill the cup of the person who will be leading birkat hamazon, as an expression of freedom.

The leader should raise his cup, but the other participants do not need to do so (although some have the custom that the other participants should hold their cups without raising them).

It is preferable to have three or more males above the age of Bar Mitzvah for

◂ the

בָּרוּךְ אַתָּה יְהֹוָה אֱלֹהֵינוּ מֶלֶךְ הָעוֹלָם, הַזָּן אֶת הָעוֹלָם כֻּלּוֹ בְּטוּבוֹ, בְּחֵן, בְּחֶסֶד וּבְרַחֲמִים. הוּא נוֹתֵן לֶחֶם לְכָל בָּשָׂר כִּי לְעוֹלָם חַסְדּוֹ. וּבְטוּבוֹ הַגָּדוֹל תָּמִיד לֹא חָסַר לָנוּ, וְאַל יֶחְסַר לָנוּ מָזוֹן לְעוֹלָם וָעֶד, בַּעֲבוּר שְׁמוֹ הַגָּדוֹל, כִּי הוּא אֵל זָן וּמְפַרְנֵס לַכֹּל וּמֵטִיב לַכֹּל וּמֵכִין מָזוֹן לְכָל בְּרִיּוֹתָיו אֲשֶׁר בָּרָא. בָּרוּךְ אַתָּה יְהֹוָה, הַזָּן אֶת הַכֹּל.

נוֹדֶה לְךָ יְהֹוָה אֱלֹהֵינוּ עַל שֶׁהִנְחַלְתָּ לַאֲבוֹתֵינוּ אֶרֶץ חֶמְדָּה טוֹבָה וּרְחָבָה, וְעַל שֶׁהוֹצֵאתָנוּ יְהֹוָה אֱלֹהֵינוּ מֵאֶרֶץ מִצְרַיִם, וּפְדִיתָנוּ מִבֵּית עֲבָדִים, וְעַל בְּרִיתְךָ שֶׁחָתַמְתָּ בִּבְשָׂרֵנוּ, וְעַל תּוֹרָתְךָ שֶׁלִּמַּדְתָּנוּ, וְעַל חֻקֶּיךָ שֶׁהוֹדַעְתָּנוּ, וְעַל חַיִּים, חֵן וָחֶסֶד שֶׁחוֹנַנְתָּנוּ, וְעַל אֲכִילַת מָזוֹן שָׁאַתָּה זָן וּמְפַרְנֵס אוֹתָנוּ תָּמִיד בְּכָל יוֹם וּבְכָל עֵת וּבְכָל שָׁעָה.

וְעַל הַכֹּל יְהֹוָה אֱלֹהֵינוּ, אֲנַחְנוּ מוֹדִים לָךְ, וּמְבָרְכִים אוֹתָךְ, יִתְבָּרַךְ שִׁמְךָ בְּפִי כָּל חַי תָּמִיד לְעוֹלָם וָעֶד. כַּכָּתוּב: וְאָכַלְתָּ וְשָׂבָעְתָּ, וּבֵרַכְתָּ אֶת יְהֹוָה אֱלֹהֶיךָ עַל הָאָרֶץ הַטֹּבָה אֲשֶׁר נָתַן לָךְ. בָּרוּךְ אַתָּה יְהֹוָה, עַל הָאָרֶץ וְעַל הַמָּזוֹן.

רַחֵם נָא יְהֹוָה אֱלֹהֵינוּ עַל יִשְׂרָאֵל עַמֶּךָ, וְעַל יְרוּשָׁלַיִם עִירֶךָ, וְעַל צִיּוֹן מִשְׁכַּן כְּבוֹדֶךָ, וְעַל מַלְכוּת בֵּית דָּוִד מְשִׁיחֶךָ, וְעַל הַבַּיִת הַגָּדוֹל וְהַקָּדוֹשׁ

---

the communal birkat hamazon, so that they can then say hallel together.

One does not lean while reciting birkat hamazon. Birkat hamazon is recited with joy and thanks for all the good that God has given us. ▪

BLESSED ARE YOU, LORD OUR GOD, King of the universe, who, in His goodness, nourishes the whole world with grace, with kindness, and with compassion. He gives nourishment to all flesh, for His kindness is eternal. And through His great goodness we have never lacked, and may we never lack food forever – for the sake of His great Name. For He is God who provides and sustains all, does good to all, and prepares food for all His creatures whom He has created. Blessed are You, Lord, who provides food for all.

WE THANK YOU, LORD OUR GOD, FOR having given as an inheritance to our fathers a desirable, good and spacious land; for having brought us out, Lord our God, from the land of Egypt and redeemed us from the house of slavery; for Your covenant that You have sealed in our flesh; for Your Torah that You have taught us; for Your statutes that You have made known to us; for the life, favor and kindness that You have graciously bestowed upon us; and for the food that You provide for us and sustain us constantly, in every day, in every season, and in every hour.

AND FOR ALL OF THIS, LORD OUR GOD, we thank You and bless You. May Your Name be blessed by the mouth of every living being, constantly and forever. As it is written: "When you have eaten and are satiated, you shall bless the Lord your God, for the good land that He has given you." Blessed are You, Lord, for the land and for the food.

HAVE MERCY LORD OUR GOD, UPON Israel Your people, upon Jerusalem Your city, upon Zion the abode of Your glory, upon the kingship of the house of David, Your anointed; and upon the great and holy House upon which

שֶׁנִּקְרָא שִׁמְךָ עָלָיו. אֱלֹהֵינוּ אָבִינוּ, רְעֵנוּ, זוּנֵנוּ, פַּרְנְסֵנוּ, וְכַלְכְּלֵנוּ, וְהַרְוִיחֵנוּ, וְהַרְוַח לָנוּ יְהֹוָה אֱלֹהֵינוּ מְהֵרָה מִכָּל צָרוֹתֵינוּ, וְנָא אַל תַּצְרִיכֵנוּ יְהֹוָה אֱלֹהֵינוּ לֹא לִידֵי מַתְּנַת בָּשָׂר וָדָם וְלֹא לִידֵי הַלְוָאָתָם, כִּי אִם לְיָדְךָ הַמְּלֵאָה, הַפְּתוּחָה, הַקְּדוֹשָׁה וְהָרְחָבָה, שֶׁלֹּא נֵבוֹשׁ וְלֹא נִכָּלֵם לְעוֹלָם וָעֶד.

בשבת: **רְצֵה** וְהַחֲלִיצֵנוּ יְהֹוָה אֱלֹהֵינוּ בְּמִצְוֹתֶיךָ וּבְמִצְוַת יוֹם הַשְּׁבִיעִי, הַשַּׁבָּת הַגָּדוֹל וְהַקָּדוֹשׁ הַזֶּה, כִּי יוֹם זֶה גָּדוֹל וְקָדוֹשׁ הוּא לְפָנֶיךָ לִשְׁבָּת בּוֹ וְלָנוּחַ בּוֹ בְּאַהֲבָה כְּמִצְוַת רְצוֹנֶךָ, וּבִרְצוֹנְךָ הָנִיחַ לָנוּ יְהֹוָה אֱלֹהֵינוּ, שֶׁלֹּא תְהֵא צָרָה וְיָגוֹן וַאֲנָחָה בְּיוֹם מְנוּחָתֵנוּ, וְהַרְאֵנוּ יְהֹוָה אֱלֹהֵינוּ בְּנֶחָמַת צִיּוֹן עִירֶךָ, וּבְבִנְיַן יְרוּשָׁלַיִם עִיר קָדְשֶׁךָ, כִּי אַתָּה הוּא בַּעַל הַיְשׁוּעוֹת וּבַעַל הַנֶּחָמוֹת.

אֱלֹהֵינוּ וֵאלֹהֵי אֲבוֹתֵינוּ, יַעֲלֶה וְיָבֹא וְיַגִּיעַ וְיֵרָאֶה וְיֵרָצֶה וְיִשָּׁמַע וְיִפָּקֵד וְיִזָּכֵר זִכְרוֹנֵנוּ וּפִקְדוֹנֵנוּ, וְזִכְרוֹן אֲבוֹתֵינוּ, וְזִכְרוֹן מָשִׁיחַ בֶּן דָּוִד עַבְדֶּךָ, וְזִכְרוֹן יְרוּשָׁלַיִם עִיר קָדְשֶׁךָ, וְזִכְרוֹן כָּל עַמְּךָ בֵּית יִשְׂרָאֵל לְפָנֶיךָ, לִפְלֵיטָה, לְטוֹבָה, לְחֵן וּלְחֶסֶד וּלְרַחֲמִים, לְחַיִּים וּלְשָׁלוֹם, בְּיוֹם חַג הַמַּצּוֹת הַזֶּה. זָכְרֵנוּ יְהֹוָה אֱלֹהֵינוּ בּוֹ לְטוֹבָה, וּפָקְדֵנוּ בוֹ לִבְרָכָה, וְהוֹשִׁיעֵנוּ בוֹ לְחַיִּים. וּבִדְבַר יְשׁוּעָה וְרַחֲמִים, חוּס וְחָנֵּנוּ, וְרַחֵם עָלֵינוּ וְהוֹשִׁיעֵנוּ, כִּי אֵלֶיךָ עֵינֵינוּ כִּי אֵל מֶלֶךְ חַנּוּן וְרַחוּם אָתָּה.

וּבְנֵה יְרוּשָׁלַיִם עִיר הַקֹּדֶשׁ בִּמְהֵרָה בְיָמֵינוּ. בָּרוּךְ אַתָּה יְהֹוָה, בּוֹנֵה בְרַחֲמָיו יְרוּשָׁלָיִם, אָמֵן.

Your Name is called. Our God, our Father, our Shepherd, tend us, provide for us, sustain us, support us, and speedily grant us, Lord our God, relief from all our troubles. Lord our God, please do not make us dependent upon the gifts of mortal men nor upon their loans, but only upon Your full, open, holy and generous hand, that we may not be shamed or disgraced forever and ever.

On Shabbat: May it please You, God, our Lord, to give us rest, through Your mitzvot and through the mitzvah of the seventh day, this great and holy Shabbat. For this day is great and holy before You, to refrain from work on it and to rest on it with love, in accordance with Your will. May it be Your will, God our Lord, to grant us rest, that there shall be no distress, grief, or moaning on this day of our rest. And show us, God our Lord, the consolation of Zion Your city, and the rebuilding of Jerusalem Your holy city, for You are the Master of salvation and the Master of consolation.

OUR GOD AND GOD OF OUR FATHERS, may the remembrance and consideration of us; the remembrance of our fathers; the remembrance of the Mashiach, son of David, Your servant; the remembrance of Jerusalem, the city of your holiness; and the remembrance of all your people, the House of Israel, ascend, come and reach, be seen, accepted, heard, considered, and remembered before You, for deliverance, for goodness, for grace, for kindness, for compassion, for life, and for peace, on this day of the Festival of Matzot. Remember us, Lord our God, on this day for goodness; consider us on it for blessing; and save us on it for life. And with Your word of salvation and mercy, pity us, be gracious and compassionate with us, and save us, for our eyes are turned to You, because You are a gracious and compassionate God and King.

REBUILD JERUSALEM, THE HOLY CITY, speedily in our days. Blessed are You, Lord, Who in His mercy rebuilds Jerusalem. Amen.

בָּרוּךְ אַתָּה יְהוָֹה אֱלֹהֵינוּ מֶלֶךְ הָעוֹלָם, הָאֵל, אָבִינוּ, מַלְכֵּנוּ, אַדִּירֵנוּ, בּוֹרְאֵנוּ, גּוֹאֲלֵנוּ, יוֹצְרֵנוּ, קְדוֹשֵׁנוּ, קְדוֹשׁ יַעֲקֹב, רוֹעֵנוּ, רוֹעֵה יִשְׂרָאֵל, הַמֶּלֶךְ הַטּוֹב וְהַמֵּיטִיב לַכֹּל, שֶׁבְּכָל יוֹם וָיוֹם הוּא הֵיטִיב הוּא מֵיטִיב הוּא יֵיטִיב לָנוּ. הוּא גְמָלָנוּ, הוּא גוֹמְלֵנוּ, הוּא יִגְמְלֵנוּ לָעַד, לְחֵן וּלְחֶסֶד וּלְרַחֲמִים וּלְרֶוַח, הַצָּלָה וְהַצְלָחָה, בְּרָכָה וִישׁוּעָה, נֶחָמָה, פַּרְנָסָה וְכַלְכָּלָה, וְרַחֲמִים וְחַיִּים וְשָׁלוֹם וְכָל טוֹב. וּמִכָּל טוּב לְעוֹלָם אַל יְחַסְּרֵנוּ.

הָרַחֲמָן הוּא יִמְלֹךְ עָלֵינוּ לְעוֹלָם וָעֶד. הָרַחֲמָן הוּא יִתְבָּרַךְ בַּשָּׁמַיִם וּבָאָרֶץ. הָרַחֲמָן הוּא יִשְׁתַּבַּח לְדוֹר דּוֹרִים, וְיִתְפָּאַר בָּנוּ לָעַד וּלְנֵצַח נְצָחִים, וְיִתְהַדַּר בָּנוּ לָעַד וּלְעוֹלְמֵי עוֹלָמִים. הָרַחֲמָן הוּא יְפַרְנְסֵנוּ בְּכָבוֹד. הָרַחֲמָן הוּא יִשְׁבֹּר עֻלֵּנוּ מֵעַל צַוָּארֵנוּ וְהוּא יוֹלִיכֵנוּ קוֹמְמִיּוּת לְאַרְצֵנוּ. הָרַחֲמָן הוּא יִשְׁלַח לָנוּ בְּרָכָה מְרֻבָּה בַּבַּיִת הַזֶּה וְעַל שֻׁלְחָן זֶה שֶׁאָכַלְנוּ עָלָיו. הָרַחֲמָן הוּא יִשְׁלַח לָנוּ אֶת אֵלִיָּהוּ הַנָּבִיא זָכוּר לַטּוֹב, וִיבַשֶּׂר לָנוּ בְּשׂוֹרוֹת טוֹבוֹת יְשׁוּעוֹת וְנֶחָמוֹת.

ברכת האורח: יְהִי רָצוֹן, שֶׁלֹּא יֵבוֹשׁ וְלֹא יִכָּלֵם בַּעַל הַבַּיִת הַזֶּה לֹא בָּעוֹלָם הַזֶּה וְלֹא בָּעוֹלָם הַבָּא, וְיַצְלִיחַ בְּכָל נְכָסָיו, וְיִהְיוּ נְכָסָיו מוּצְלָחִים וּקְרוֹבִים לָעִיר, וְלֹא יִשְׁלוֹט שָׂטָן בְּמַעֲשֵׂי יָדָיו, וְאַל יִזְדַּקֵּק לְפָנָיו שׁוּם דְּבַר חֵטְא וְהִרְהוּר עָוֹן מֵעַתָּה וְעַד עוֹלָם.

BLESSED ARE YOU, LORD OUR GOD, KING of the Universe, God our Father, our King, our Sovereign, our Creator, our Redeemer, our Maker, our Holy One, the Holy One of Jacob, our Shepherd, the Shepherd of Israel, the King Who is good and Who continually does good to all. Each and every day He has done good for us, He does good for us, and He will [continue to] do good for us; He was bountiful to us, He is bountiful to us, and He will be bountiful to us forever, with grace, kindness, and mercy, and with relief, salvation and success, blessing and help, consolation, sustenance and support, and with compassion and life and peace, and all goodness; and may He never deprive us of all good things.

MAY THE MERCIFUL ONE REIGN OVER US forever and ever. May the Merciful One be blessed in heaven and on earth. May the Merciful One be praised for all generations, and be glorified through us forever and all eternity, and be honored through us forever and ever. May the Merciful One sustain us in honor. May the Merciful One break the yoke of exile from our neck, and may He lead us upright to our land. May the Merciful One send to us abundant blessing into this house and upon this table at which we have eaten. May the Merciful One send us Elijah the Prophet, who is remembered for good, and let him bring us good tidings, salvation and consolation.

The guest's blessing:

May it be Your will, that the head of this household will never be ashamed or abashed, neither in this world nor in the World to Come, and may he succeed in all his ventures, and may his ventures be successful and close to the city. and may Satan not control his actions, and may he never be involved in any sin or sinful thought from now and eternally.

הָרַחֲמָן הוּא יְבָרֵךְ אֶת (אם הוא סמוך על שולחן אביו ואמו יאמר: אָבִי מוֹרִי) בַּעַל הַבַּיִת הַזֶּה, וְאֶת (אִמִּי מוֹרָתִי) בַּעֲלַת הַבַּיִת הַזֶּה, אוֹתָם וְאֶת בֵּיתָם וְאֶת זַרְעָם וְאֶת כָּל אֲשֶׁר לָהֶם, (ואם הוא נשוי יאמר: אוֹתִי וְאֶת אִשְׁתִּי וְאֶת זַרְעִי וְאֶת כָּל אֲשֶׁר לִי), אוֹתָנוּ וְאֶת כָּל אֲשֶׁר לָנוּ. כְּמוֹ שֶׁנִּתְבָּרְכוּ אֲבוֹתֵינוּ אַבְרָהָם יִצְחָק וְיַעֲקֹב: בַּכֹּל מִכֹּל כֹּל, כֵּן יְבָרֵךְ אוֹתָנוּ כֻּלָּנוּ יַחַד בִּבְרָכָה שְׁלֵמָה, וְנֹאמַר אָמֵן.

בַּמָּרוֹם יְלַמְּדוּ עֲלֵיהֶם וְעָלֵינוּ זְכוּת שֶׁתְּהֵא לְמִשְׁמֶרֶת שָׁלוֹם, וְנִשָּׂא בְרָכָה מֵאֵת יְהֹוָה, וּצְדָקָה מֵאֱלֹהֵי יִשְׁעֵנוּ. וְנִמְצָא חֵן וְשֵׂכֶל טוֹב בְּעֵינֵי אֱלֹהִים וְאָדָם.

בשבת: הָרַחֲמָן הוּא יַנְחִילֵנוּ יוֹם שֶׁכֻּלּוֹ שַׁבָּת וּמְנוּחָה לְחַיֵּי הָעוֹלָמִים.

הָרַחֲמָן הוּא יַנְחִילֵנוּ יוֹם שֶׁכֻּלּוֹ טוֹב, יוֹם שֶׁכֻּלּוֹ אָרוֹךְ, יוֹם שֶׁצַּדִּיקִים יוֹשְׁבִים וְעַטְרוֹתֵיהֶם בְּרָאשֵׁיהֶם וְנֶהֱנִים מִזִּיו הַשְּׁכִינָה, וִיהִי חֶלְקֵנוּ עִמָּהֶם. הָרַחֲמָן הוּא יְזַכֵּנוּ לִימוֹת הַמָּשִׁיחַ וּלְחַיֵּי הָעוֹלָם הַבָּא. מִגְדּוֹל יְשׁוּעוֹת מַלְכּוֹ וְעֹשֶׂה חֶסֶד לִמְשִׁיחוֹ, לְדָוִד וּלְזַרְעוֹ עַד עוֹלָם. עֹשֶׂה שָׁלוֹם בִּמְרוֹמָיו, הוּא יַעֲשֶׂה שָׁלוֹם עָלֵינוּ וְעַל כָּל יִשְׂרָאֵל, וְאִמְרוּ אָמֵן.

יְראוּ אֶת יְהֹוָה קְדֹשָׁיו, כִּי אֵין מַחְסוֹר לִירֵאָיו. כְּפִירִים רָשׁוּ וְרָעֵבוּ, וְדֹרְשֵׁי יְהֹוָה לֹא יַחְסְרוּ כָל טוֹב. הוֹדוּ לַיהֹוָה כִּי טוֹב, כִּי לְעוֹלָם חַסְדּוֹ. פּוֹתֵחַ אֶת יָדֶךָ, וּמַשְׂבִּיעַ לְכָל חַי רָצוֹן. בָּרוּךְ הַגֶּבֶר אֲשֶׁר יִבְטַח בַּיהֹוָה, וְהָיָה יְהֹוָה מִבְטַחוֹ. נַעַר הָיִיתִי גַּם זָקַנְתִּי, וְלֹא רָאִיתִי צַדִּיק נֶעֱזָב, וְזַרְעוֹ מְבַקֶּשׁ לָחֶם. יְהֹוָה עֹז לְעַמּוֹ יִתֵּן, יְהֹוָה יְבָרֵךְ אֶת עַמּוֹ בַשָּׁלוֹם.

May He bless (if eating at his parents' table: my father and teacher) the master of this house, and (my mother and teacher) the mistress of this house – them, their household, their children, and all that is theirs. (If he is married: May the Merciful One bless me, my wife/husband, and my children, and all that is mine). May He bless us and all that is ours – just as our forefathers, Abraham, Isaac, and Jacob were blessed in everything, above everything, and with everything. So may He bless us all together with a perfect blessing, and let us say, Amen.

IN HEAVEN, MAY THEIR MERIT AND OUR MERIT be invoked as a safeguarding of peace. May we receive blessing from the Lord, and righteousness from the God of our salvation, and may we find favor and understanding in the eyes of God and man.

On Shabbat: May the Merciful One grant us to inherit a day that is entirely Shabbat and eternal rest.

May the Merciful One cause us to inherit a day that is entirely good, one that is entirely long, a day where the righteous sit with their crowns on their heads and rejoice in the radiance of the Divine Presence, and may our portion be with them. May the Merciful One grant us the privilege of reaching the days of Mashiach and the life of the World to Come. He is a tower of salvation to His king, and bestows kindness upon His anointed, to David and his descendants forever. May He who makes peace in His heights make peace for us and all of Israel, and say Amen.

FEAR THE LORD, HIS HOLY ONES, FOR THERE IS no lack for those who fear Him. Young lions are in need and go hungry, but those who seek the Lord shall not lack any good. Praise the Lord because He is good, for His mercy is everlasting. You open Your hand and supply all with their needs. Blessed is the man who trusts in the Lord, whose trust is in the Lord alone. I was a youth and also have aged, and I have not seen a righteous man forsaken and his children begging for bread. The Lord will give His people strength, the Lord will bless His people with peace.

מברכים 'בורא פרי הגפן' ושותים את הכוס השלישית בהסבה.

יש נוהגים לומר לפני ברכת "בורא פרי הגפן":

הִנְנִי מוּכָן וּמְזֻמָּן לְקַיֵּם מִצְוַת כּוֹס שְׁלִישִׁי שֶׁל אַרְבַּע כּוֹסוֹת. לְשֵׁם יִחוּד קוּדְשָׁא בְּרִיךְ הוּא וּשְׁכִינְתֵּיהּ עַל יְדֵי הַהוּא טָמִיר וְנֶעְלָם בְּשֵׁם כָּל יִשְׂרָאֵל. וִיהִי נֹעַם אֲדֹנָי אֱלֹהֵינוּ עָלֵינוּ וּמַעֲשֵׂה יָדֵינוּ כּוֹנְנָה עָלֵינוּ וּמַעֲשֵׂה יָדֵינוּ כּוֹנְנֵהוּ.

בָּרוּךְ אַתָּה יְהֹוָה אֱלֹהֵינוּ מֶלֶךְ הָעוֹלָם, בּוֹרֵא פְּרִי הַגָּפֶן.

אין מברכים ברכה אחרונה.

Food For Thought

Elijah's cup

The Talmud (118a) states:

> Our Rabbis taught: Over the fourth [cup] he concludes hallel and recites the Great Hallel – this is the view of Rabbi Tarfon…

This version of the text, our version, is that of Rashi, Tosafot (117a, *Revi'i*) and Rashbam (*ibid.*). However, the text in Seder Rav Amram Gaon reads "Over the *fifth* [cup] he concludes hallel" (and that is also the view of Maharam, *Maharam Chalavah*, and Me'iri *ibid.*).

The Rishonim differ as to what one should do in practice. The problem is that if one adopts the stringent view and drinks five cups of wine, it might appear as if one is drinking more than the required number of cups.

Indeed, Shulchan Aruch (481:1) ruled: "After the four cups one is not permitted to drink wine, but only water." Rama, though, differed with this ruling and writes:

> One who is fastidious or is very thirsty can drink a fifth cup and recite the Great Hallel over it (*Mordechai*).

According to Rama, one may drink a fifth cup. Indeed, there are those who rule that way, deeming it a worthy custom, in accordance with the fifth verb of redemption, "I will bring you to the land" (Maharal, cited in *Haggadah Divrei Negidim*. See the section above, "Why was the fifth language of redemption – 'I will bring you' – omitted?" on p. 222). Indeed, the link between this cup, known as the "cup of Elijah," and the verse of "I will bring you" is most appropriate, for it is the prophet Elijah who will herald the final redemption and the ingathering of the scattered Jews throughout the world.

◂ However,

One recites the blessing over wine and drinks the third cup of wine while leaning.

There are those who say the following before reciting the blessing over wine:

I am prepared and ready to fulfill the mitzvah of the third cup of four cups. For the sake of the unification of the Holy One, Blessed be He, and His Presence, in the name of all Israel. And may the pleasantness of the Lord our God be upon us, and may the work of our hands establish for us, and may the work of our hands establish it.

BLESSED ARE YOU, LORD OUR GOD, KING of the universe, who creates the fruit of the vine.

One does not recite the concluding blessing on the wine.

However, the accepted custom is *to pour it but not to drink it*. This emerges from the words of Rambam (8:10), who writes:

> One must *pour* the fifth cup and recite the Great Hallel on it, from "*Hodu LaShem ki tov*" to "*Al naharot Bavel*," and this cup is not obligatory, unlike the other four cups.

Rambam speaks about *pouring* and does not mention drinking, but he does mention drinking in regard to the other four cups. Likewise, Rambam continues: "*And he does not taste anything else that whole night, except for water.*" It is thus clear that one does not drink the fifth cup, but merely *pours* it. There are those, though, who do not have the custom of Elijah's cup and do not even pour it (see *Chayei Adam*, 130:19; *Haggadat Pesach Meubin*).

It is the custom to leave the cup until the next day (after covering it), and then use it for kiddush in the morning, or to pour it back into the bottle (*Minhagei Chatam Sofer*, 10:7; *VaYaged Moshe*, 30:5, writes that this is the custom of many people). Some have the custom of not completely filling the fourth cup for each person, and after *shefoch chamatcha* adding the wine from Elijah's cup to fill the cup of each person (*Chayei Adam*, 130:19. Some fill the fourth cup only after *shefoch chamatcha*, and can then use Elijah's cup not only to top off the other cups but actually to fill them from Elijah's Cup, which had been filled before *shefoch chamatcha*, and then to fill the rest from other wine – *VaYaged Moshe ibid.*).

Why is this cup known as "Elijah's cup?" The simple reason is that it represents the future redemption, that of "I will bring you." It is appropriate to be Elijah's cup, for it is Elijah who will herald the final redemption (see Mishnah Berurah 480:10. Because of the importance of the cup, it is the custom for the head of the household himself to fill it – *VaYaged Moshe* 30:4, in the name of *Si'ach Avot, Minhagim* 66).

Gra (quoted in *Sefer HaAruch*,

◂ Part

מוזגים כוס רביעית.

פותחים את הדלת (עד סוף הקטע של 'שפוך חמתך'), כדי לזכור שליל שימורים הוא (הרמ"א, ת"פ, א), ושהקב"ה הוא המגן האמיתי עלינו. רבים נוהגים לעמוד באמירת קטע זה (ערוך השולחן, ת"פ, א).

נוהגים למזוג כוס נוספת (חמישית), וקוראים לה 'כוס של אליהו' (ויש שאינם מוזגים כוס זו). כוס זו מוזגים אך לא שותים, והיא מסמלת את האמונה בגאולה, והאמונה שהרחמן הוא ישלח לנו במהרה את אליהו הנביא זכור לטוב (משנה ברורה, ת"פ, ס"ק י).

שְׁפֹךְ חֲמָתְךָ אֶל הַגּוֹיִם אֲשֶׁר לֹא יְדָעוּךָ וְעַל מַמְלָכוֹת אֲשֶׁר בְּשִׁמְךָ לֹא קָרָאוּ. כִּי אָכַל אֶת יַעֲקֹב וְאֶת נָוֵהוּ הֵשַׁמּוּ (תהלים ע"ט, ו-ז). שְׁפָךְ עֲלֵיהֶם זַעְמֶךָ וַחֲרוֹן אַפְּךָ יַשִּׂיגֵם (שם ס"ט, כה). תִּרְדֹּף בְּאַף וְתַשְׁמִידֵם מִתַּחַת שְׁמֵי יְהֹוָה (איכה ג', סו).

סוגרים את הדלת.

Part II, p. 263) explains this in an original way. Since there is a dispute as to whether one drinks the fifth cup, we pour it but do not drink it, and we await the arrival of Elijah, who will rule as to whether that cup is to be drunk. ▪

Food For Thought

Pour out Your wrath upon the nations that do not acknowledge You

Many explanations have been given for the meaning of this section, whose importance is emphasized by the custom most have to stand while reciting it (Aruch HaShulchan 480:1).

Ran (19a of Rif) and Me'iri (99b) explain that the four cups represent the four kingdoms that enslaved Israel, and, therefore, when we pour the fifth cup, we ask God to pour out His wrath on them.

Another reason could be that the main theme of the haggadah, until the meal, is the Exodus from Egypt. Now, after the meal, we continue to thank God for the Exodus, but we also include thanks to God for all *the times He has saved Am Yisrael over the generations.* At the same time, we remember the Crusades, the Inquisition, the Holocaust, and the other pogroms

◂ throughout

The fourth cup is poured.

The door is opened (until the end of the *shefoch chamatcha* paragraph), in order to remember that this is a night of being guarded (Rama 480:1) and that God is our true defender. Many people have the custom of standing when saying this section (Aruch HaShulchan 480:1).

It is the custom to pour another cup (the fifth), and this is referred to as "Elijah's cup" (some do not pour this cup). This cup is poured but not drunk, and it symbolizes our belief in the final redemption and our faith that God will soon send us the prophet Elijah (Mishnah Berurah 480:10).

POUR OUT YOUR WRATH UPON THE nations that do not acknowledge You and upon the kingdoms that do not cry out Your Name. For they have devoured Jacob and destroyed his habitation (Psalms 79:6–7). Pour out Your anger upon them, and let Your wrath overtake them (Psalms 69:25). Pursue them with wrath and annihilate them from beneath the heavens of the Lord (Lamentations 3:66).

The door is closed.

---

throughout history, and we ask God to exact retribution from our enemies.

This request is like the paragraph we say each Shabbat morning, which was composed following the Crusades:

> And by the hands of Your servants, the prophets, it is written saying, "I will cleanse their blood that I have not yet cleansed, for the Lord dwells in Zion." And in the Holy Writings it is said, "Why should the nations say, Where is their God? Let it be known among the nations in our sight the revenging of the blood of Your servants that has been shed." And it is said, "For He who avenges blood remembers them; He has not forgotten the cry of the humble." And it is further said, "He will judge among the nations, and, as a result, the land will be full of corpses: He smites their heads stretching over a wide area of land. He drinks of the brook [of their blood] along the way; therefore, He will raise up our head."

When we say this section we open the door, as a symbol of our faith in God and our trust that He will rescue us from all those in each generation who seek to destroy us (based on Rama, end of 480).

What do they want from us?

Throughout history, non-Jews have killed and slaughtered Jews. Anti-Semitism still exists today, although it has changed form. Whenever the State of Israel acts morally against terrorists

◂ and

and saboteurs, the world screams out against us. Doesn't the world realize that we are trying to defend our citizens?

Why do they all claim that we are immoral, when our morality in dealing with our enemies is far superior to that of other nations? This is the anti-Semitism of our time. We can clarify this with a story I heard from Rav Yehuda Amital, of blessed memory.

Once, on the day before Rosh Hashanah, when the longest selichot of the year are said by Ashkenazi Jews, Reb Yaakov, the shamash, worked the whole night in the synagogue, arranging the chairs, preparing the prayer books, and cleaning the synagogue. At 3 A.M., he went from home to home to wake the men for the selichot prayers: "Arise those who are sleeping, wake up from your slumber; come worship the Creator."

All came to the synagogue, among them the children and youths. After they began the selichot, Reb Yaakov fell asleep, and his head began to droop. The children gathered pieces of paper, rolled them into a ball, and threw them at Reb Yaakov's face. Reb Yaakov woke up and continued to recite the selichot, but soon fell asleep again. Again the children threw a ball of paper at his face, and he again woke up and recited the selichot, but soon fell asleep again. The children woke him another time. He then turned to the children and said to them, "Aren't you ashamed? I was up the whole night, fixing up the synagogue and arranging everything. Aren't you ashamed to wake me in that way?" The children answered him, "Reb Yaakov, we were sleeping peacefully at home, and you woke us up. Now you want to sleep?"

That is the relationship Israel has with the other nations. Until Am Yisrael arrived, the other nations could behave in a barbaric manner, without any moral rules. The appearance of Am Yisrael in the world brought the Torah to the world, along with ethical behavior and humanitarian rules. That is why the other nations are constantly testing us to see if we are ethical in all our actions, as they know that Am Yisrael was the one that brought morality to the world.

Deep down, the other nations of the world realize our nature – that we are

◄ the

Riddles

83. What does God pour on nations that do not act properly?

Topic for Discussion

p. One can ask from a grandfather or grandmother, or one's parents or anyone else at the meal, to tell a personal or family story about rescue and survival in the Holocaust. Based on this, one can ask and discuss how one can preserve his freedom and faith in such very difficult times.

the most moral nation. The fact that the other nations do not act that way – but demand that we do – shows that the world understands that Am Yisrael is more moral than they are, and that based on our spiritual level our ethical standards must be higher than the rest of the world.

We will continue to strive for moral perfection. We will remember our role as a teacher of values to the whole world. We must hold fast to what we know is right and not bend to foreign pressures. We must remember the value that dictates that "if one comes to kill you, kill him before he manages to do so" (Numbers Rabbah 21:4). Sometimes, the most moral action is one of destruction. In order to preserve the safety and value system of the world we must show that we do not tolerate terrorism. However, we must always remember that our goal is to reach a time when force is no longer necessary, when the world will join us in a time of morality and peace. ▪

Miniature Torah finial, Persia, 19th century, silver
The Wolfson Museum, Hechal Shlomo

Hallel

Our main obligation on the Seder night is to thank and praise God. Before the meal we praised Him for the Exodus from Egypt in particular. Now, we praise Him for all the kindness and good that He bestows upon us – in the past, in the present, and in the future as well.

לֹא לָנוּ יְהֹוָה, לֹא לָנוּ, כִּי לְשִׁמְךָ תֵּן כָּבוֹד, עַל חַסְדְּךָ עַל אֲמִתֶּךָ. לָמָּה יֹאמְרוּ הַגּוֹיִם, אַיֵּה נָא אֱלֹהֵיהֶם. וֵאלֹהֵינוּ בַשָּׁמָיִם, כֹּל אֲשֶׁר חָפֵץ עָשָׂה. עֲצַבֵּיהֶם כֶּסֶף וְזָהָב, מַעֲשֵׂה יְדֵי אָדָם. פֶּה לָהֶם וְלֹא יְדַבֵּרוּ, עֵינַיִם לָהֶם וְלֹא יִרְאוּ. אָזְנַיִם לָהֶם וְלֹא יִשְׁמָעוּ, אַף לָהֶם וְלֹא יְרִיחוּן. יְדֵיהֶם וְלֹא יְמִישׁוּן, רַגְלֵיהֶם וְלֹא יְהַלֵּכוּ, לֹא יֶהְגּוּ בִּגְרוֹנָם. כְּמוֹהֶם יִהְיוּ עֹשֵׂיהֶם, כֹּל אֲשֶׁר בֹּטֵחַ בָּהֶם. יִשְׂרָאֵל בְּטַח בַּיהֹוָה, עֶזְרָם וּמָגִנָּם הוּא. בֵּית אַהֲרֹן בִּטְחוּ בַיהֹוָה, עֶזְרָם וּמָגִנָּם הוּא. יִרְאֵי יְהֹוָה בִּטְחוּ בַיהֹוָה, עֶזְרָם וּמָגִנָּם הוּא. (תהלים קט"ו)

יְהֹוָה זְכָרָנוּ יְבָרֵךְ, יְבָרֵךְ אֶת בֵּית יִשְׂרָאֵל, יְבָרֵךְ אֶת בֵּית אַהֲרֹן. יְבָרֵךְ יִרְאֵי יְהֹוָה, הַקְּטַנִּים עִם הַגְּדֹלִים. יֹסֵף יְהֹוָה עֲלֵיכֶם, עֲלֵיכֶם וְעַל בְּנֵיכֶם. בְּרוּכִים אַתֶּם לַיהֹוָה, עֹשֵׂה שָׁמַיִם וָאָרֶץ. הַשָּׁמַיִם שָׁמַיִם לַיהֹוָה, וְהָאָרֶץ נָתַן לִבְנֵי אָדָם. לֹא הַמֵּתִים יְהַלְלוּ יָהּ, וְלֹא כָּל יֹרְדֵי דוּמָה. וַאֲנַחְנוּ נְבָרֵךְ יָהּ, מֵעַתָּה וְעַד עוֹלָם, הַלְלוּיָהּ.

Halachic Summary

We have already recited two of the psalms of hallel before the meal. Now we continue to say the rest (without a blessing). Hallel is a central part of this night: to thank and praise God for all the miracles that He performed for us. The verses of *hodu* and ana should be said by one of the participants, and the others should answer him, as in the synagogue. It is proper to sing these (rather than just recite them). ▪

NOT FOR US, LORD, NOT FOR US, BUT for Your Name's sake give honor, for Your kindness and Your truth. Why should the nations say, "Where is their God?" Our God is in the heavens, whatever He wills, He does. Their idols are of silver and gold, the product of human hands. They have a mouth, but cannot speak; they have eyes, but cannot see. They have ears, but cannot hear; they have a nose, but cannot smell; their hands cannot feel; their feet cannot walk; they can make no sound with their throat. Let those who make them become like them, whoever trusts in them! Israel, trust in the Lord! He is their help and their shield. House of Aaron, trust in the Lord! He is their help and their shield. Those who fear the Lord, trust in the Lord! He is their help and their shield (Psalms 115).

THE LORD, WHO HAS BEEN MINDFUL OF us, will bless – He will bless the House of Israel; He will bless the House of Aaron; He will bless those who revere the Lord, the small with the great. May the Lord increase you, you and your children. Blessed are you to the Lord, Maker of heaven and earth. The heavens are the heavens of the Lord, but the earth, He has given to mankind. The dead cannot praise God, nor any who go down into the silence of the grave. But we will bless God, from now to eternity. Halleluyah.

Food For Thought

Give thanks to the Lord for He is good

The psalms that conclude hallel focus on the act of thanking God. After we have described the great miracles and our faith in God's supervision over us, *we call upon the entire world to join us, and to praise God* (Psalms 117).

The last psalm we say here, psalm 118, is also one of thanksgiving to God:

◂ it begins

אָהַבְתִּי כִּי יִשְׁמַע יְהֹוָה, אֶת קוֹלִי תַּחֲנוּנָי. כִּי הִטָּה אָזְנוֹ לִי, וּבְיָמַי אֶקְרָא. אֲפָפוּנִי חֶבְלֵי מָוֶת, וּמְצָרֵי שְׁאוֹל מְצָאוּנִי, צָרָה וְיָגוֹן אֶמְצָא. וּבְשֵׁם יְהֹוָה אֶקְרָא, אָנָּה יְהֹוָה מַלְּטָה נַפְשִׁי. חַנּוּן יְהֹוָה וְצַדִּיק, וֵאלֹהֵינוּ מְרַחֵם. שֹׁמֵר פְּתָאִים יְהֹוָה, דַּלֹּתִי וְלִי יְהוֹשִׁיעַ. שׁוּבִי נַפְשִׁי לִמְנוּחָיְכִי, כִּי יְהֹוָה גָּמַל עָלָיְכִי. כִּי חִלַּצְתָּ נַפְשִׁי מִמָּוֶת, אֶת עֵינִי מִן דִּמְעָה, אֶת רַגְלִי מִדֶּחִי. אֶתְהַלֵּךְ לִפְנֵי יְהֹוָה, בְּאַרְצוֹת הַחַיִּים. הֶאֱמַנְתִּי כִּי אֲדַבֵּר, אֲנִי עָנִיתִי מְאֹד. אֲנִי אָמַרְתִּי בְחָפְזִי, כָּל הָאָדָם כֹּזֵב. (תהלים קט״ז)

מָה אָשִׁיב לַיהֹוָה, כָּל תַּגְמוּלוֹהִי עָלָי. כּוֹס יְשׁוּעוֹת אֶשָּׂא, וּבְשֵׁם יְהֹוָה אֶקְרָא. נְדָרַי לַיהֹוָה אֲשַׁלֵּם, נֶגְדָה נָּא לְכָל עַמּוֹ. יָקָר בְּעֵינֵי יְהֹוָה, הַמָּוְתָה לַחֲסִידָיו. אָנָּה יְהֹוָה כִּי אֲנִי עַבְדֶּךָ, אֲנִי עַבְדְּךָ בֶּן אֲמָתֶךָ, פִּתַּחְתָּ לְמוֹסֵרָי. לְךָ אֶזְבַּח זֶבַח תּוֹדָה, וּבְשֵׁם יְהֹוָה אֶקְרָא. נְדָרַי לַיהֹוָה אֲשַׁלֵּם, נֶגְדָה נָּא לְכָל עַמּוֹ. בְּחַצְרוֹת בֵּית יְהֹוָה, בְּתוֹכֵכִי יְרוּשָׁלָיִם, הַלְלוּיָהּ.

---

it begins with, "Give thanks to the Lord for He is good; His kindness is everlasting," and it ends with "Give thanks to the Lord for He is good; His kindness is everlasting."

This psalm covers a number of topics that were mentioned in previous psalms and in other places in Tanach.

This psalm is *a culmination of thanksgiving of all the generations, after their redemption from various troubles.* This is also reflected in the words of the Sages regarding the entire hallel:

> Our Rabbis taught: Who uttered this hallel? Rabbi Eliezer said: Moses and Israel uttered it when they stood by the Sea…

◂ Rabbi

I LOVE IT WHEN THE LORD HEARS MY voice, my prayers. For He has inclined His ear to me; and in my own days I will call upon Him. The pains of death encompassed me, and the confines of the grave have found me, trouble and sorrow I encountered and I called upon the Name of the Lord: "Please, Lord, deliver my soul!" The Lord is gracious and just, our God is compassionate. The Lord watches over the simple; I was brought low, but He saved me. Return, my soul, to your resting place, for the Lord has dealt kindly with you. For You have delivered my soul from death, my eyes from tears, my feet from stumbling. I shall walk before the Lord in the land of the living. I had faith even while speaking of how I suffer so much [even though] I said in haste, "All mankind is deceitful" (Psalms 116).

HOW CAN I REPAY THE LORD FOR ALL His kindnesses to me? I will raise the cup of salvation and call upon the Name of the Lord. I will pay my vows to the Lord in the presence of all His people. Precious in the eyes of the Lord is the death of His devout ones. Please, Lord, for I am Your servant, I am Your servant the son of Your handmaid: You have released my bonds. To You I will bring an offering of thanksgiving, and I will call upon the Name of the Lord. I will pay my vows to the Lord in the presence of all His people, in the courtyards of the House of the Lord, in the midst of Jerusalem. Halleluyah.

Rabbi Yehudah said: Joshua and Israel uttered it when the kings of Canaan attacked them…

Rabbi Elazar the Modiite said: Deborah and Barak uttered it when Sisera attacked them…

Rabbi Elazar ben Azariah said: Hezekiah and his companions uttered it when Sennacherib attacked them…

Rabbi Akiva said: Hananiah, Mishael and Azariah uttered it

◂ when

הַלְלוּ אֶת יְהֹוָה כָּל גּוֹיִם, שַׁבְּחוּהוּ כָּל הָאֻמִּים. כִּי גָבַר עָלֵינוּ חַסְדּוֹ, וֶאֱמֶת יְהֹוָה לְעוֹלָם, הַלְלוּיָהּ. (תהלים קי״ז)

הוֹדוּ לַיהֹוָה כִּי טוֹב כִּי לְעוֹלָם חַסְדּוֹ.
יֹאמַר נָא יִשְׂרָאֵל כִּי לְעוֹלָם חַסְדּוֹ.
יֹאמְרוּ נָא בֵית אַהֲרֹן כִּי לְעוֹלָם חַסְדּוֹ.
יֹאמְרוּ נָא יִרְאֵי יְהֹוָה כִּי לְעוֹלָם חַסְדּוֹ. (תהלים קי״ח)

מִן הַמֵּצַר קָרָאתִי יָּהּ, עָנָנִי בַמֶּרְחָב יָהּ. יְהֹוָה לִי לֹא אִירָא, מַה יַּעֲשֶׂה לִי אָדָם. יְהֹוָה לִי בְּעֹזְרָי, וַאֲנִי אֶרְאֶה בְשֹׂנְאָי. טוֹב לַחֲסוֹת בַּיהֹוָה, מִבְּטֹחַ בָּאָדָם. טוֹב לַחֲסוֹת בַּיהֹוָה, מִבְּטֹחַ בִּנְדִיבִים. כָּל גּוֹיִם סְבָבוּנִי, בְּשֵׁם יְהֹוָה כִּי אֲמִילַם. סַבּוּנִי גַם סְבָבוּנִי, בְּשֵׁם יְהֹוָה כִּי אֲמִילַם. סַבּוּנִי כִדְבוֹרִים, דֹּעֲכוּ כְּאֵשׁ קוֹצִים, בְּשֵׁם יְהֹוָה כִּי אֲמִילַם. דָּחֹה דְחִיתַנִי לִנְפֹּל, וַיהֹוָה עֲזָרָנִי. עָזִּי וְזִמְרָת יָהּ, וַיְהִי לִי לִישׁוּעָה. קוֹל רִנָּה וִישׁוּעָה בְּאָהֳלֵי צַדִּיקִים, יְמִין יְהֹוָה עֹשָׂה חָיִל. יְמִין יְהֹוָה רוֹמֵמָה, יְמִין יְהֹוָה עֹשָׂה חָיִל. לֹא אָמוּת כִּי אֶחְיֶה, וַאֲסַפֵּר מַעֲשֵׂי יָהּ. יַסֹּר יִסְּרַנִּי יָּהּ, וְלַמָּוֶת לֹא נְתָנָנִי. פִּתְחוּ לִי שַׁעֲרֵי צֶדֶק, אָבֹא בָם אוֹדֶה יָהּ. זֶה הַשַּׁעַר לַיהֹוָה, צַדִּיקִים יָבֹאוּ בוֹ.

Esther uttered it when the wicked Haman rose against them…

And the Sages maintain: The prophets among them decreed that Israel ◂ should

when the wicked Nebuchadnezzar rose against them…

Rabbi Yossi the Galilean said: Mordecai and

PRAISE THE LORD, ALL NATIONS! EXTOL Him, all peoples! For His kindness has overwhelmed us, and the truth of the Lord is everlasting. Halleluyah (Psalms 117).

Give thanks to the Lord
for He is good: HIS KINDNESS IS EVERLASTING.
Let Israel say: HIS KINDNESS IS EVERLASTING.
Let the House of Aaron say: HIS KINDNESS IS EVERLASTING.
Let those who revere the Lord say:
HIS KINDNESS IS EVERLASTING.
(Psalms 118)

OUT OF NARROW CONFINES I CALLED to God; God answered me with abundance... The Lord is with me, I will not fear – what can man do to me? The Lord is with me, through my helpers, and I can face my enemies. It is better to rely on the Lord than to trust in man. It is better to rely on the Lord than to trust in nobles. All the nations surround me; in the name of the Lord I cut them down! They surround me and encircle me; in the name of the Lord I cut them down. They encircle me like bees, but they are quenched like a fire of thorns; in the name of the Lord I cut them down. You pushed me again and again that I might fall, but the Lord helped me. God is my strength and song, and He was for me, my salvation. The sound of joyous song and salvation is in the tents of the righteous. The right hand of the Lord performs deeds of valor. The Lord's right hand is exalted; the right hand of the Lord performs deeds of valor! I shall not die, but I shall live and relate the deeds of God. God has chastised me, but He did not let me die. Open for me the gates of righteousness – I will enter them and thank God. This is the gate of the Lord, the righteous will enter it.

אוֹדְךָ כִּי עֲנִיתָנִי, וַתְּהִי לִי לִישׁוּעָה.
אוֹדְךָ כִּי עֲנִיתָנִי, וַתְּהִי לִי לִישׁוּעָה.

אֶבֶן מָאֲסוּ הַבּוֹנִים, הָיְתָה לְרֹאשׁ פִּנָּה.
אֶבֶן מָאֲסוּ הַבּוֹנִים, הָיְתָה לְרֹאשׁ פִּנָּה.

מֵאֵת יְהֹוָה הָיְתָה זֹּאת, הִיא נִפְלָאת בְּעֵינֵינוּ.
מֵאֵת יְהֹוָה הָיְתָה זֹּאת, הִיא נִפְלָאת בְּעֵינֵינוּ.

זֶה הַיּוֹם עָשָׂה יְהֹוָה, נָגִילָה וְנִשְׂמְחָה בוֹ.
זֶה הַיּוֹם עָשָׂה יְהֹוָה, נָגִילָה וְנִשְׂמְחָה בוֹ.

אָנָּא יְהֹוָה הוֹשִׁיעָה נָּא.
אָנָּא יְהֹוָה הוֹשִׁיעָה נָּא.
אָנָּא יְהֹוָה הַצְלִיחָה נָא.
אָנָּא יְהֹוָה הַצְלִיחָה נָא.

should recite it at every epoch and at every trouble – may it not come to them! – and when they are redeemed, they recite it [in thankfulness] for their delivery.

This passage expresses the timeless nature of hallel. When we say these words, we are participating in a legacy of thanksgiving – this is hallel of all the generations.

The Amora'im in the Talmud (117a–b) differ as to whether "Halleluyah" is the end of the previous psalm or is the beginning of the following one, and there is no definite conclusion. In Keter Aram Zova the word is found between the two psalms. It is possible that this is a statement that it belongs to both psalms, both as the end of the preceding one and the beginning of the next one, and through it, all "Halleluyahs" merge into a continuous outpouring of thanks.

Furthermore, hallel begins with the *Exodus from Egypt,* but, as we saw, there are hints later on to various other

◂ eras,

I THANK YOU FOR YOU HAVE ANSWERED ME,
and You will become my salvation.
I thank You, for You have answered me
and will become my salvation.

The stone scorned by the builders
has become the cornerstone.
The stone scorned by the builders
has become the cornerstone.

This thing is from the Lord, it is wondrous in our eyes.
This thing is from the Lord, it is wondrous in our eyes.

This is the day that the Lord has made,
let us be glad and rejoice on it.
This is the day that the Lord has made,
let us be glad and rejoice on it.

O LORD, PLEASE SAVE US!
O Lord, please save us!
O Lord, please grant us success!
O Lord, please grant us success!

---

eras, and that way all our thanks are joined together. One can learn from this that *all the praise and all the rescues throughout all the generations stem from the Exodus from Egypt.* The Exodus from Egypt is the precedent for all the times we were rescued by God. That is why there are parallels between this psalm of praise and the Song of the Sea. Everything can be traced back to the redemption from Egypt.

The prophet Jeremiah (33:10–11) used expressions from psalm 118 to describe the future redemption: "There shall again be heard in this place… the sound of mirth and the sound of joy… the sound of those saying, 'Thank the Lord of Hosts, for He is good: His kindness is everlasting.'" One can learn from this that there is special importance for our generation, the generation of the beginning of the

◂ redemption

בָּרוּךְ הַבָּא בְּשֵׁם יְהֹוָה, בֵּרַכְנוּכֶם מִבֵּית יְהֹוָה.
בָּרוּךְ הַבָּא בְּשֵׁם יְהֹוָה, בֵּרַכְנוּכֶם מִבֵּית יְהֹוָה.

אֵל יְהֹוָה וַיָּאֶר לָנוּ, אִסְרוּ חַג בַּעֲבֹתִים, עַד קַרְנוֹת הַמִּזְבֵּחַ.
אֵל יְהֹוָה וַיָּאֶר לָנוּ, אִסְרוּ חַג בַּעֲבֹתִים, עַד קַרְנוֹת הַמִּזְבֵּחַ.

אֵלִי אַתָּה וְאוֹדֶךָּ, אֱלֹהַי אֲרוֹמְמֶךָּ.
אֵלִי אַתָּה וְאוֹדֶךָּ, אֱלֹהַי אֲרוֹמְמֶךָּ.

הוֹדוּ לַיהֹוָה כִּי טוֹב, כִּי לְעוֹלָם חַסְדּוֹ.
הוֹדוּ לַיהֹוָה כִּי טוֹב, כִּי לְעוֹלָם חַסְדּוֹ. (תהלים קי״ח)

בנוסח אשכנז אומרים כאן 'יהללוך' ללא חתימה. ואילו בנוסח ספרד, אין אומרים אותו כאן, אלא אומרים אותו בהמשך, וחותמים איתו את ברכת 'ישתבח' (ביאור המחלוקת יובא להלן, לפני 'נשמת').

יְהַלְלוּךָ יְהֹוָה אֱלֹהֵינוּ כָּל מַעֲשֶׂיךָ, וַחֲסִידֶיךָ צַדִּיקִים עוֹשֵׂי רְצוֹנֶךָ, וְכָל עַמְּךָ בֵּית יִשְׂרָאֵל, בְּרִנָּה יוֹדוּ וִיבָרְכוּ וִישַׁבְּחוּ וִיפָאֲרוּ וִירוֹמְמוּ וְיַעֲרִיצוּ וְיַקְדִּישׁוּ וְיַמְלִיכוּ אֶת שִׁמְךָ מַלְכֵּנוּ, כִּי לְךָ טוֹב לְהוֹדוֹת וּלְשִׁמְךָ נָאֶה לְזַמֵּר, כִּי מֵעוֹלָם וְעַד עוֹלָם אַתָּה אֵל.

redemption in Israel itself, to have this special connection to the ongoing thanks of all the generations. May it be God's will that we prove to be worthy *of thanking Him for all the good that we have received, and that we be privileged to sing a spontaneous song of hallel for the full redemption, in our days.* ▪

Elijah's cup, Bohemia, 17th–18th century, cup
The Wolfson Museum, Hechal Shlomo, Golnitzki Collection

BLESSED IS HE WHO COMES
in the Name of the Lord;
we bless you from the House of the Lord.
Blessed is he who comes in the Name of the Lord;
we bless you from the House of the Lord.

The Lord is Almighty, He gave us light;
bring the festival offering, bound with cords,
to the corners of the altar.
The Lord is Almighty, He gave us light;
bring the festival offering, bound with cords,
to the corners of the altar.

You are my God and I will thank You;
my God and I will exalt You.
You are my God and I will thank You;
my God and I will exalt You.

Give thanks to the Lord, for He is good:
His kindness is everlasting.
Give thanks to the Lord, for He is good:
His kindness is everlasting. (Psalms 118)

Ashkenazim recite "Lord our God, all Your creations shall praise You..." here, without a concluding blessing, whereas according to the Ashkenazi tradition, one does not say it here but later on, and concludes it with the blessing of yishtabach – "May Your Name be praised forever" (the explanation of the dispute will appear later, before *Nishmat* – "The soul of every living being shall bless Your Name").

LORD OUR GOD, ALL YOUR CREATIONS shall praise You; Your devout ones, the righteous who do Your will, and Your entire nation the House of Israel, with joyous song will thank and bless, laud and glorify, exalt and adore, sanctify and proclaim the sovereignty of Your Name, our King. For it is good to thank You, and befitting to sing to Your Name, for now and forever You are Almighty God.

הַלֵּל הַגָּדוֹל

הוֹדוּ לַיהֹוָה כִּי טוֹב כִּי לְעוֹלָם חַסְדּוֹ.
הוֹדוּ לֵאלֹהֵי הָאֱלֹהִים כִּי לְעוֹלָם חַסְדּוֹ.
הוֹדוּ לַאֲדֹנֵי הָאֲדֹנִים כִּי לְעוֹלָם חַסְדּוֹ.
לְעֹשֵׂה נִפְלָאוֹת גְּדֹלוֹת לְבַדּוֹ כִּי לְעוֹלָם חַסְדּוֹ.
לְעֹשֵׂה הַשָּׁמַיִם בִּתְבוּנָה כִּי לְעוֹלָם חַסְדּוֹ.
לְרֹקַע הָאָרֶץ עַל הַמָּיִם כִּי לְעוֹלָם חַסְדּוֹ.
לְעֹשֵׂה אוֹרִים גְּדֹלִים כִּי לְעוֹלָם חַסְדּוֹ.
אֶת הַשֶּׁמֶשׁ לְמֶמְשֶׁלֶת בַּיּוֹם כִּי לְעוֹלָם חַסְדּוֹ.
אֶת הַיָּרֵחַ וְכוֹכָבִים לְמֶמְשְׁלוֹת בַּלָּיְלָה כִּי לְעוֹלָם חַסְדּוֹ.
לְמַכֵּה מִצְרַיִם בִּבְכוֹרֵיהֶם כִּי לְעוֹלָם חַסְדּוֹ.
וַיּוֹצֵא יִשְׂרָאֵל מִתּוֹכָם כִּי לְעוֹלָם חַסְדּוֹ.
בְּיָד חֲזָקָה וּבִזְרוֹעַ נְטוּיָה כִּי לְעוֹלָם חַסְדּוֹ.
לְגֹזֵר יַם סוּף לִגְזָרִים כִּי לְעוֹלָם חַסְדּוֹ.
וְהֶעֱבִיר יִשְׂרָאֵל בְּתוֹכוֹ כִּי לְעוֹלָם חַסְדּוֹ.
וְנִעֵר פַּרְעֹה וְחֵילוֹ בְיַם סוּף כִּי לְעוֹלָם חַסְדּוֹ.
לְמוֹלִיךְ עַמּוֹ בַּמִּדְבָּר כִּי לְעוֹלָם חַסְדּוֹ.
לְמַכֵּה מְלָכִים גְּדֹלִים כִּי לְעוֹלָם חַסְדּוֹ.

Havdalah plate, 19th century, porcelain
The Wolfson Museum, Hechal Shlomo

HALLEL HAGADOL – THE GREAT HALLEL

Give thanks to the Lord, for He is good
FOR HIS KINDNESS IS EVERLASTING.
Give thanks to the God of gods
FOR HIS KINDNESS IS EVERLASTING.
Give thanks to the Master of masters
FOR HIS KINDNESS IS EVERLASTING.
To Him who alone does great wonders
FOR HIS KINDNESS IS EVERLASTING.
To Him who made the heavens with understanding
FOR HIS KINDNESS IS EVERLASTING.
To Him who spread out the earth upon the waters
FOR HIS KINDNESS IS EVERLASTING.
To Him who made great lights
FOR HIS KINDNESS IS EVERLASTING.
The sun, to rule by day FOR HIS KINDNESS IS EVERLASTING.
The moon and stars, to rule by night
FOR HIS KINDNESS IS EVERLASTING.
To Him who smote Egypt through their firstborn
FOR HIS KINDNESS IS EVERLASTING.
And brought Israel out of their midst
FOR HIS KINDNESS IS EVERLASTING.
With a strong hand and with an outstretched arm
FOR HIS KINDNESS IS EVERLASTING.
To Him who split the Sea of Reeds into sections
FOR HIS KINDNESS IS EVERLASTING.
And led Israel through it
FOR HIS KINDNESS IS EVERLASTING.
And cast Pharaoh and his army into the Sea of Reeds
FOR HIS KINDNESS IS EVERLASTING.

וַיַּהֲרֹג מְלָכִים אַדִּירִים כִּי לְעוֹלָם חַסְדּוֹ.
לְסִיחוֹן מֶלֶךְ הָאֱמֹרִי כִּי לְעוֹלָם חַסְדּוֹ.
וּלְעוֹג מֶלֶךְ הַבָּשָׁן כִּי לְעוֹלָם חַסְדּוֹ.
וְנָתַן אַרְצָם לְנַחֲלָה כִּי לְעוֹלָם חַסְדּוֹ.
נַחֲלָה לְיִשְׂרָאֵל עַבְדּוֹ כִּי לְעוֹלָם חַסְדּוֹ.
שֶׁבְּשִׁפְלֵנוּ זָכַר לָנוּ כִּי לְעוֹלָם חַסְדּוֹ.
וַיִּפְרְקֵנוּ מִצָּרֵינוּ כִּי לְעוֹלָם חַסְדּוֹ.
נֹתֵן לֶחֶם לְכָל בָּשָׂר כִּי לְעוֹלָם חַסְדּוֹ.
הוֹדוּ לְאֵל הַשָּׁמָיִם כִּי לְעוֹלָם חַסְדּוֹ.

Spice box in the shape of a bird, Germany, 17th century, silver
The Wolfson Museum, Hechal Shlomo

To Him, He who led His people through the wilderness
FOR HIS KINDNESS IS EVERLASTING.
To Him, He who smote great kings
FOR HIS KINDNESS IS EVERLASTING.
And slew mighty kings FOR HIS KINDNESS IS EVERLASTING.
Sichon, king of the Amorites
FOR HIS KINDNESS IS EVERLASTING.
And Og, king of Bashan
FOR HIS KINDNESS IS EVERLASTING.
And gave us their land as an inheritance
FOR HIS KINDNESS IS EVERLASTING.
An inheritance to Israel, His servant
FOR HIS KINDNESS IS EVERLASTING.
Who remembered us in our lowliness
FOR HIS KINDNESS IS EVERLASTING.
And delivered us from our oppressors
FOR HIS KINDNESS IS EVERLASTING.
Who gives food to all flesh
FOR HIS KINDNESS IS EVERLASTING.
Give thanks to the God of heavens
FOR HIS KINDNESS IS EVERLASTING.

נִשְׁמַת כָּל חַי תְּבָרֵךְ אֶת שִׁמְךָ יְהוָֹה אֱלֹהֵינוּ, וְרוּחַ כָּל בָּשָׂר תְּפָאֵר וּתְרוֹמֵם זִכְרְךָ מַלְכֵּנוּ תָּמִיד. מִן הָעוֹלָם וְעַד הָעוֹלָם אַתָּה אֵל, וּמִבַּלְעָדֶיךָ אֵין לָנוּ מֶלֶךְ גּוֹאֵל וּמוֹשִׁיעַ, פּוֹדֶה וּמַצִּיל וּמְפַרְנֵס וּמְרַחֵם בְּכָל עֵת צָרָה וְצוּקָה. אֵין לָנוּ מֶלֶךְ אֶלָּא אָתָּה, אֱלֹהֵי הָרִאשׁוֹנִים וְהָאַחֲרוֹנִים, אֱלוֹהַּ כָּל בְּרִיּוֹת, אֲדוֹן כָּל תּוֹלָדוֹת, הַמְהֻלָּל בְּרוֹב הַתִּשְׁבָּחוֹת, הַמְנַהֵג עוֹלָמוֹ בְּחֶסֶד וּבְרִיּוֹתָיו בְּרַחֲמִים. וַיהוָֹה לֹא יָנוּם וְלֹא יִישָׁן, הַמְעוֹרֵר יְשֵׁנִים, וְהַמֵּקִיץ נִרְדָּמִים, וְהַמֵּשִׂיחַ אִלְּמִים, וְהַמַּתִּיר אֲסוּרִים, וְהַסּוֹמֵךְ נוֹפְלִים, וְהַזּוֹקֵף כְּפוּפִים. וּלְךָ לְבַדְּךָ אֲנַחְנוּ מוֹדִים.

אִלּוּ פִינוּ מָלֵא שִׁירָה כַּיָּם,
וּלְשׁוֹנֵנוּ רִנָּה כַּהֲמוֹן גַּלָּיו,

Food For Thought

Nishmat kol chai – the praise of the soul!

The Zohar (*Vayakhel* p. 205a) refers to the *Nishmat kol chai* prayer as "*the praise of the soul*" (that is why it is recited on Shabbat, the day upon which we are given an additional soul, and the day that one should spend in prayer and song to God).

The focal point of the Nishmat prayer is to thank God! We thank God for the overwhelming good that He grants us, and to proclaim – we do not have enough words to thank God for everything!

Gratitude is a fundamental value in Judaism – our very name, *Yehudim*, Jews, Judaism comes from the word *todah* – Leah named her son Yehudah – Judah – "This time, I will thank (*odeh*) the Lord! Therefore, she named him Judah" (Genesis 29:35). Tractate

◄ Berachot

THE SOUL OF EVERY LIVING BEING shall bless Your name, Lord, our God; the spirit of all flesh shall always glorify and exalt Your remembrance, our King. In this world and for eternity You are God, and besides You we have no King, Redeemer and Savior who delivers, rescues, saves, sustains, and is merciful in every time of trouble and distress; we have no King but You. You are the God of the first and of the last, God of all creatures, Lord of all generations, who is extolled with manifold praises, who directs His world with kindness and His creatures with compassion. Behold, the Lord neither slumbers nor sleeps. He arouses the sleepers and awakens the slumbering, gives speech to the mute, releases the bound, supports the fallen and raises up the bent. To You alone we give thanks.

WERE OUR MOUTHS AS FULL OF SONG AS THE SEA,
AND OUR TONGUES WITH JOYOUS SINGING
LIKE THE MULTITUDES OF ITS WAVES,

Berachot (7b) explains that this was the first time a person thanked God. That is why the word todah is an underlying basis of the Jewish world. We begin each day with the words *Modeh ani* – I thank You.

Rav Avraham Yitzchak Kook (*Olat Re'iyah*, on *Modeh ani*) explains that saying *Modeh ani* is not only an expression of thanks, but it is also the *acknowledgment of the truth,* and the realization that whatever we have is from God. When a person understands this, he realizes that whatever he has been given should not be taken for granted, and it follows that he must *thank* God for whatever He gave him. This expression of thanks *gives him special joy* when he realizes how much good God does for His creations. Only when a person *acknowledges* (*modeh*) and understands the source of all, can he say "I" (*ani*). Only with this understanding is there significance to the existence of humankind.

Giving thanks is not only an obligation, but also a privilege – the privilege to be aware of God's supervision over us, and His love and great influence on us. Therefore, we have to thank God for

◂ the

וְשִׂפְתוֹתֵינוּ שֶׁבַח כְּמֶרְחֲבֵי רָקִיעַ, וְעֵינֵינוּ מְאִירוֹת כַּשֶּׁמֶשׁ וְכַיָּרֵחַ,
וְיָדֵינוּ פְרוּשׂוֹת כְּנִשְׁרֵי שָׁמָיִם, וְרַגְלֵינוּ קַלּוֹת כָּאַיָּלוֹת. אֵין אֲנַחְנוּ
מַסְפִּיקִים לְהוֹדוֹת לְךָ יְהוָה אֱלֹהֵינוּ וֵאלֹהֵי אֲבוֹתֵינוּ, וּלְבָרֵךְ
אֶת שְׁמֶךָ עַל אַחַת מֵאָלֶף אֶלֶף אַלְפֵי אֲלָפִים וְרִבֵּי רְבָבוֹת
פְּעָמִים, הַטּוֹבוֹת שֶׁעָשִׂיתָ עִם אֲבוֹתֵינוּ וְעִמָּנוּ. מִמִּצְרַיִם גְּאַלְתָּנוּ
יְהוָה אֱלֹהֵינוּ, וּמִבֵּית עֲבָדִים פְּדִיתָנוּ, בְּרָעָב זַנְתָּנוּ וּבְשָׂבָע
כִּלְכַּלְתָּנוּ, מֵחֶרֶב הִצַּלְתָּנוּ וּמִדֶּבֶר מִלַּטְתָּנוּ, וּמֵחֳלָיִם רָעִים
וְנֶאֱמָנִים דִּלִּיתָנוּ. עַד הֵנָּה עֲזָרוּנוּ רַחֲמֶיךָ וְלֹא עֲזָבוּנוּ חֲסָדֶיךָ
וְאַל תִּטְּשֵׁנוּ יְהוָה אֱלֹהֵינוּ לָנֶצַח.

---

the privilege of praising and thanking Him: "We thank You… for [the fact that] we thank You" (from *Modim de-Rabbanan* – Sotah 40a). Rashi explains the significance of this thanking (Sotah ibid., *al she'anu modim lach*): "that You put into our hearts to *cling to You and thank You.*"

By our very nature, our souls long to praise Him and cling to Him. Sometimes the impediments in our bodies do not enable our souls to attain the heights of praise and thanks. However, there are times when the soul manages to overcome these impediments – on Shabbat, where we have an additional soul, and toward the end of the Seder night, when we understand what true freedom really is. *At such times, the soul bursts through all these impediments, and becomes totally involved in praising and thanking God!* "The soul of every living being shall bless Your name, Lord, our God; the spirit of all flesh shall always glorify and exalt Your remembrance, our King."

Can we ever thank God enough?

The Talmud in Tractate Horiyot (13b) says:

> "Who can express the mighty acts of the Lord; make all His praise to be heard?" (Psalms 106). For whom is it becoming to express the mighty acts of the Lord? For he who can make all His praise to be heard!

The Talmud states that only a person who can express *all of God's praises* is able to sing praises of Him. There is a great deal of logic in this statement, because one who is not able to list all

◂ of God's

and our lips with praise like the expanse of the sky; and our eyes shining like the sun and the moon, and our hands spread out like the eagles of heaven, and our feet swift like deer we would still be unable to thank You Lord, our God and God of our fathers, and to bless Your name, for even one of the thousands and myriads of favors that You have done for us and for our fathers before us. Lord our God, You have redeemed us from Egypt, You have freed us from the house of bondage, You have fed us in famine and nourished us in times of plenty; You have saved us from the sword and delivered us from pestilence, and rescued us from evil and lasting diseases. Until now Your mercies have helped us, and Your kindnesses have not forsaken us; and do not abandon us, Lord our God, forever!

---

of God's praises is liable to diminish God's praise and honor, and, therefore, it is preferable not to deal with them at all. However, according to this, how can we praise God? How did the Men of the Great Assembly, who instituted the prayers, include praises to God in the prayers? Are we able to praise Him sufficiently?

Case for Esther scroll,
Europe, 19th century, silver
The Wolfson Museum, Hechal Shlomo

Ben Ish Chai has a wonderful answer to this (in his *Benayahu*, Megillah 18a), explaining that the Men of the Great Assembly first instituted *Nishmat.* In this prayer, we announce that *we do not have enough words to thank God.*

> Were our mouths as full of song as the sea, and our tongues with joyous singing like the multitudes of its waves…*we would still be unable to thank You Lord, our God and God of our fathers,* and to bless Your name, for even one of the thousands, and myriads of favors that You have done for us and our fathers before us.

With these words we announce: even if we would try to say all the praises in the world, we would not succeed in

◂ truly

עַל כֵּן אֵבָרִים שֶׁפִּלַּגְתָּ בָּנוּ, וְרוּחַ וּנְשָׁמָה שֶׁנָּפַחְתָּ בְּאַפֵּינוּ, וְלָשׁוֹן אֲשֶׁר שַׂמְתָּ בְּפִינוּ, הֵן הֵם יוֹדוּ וִיבָרְכוּ וִישַׁבְּחוּ וִיפָאֲרוּ וִירוֹמְמוּ וְיַעֲרִיצוּ וְיַקְדִּישׁוּ וְיַמְלִיכוּ אֶת שִׁמְךָ מַלְכֵּנוּ. כִּי כָל פֶּה לְךָ יוֹדֶה, וְכָל לָשׁוֹן לְךָ תִשָּׁבַע, וְכָל בֶּרֶךְ לְךָ תִכְרַע, וְכָל קוֹמָה לְפָנֶיךָ תִשְׁתַּחֲוֶה. וְכָל לְבָבוֹת יִירָאוּךָ, וְכָל קֶרֶב וּכְלָיוֹת יְזַמְּרוּ לִשְׁמֶךָ. כַּדָּבָר שֶׁכָּתוּב: כָּל עַצְמוֹתַי תֹּאמַרְנָה יְהֹוָה מִי כָמוֹךָ, מַצִּיל עָנִי מֵחָזָק מִמֶּנּוּ וְעָנִי וְאֶבְיוֹן מִגּוֹזְלוֹ. מִי יִדְמֶה לָּךְ וּמִי יִשְׁוֶה לָּךְ וּמִי יַעֲרָךְ לָךְ, הָאֵל הַגָּדוֹל הַגִּבּוֹר וְהַנּוֹרָא, אֵל עֶלְיוֹן, קוֹנֵה שָׁמַיִם וָאָרֶץ. נְהַלֶּלְךָ וּנְשַׁבֵּחֲךָ וּנְפָאֶרְךָ וּנְבָרֵךְ אֶת שֵׁם קָדְשֶׁךָ. כָּאָמוּר: לְדָוִד, בָּרְכִי נַפְשִׁי אֶת יְהֹוָה וְכָל קְרָבַי אֶת שֵׁם קָדְשׁוֹ.

הָאֵל בְּתַעֲצֻמוֹת עֻזֶּךָ, הַגָּדוֹל בִּכְבוֹד שְׁמֶךָ, הַגִּבּוֹר לָנֶצַח וְהַנּוֹרָא בְּנוֹרְאוֹתֶיךָ. הַמֶּלֶךְ הַיּוֹשֵׁב עַל כִּסֵּא רָם וְנִשָּׂא. שׁוֹכֵן עַד מָרוֹם וְקָדוֹשׁ שְׁמוֹ. וְכָתוּב: רַנְּנוּ צַדִּיקִים בַּיהֹוָה, לַיְשָׁרִים נָאוָה תְהִלָּה.

בְּפִי יְשָׁרִים תִּתְהַלָּל.
וּבְדִבְרֵי צַדִּיקִים תִּתְבָּרַךְ.
וּבִלְשׁוֹן חֲסִידִים תִּתְרוֹמָם.
וּבְקֶרֶב קְדוֹשִׁים תִּתְקַדָּשׁ.

---

truly thanking God for all the good that He has done for us. Therefore, after that introduction, *we are permitted to continue to praise God! Only after we recognize that praise of God is inherently partial, are we permitted and even obligated to recite God's praises.*

We say *Nishmat* at the end of the haggadah, after we have concluded hallel. Maharal (*Gevurot Hashem* 65) explains that this prayer is referred to as "the blessing of the song" (Pesachim 118a) as it is said after hallel, and there is an obligation to sing after hallel. This would seem to be very surprising: after all, in reciting hallel we have praised God.

Therefore, the limbs that You have formed for us, and the spirit and soul that You have breathed into our nostrils, and the tongue that You have placed in our mouth all shall thank, bless, praise, glorify, exalt, adore, sanctify and proclaim the sovereignty of Your name, our King. For every mouth shall offer thanks to You, every tongue shall swear loyalty to You, every knee shall bend to You, all who stand erect shall bow down before You, all hearts shall fear You, and every innermost part shall sing praise to Your name, as it is written: "All my bones will say, Lord, who is like You; You save the poor from one stronger than he [is], the poor and the needy from one who would rob him!" Who can be likened to You, who is equal to You, who can be compared to You, the great, mighty, awesome God, God most high, Possessor of heaven and earth! We will laud You, praise You and glorify You, and we will bless Your holy name, as it says: "A Psalm of David; bless the Lord, O my soul, and all that is within me bless His holy name."

You are the Almighty God in the power of Your strength; great in the glory of Your name; mighty forever, and awe-inspiring in Your awesome deeds; the King who sits upon a lofty and exalted throne. He who dwells for eternity, lofty and holy is His name. And it is written: "Exult, righteous ones, before God; for the upright praise is fitting."

By the mouth of the upright
You shall be praised;
and by the word of the righteous
You shall be blessed;
and by the tongue of the devout
You shall be exalted;
and among the holy ones
You shall be sanctified.

וּבְמַקְהֲלוֹת רִבְבוֹת עַמְּךָ בֵּית יִשְׂרָאֵל, בְּרִנָּה יִתְפָּאַר שִׁמְךָ מַלְכֵּנוּ בְּכָל דּוֹר וָדוֹר, שֶׁכֵּן חוֹבַת כָּל הַיְצוּרִים, לְפָנֶיךָ יְהוָה אֱלֹהֵינוּ וֵאלֹהֵי אֲבוֹתֵינוּ, לְהוֹדוֹת, לְהַלֵּל, לְשַׁבֵּחַ, לְפָאֵר, לְרוֹמֵם, לְהַדֵּר, לְבָרֵךְ, לְעַלֵּה וּלְקַלֵּס, עַל כָּל דִּבְרֵי שִׁירוֹת וְתִשְׁבְּחוֹת דָּוִד בֶּן יִשַׁי עַבְדְּךָ מְשִׁיחֶךָ.

יִשְׁתַּבַּח שִׁמְךָ לָעַד מַלְכֵּנוּ, הָאֵל, הַמֶּלֶךְ הַגָּדוֹל וְהַקָּדוֹשׁ בַּשָּׁמַיִם וּבָאָרֶץ. כִּי לְךָ נָאֶה יְהוָה אֱלֹהֵינוּ וֵאלֹהֵי אֲבוֹתֵינוּ, שִׁיר וּשְׁבָחָה, הַלֵּל וְזִמְרָה, עֹז וּמֶמְשָׁלָה, נֶצַח, גְּדֻלָּה וּגְבוּרָה, תְּהִלָּה וְתִפְאֶרֶת, קְדֻשָּׁה וּמַלְכוּת, בְּרָכוֹת וְהוֹדָאוֹת, מֵעַתָּה וְעַד עוֹלָם. בָּרוּךְ אַתָּה יְהוָה, אֵל מֶלֶךְ גָּדוֹל בַּתִּשְׁבָּחוֹת, אֵל הַהוֹדָאוֹת, אֲדוֹן הַנִּפְלָאוֹת, הַבּוֹחֵר בְּשִׁירֵי זִמְרָה, מֶלֶךְ אֵל חֵי הָעוֹלָמִים.

God. What, then, does *Nishmat* add? Why do we need to have another song after hallel?

Hallel is a person's thanks, his song. *Nishmat* is the song of the soul.

At the end of hallel, after we have mentioned all the miracles and good that God did for us, and also praised and thanked Him fully with "Give thanks to the Lord, for He is good: His kindness is everlasting," our soul bursts into the song of "The soul of every living being shall bless Your name." This is an internal song, and it stems from our recognition of the fact that it is impossible to adequately praise God, but we will still try to do whatever we can. At the end of the seder, our soul announces, "Bless the Lord, O my soul; and all that is within me, bless His holy name." ▪

AND IN THE ASSEMBLED MULTITUDES of Your people, the House of Israel [be glorified with rejoicing in all generations]. For such is the obligation of all creatures before You, Lord our God and God of our fathers, to thank, to laud, to praise, to glorify, to exalt, to adore, [to bless, to elevate and to honor,] even beyond all the words of songs and praises of David, son of Yishai, Your anointed servant.

MAY YOUR NAME BE PRAISED FOREVER, our King, the great and holy God and King in heaven and on earth. To You, Lord, our God and God of our fathers, forever befits song and praise, laud and hymn, strength and dominion, victory, greatness and might, glory, splendor, holiness and sovereignty; blessings and thanksgivings for now and forever. Blessed are You, Lord, Almighty God, King, great and extolled in praises; King, God, the Life of all worlds.

Crown for Torah case, Rhodes, Greece, silver
The Wolfson Museum, Hechal Shlomo

מברכים בורא פרי הגפן, ושותים כוס רביעית בהסבה.

יש נוהגים לומר לפני ברכת "בורא פרי הגפן":

הִנְנִי מוּכָן וּמְזֻמָּן לְקַיֵּם מִצְוַת כּוֹס רְבִיעִי שֶׁל אַרְבַּע כּוֹסוֹת. לְשֵׁם יִחוּד קוּדְשָׁא בְּרִיךְ הוּא וּשְׁכִינְתֵּיהּ עַל יְדֵי הַהוּא טָמִיר וְנֶעְלָם בְּשֵׁם כָּל יִשְׂרָאֵל. וִיהִי נֹעַם אֲדֹנָי אֱלֹהֵינוּ עָלֵינוּ וּמַעֲשֵׂה יָדֵינוּ כּוֹנְנָה עָלֵינוּ וּמַעֲשֵׂה יָדֵינוּ כּוֹנְנֵהוּ.

בָּרוּךְ אַתָּה יְהֹוָה אֱלֹהֵינוּ מֶלֶךְ הָעוֹלָם, בּוֹרֵא פְּרִי הַגָּפֶן.

שותים הכוס בהסבת שמאל ומברכים ברכה אחרונה.

בָּרוּךְ אַתָּה יְהֹוָה אֱלֹהֵינוּ מֶלֶךְ הָעוֹלָם, עַל הַגֶּפֶן וְעַל פְּרִי הַגֶּפֶן וְעַל תְּנוּבַת הַשָּׂדֶה, וְעַל אֶרֶץ חֶמְדָּה טוֹבָה וּרְחָבָה שֶׁרָצִיתָ וְהִנְחַלְתָּ לַאֲבוֹתֵינוּ, לֶאֱכוֹל מִפִּרְיָהּ וְלִשְׂבּוֹעַ מִטּוּבָהּ. רַחֶם נָא יְהֹוָה אֱלֹהֵינוּ עַל יִשְׂרָאֵל עַמֶּךָ, וְעַל יְרוּשָׁלַיִם עִירֶךָ, וְעַל צִיּוֹן מִשְׁכַּן כְּבוֹדֶךָ, וְעַל מִזְבְּחֶךָ וְעַל הֵיכָלֶךָ. וּבְנֵה יְרוּשָׁלַיִם עִיר הַקֹּדֶשׁ בִּמְהֵרָה בְיָמֵינוּ, וְהַעֲלֵנוּ לְתוֹכָהּ וְשַׂמְּחֵנוּ בְּבִנְיָנָהּ, וְנֹאכַל מִפִּרְיָהּ וְנִשְׂבַּע מִטּוּבָהּ וּנְבָרֶכְךָ עָלֶיהָ בִּקְדֻשָּׁה וּבְטָהֳרָה. (בשבת: וּרְצֵה וְהַחֲלִיצֵנוּ בְּיוֹם הַשַּׁבָּת הַזֶּה), וְשַׂמְּחֵנוּ בְּיוֹם חַג הַמַּצּוֹת הַזֶּה. כִּי אַתָּה יְהֹוָה טוֹב וּמֵטִיב לַכֹּל וְנוֹדֶה לְּךָ עַל הָאָרֶץ וְעַל פְּרִי הַגָּפֶן. בָּרוּךְ אַתָּה יְהֹוָה, עַל הָאָרֶץ וְעַל פְּרִי הַגָּפֶן. (על יין של ארץ ישראל מסיימים: וְעַל פְּרִי גַּפְנָהּ.)

Goblet, London, England, end of the 19th century
The Wolfson Museum, Hechal Shlomo, Max Grundt Collection

One recites the blessing over wine and drinks the fourth cup while leaning.
There are those who say the following before reciting the blessing over wine:

I am prepared and ready to fulfill the commandment of the fourth of four cups. For the sake of the unification of the Holy One, Blessed be He, and His Presence, in the name of all Israel. And may the pleasantness of the Lord our God be upon us, and the work of our hands establish for us, and may the work of our hands establish it.

BLESSED ARE YOU, LORD OUR GOD,
King of the universe, who creates the fruit of the vine.

One drinks the wine while leaning to the left, and afterwards recites the concluding blessing on the wine.

Blessed are You, Lord our God, King of the universe, for the vine and the fruit of the vine, for the produce of the field, and for the precious, good and spacious land that You have favored to give as an inheritance to our fathers, to eat of its fruit and be satiated by its goodness. Please have mercy, Lord our God, on Israel Your people, on Jerusalem Your city, on Zion the abode of Your glory, on Your altar and on Your Temple. Rebuild Jerusalem, the holy city, speedily in our days, and bring us up into it, and make us rejoice in its rebuilding, that we may eat of its fruit and be satiated by its goodness, and we will bless You in holiness and purity. (on Shabbat: May it please You to give us rest on this Shabbat day) and let us rejoice on this day of the Festival of Matzot. For You, Lord, are good and continually do good to all, and we thank You for the land and for the fruit of the vine. Blessed are You, Lord, for the land and for the fruit of the vine (on wine made in Israel: "for the fruit of its vine").

Riddles

84. Who awaits whom?
85. God looks after the poor – how is this expressed?
86. Which words in *Nishmat* resemble the first blessing of the amidah prayer? And which words are similar to *Magen avot* that is said on Friday night?
87. The organs of the body are very active in this prayer. What does each one do?
88. In *Nishmat* we thank God in a general way for all His kindness that he has done and continues to do for us. Only one instance of kindness and rescue is mentioned specifically. What is it?

Nirtzah

We have now reached a heightened spiritual state, one in which we can hear the voice of God, and one in which our prayers are answered more readily. In the following piyyutim – liturgical hymns – we sing to God for the miracles that He performed for us. We will praise, extol, and accept God as our King and pray for the rebuilding of the Bet HaMikdash ("*ki lo na'eh,*" "*adir hu*"). Finally, we will embrace God's supremacy over all of the world ("*echad mi yodei'a,*" "*chad gadya*").

אם עשה כסדר הזה, ירצה ה׳ את פעלו ויתברך מן השמים.

חֲסַל סִדּוּר פֶּסַח כְּהִלְכָתוֹ, כְּכָל מִשְׁפָּטוֹ וְחֻקָּתוֹ.
כַּאֲשֶׁר זָכִינוּ לְסַדֵּר אוֹתוֹ, כֵּן נִזְכֶּה לַעֲשׂוֹתוֹ. זַךְ
שׁוֹכֵן מְעוֹנָה, קוֹמֵם קְהַל עֲדַת מִי מָנָה. בְּקָרוֹב נַהֵל נִטְעֵי כַנָּה,
פְּדוּיִם לְצִיּוֹן בְּרִנָּה. לְשָׁנָה הַבָּאָה בִּירוּשָׁלָיִם.

Food For Thought

Why Nirtzah?

Rav Avraham Yitzchak Kook (*Olat Re'iyah, Simanei HaSeder, Nirtzah*) noticed a difference in language style between nirtzah and the words that describe the other steps of the seder. Generally, the other words are all in the form of commands: "make kiddush," "wash," etc., whereas nirtzah ("it was accepted") is in the passive form.

This teaches us that we have undergone a significant process on the Seder night – an internal change. Now, at the end of the seder, we have attained such a high level of freedom and holiness that we are able to feel the holiness that surrounds without any action on our part. The soul itself has become so holy and pure to the extent that it naturally accepts God.

Now we are ready to sing, to feel God's supervision of the world, to feel how God lights up the darkness of the night as though it were the light of the day (the *piyyut* "*az rov nissim*"), to feel how God's hand is raised on the night of the festival ("*ometz gevuratecha*"), to anoint God as our King ("*ki lo na'eh*"), to pray for the rebuilding of the *Bet HaMikdash* ("*adir hu*"), to feel that whatever happens in the world is carried out by "*echad mi yode'a – echad Eloheinu*," and to feel God's supervision over all who wish to tear one another apart, and to feel God's Existence – "And the Holy One, Blessed be He, came…"

Next year in rebuilt Jerusalem

This sentence is appropriate for ending the passage of "The seder is now completed in accordance with all of its laws," which ends with the hope of Pesach, "soon… Zion, redeemed, with song." We are not sure whether this sentence is part of the paragraph, and in ancient haggadot it sometimes appears in other places (for example, after "*ki lo na'eh*" – laws of the haggadah in the siddur of Shelah).

Twice a year we say, "Next year in rebuilt Jerusalem" – at the end of Yom

◂ *Kippur*

If one acted in this order (seder), God will accept his actions, and he will be blessed from heaven.

THE SEDER IS NOW COMPLETED IN accordance with all of its laws, its ordinances and statutes. Just as we were found worthy to perform it, so may we be worthy to do so in the future. O pure one, who dwells on high, raise up the congregation that is without number. Soon may you guide the offshoots of Your plants to Zion, redeemed, with song. Next year in rebuilt Jerusalem!

Kippur and at the Seder night, the two times that are appropriate for our redemption (see Tractate *Rosh Hashanah* 11a, as to whether we will be redeemed in *Nissan* or *Tishrei*, and see Tosafot *ibid.* 27a, that both views are the words of the Living God). The midrash (Mechilta 14) mentions specifically that the *Seder* night is an appropriate time for redemption. "It is a night of watching to the Lord – on which they were redeemed and on which they will be redeemed in the future." During both of these times, we have the merit of being pure and holy: at the end of Yom Kippur, *after a long process of atonement and forgiveness, and on the Seder night, after we have freed ourselves from slavery, both internal and external, and have become worthy of approaching God.* Now we feel that we are ready and ask directly for "Next year in rebuilt Jerusalem."

We began the haggadah with "This year we are here; next year may we be in Eretz Yisrael." At the end of the haggadah we say something similar, but more hopeful: "Next year in rebuilt Jerusalem." It is not enough for us to be in Eretz Yisrael. We want to see Jerusalem fully rebuilt, we want God's Divine Presence to be revealed, we want the Bet HaMikdash, and we want to be closer to God – "I will dwell in the midst of Bnei Yisrael, and I will be their God" (Exodus 29:45). ▪

Seder plate, Israel, second half of 20th century, embossed copper
The Wolfson Museum, Hechal Shlomo

בחוץ לארץ אומרים פיוט זה רק בלילה הראשון.

וּבְכֵן, וַיְהִי בַּחֲצִי הַלַּיְלָה.

אָז רוֹב נִסִּים הִפְלֵאתָ בַּלַּיְלָה.
בְּרֹאשׁ אַשְׁמוֹרֶת זֶה הַלַּיְלָה.
גֵּר צֶדֶק נִצַּחְתּוֹ כְּנֶחֱלַק לוֹ לַיְלָה.
וַיְהִי בַּחֲצִי הַלַּיְלָה.

דַּנְתָּ מֶלֶךְ גְּרָר בַּחֲלוֹם הַלַּיְלָה.
הִפְחַדְתָּ אֲרַמִּי בְּאֶמֶשׁ לַיְלָה.
וְיִשְׂרָאֵל יָשַׁר לָאֵל וַיּוּכַל לוֹ לַיְלָה.
וַיְהִי בַּחֲצִי הַלַּיְלָה.

זֶרַע בְּכוֹרֵי פַּתְרוֹס מָחַצְתָּ בַּחֲצִי הַלַּיְלָה.
חֵילָם לֹא מָצְאוּ בְּקוּמָם בַּלַּיְלָה.
טִיסַת נְגִיד חֲרוֹשֶׁת סִלִּיתָ בְּכוֹכְבֵי לַיְלָה.
וַיְהִי בַּחֲצִי הַלַּיְלָה.

Food For Thought

You performed many wonders by night – why specifically at night?
This piyyut lists the different miracles throughout the history of Am Yisrael that took place at night. Midrash Rabbah (Numbers 20:12) states that all the miracles that were performed for Israel against wicked men took place at night: "And God came to Balaam at night" – This is as it is written, "It is a night of watching for the Lord, to take them out of the land of Egypt; this very night" (Numbers 12:42). All the miracles that were wrought for Israel, and the punishment of the wicked, took place at night: "And God came

◂ to Lavan

Outside of Israel, this is only said on the first night of Pesach.

AND IT CAME TO PASS AT MIDNIGHT!

Then, in times of old, You performed many wonders by NIGHT.
At the beginning of the watches of this NIGHT,
The righteous convert You gave victory by dividing for him the NIGHT.

AND IT CAME TO PASS AT MIDNIGHT!

You judged the king of Gerar in a dream at NIGHT.
You frightened the Aramean in the dark of the NIGHT.
Israel (Jacob) fought an angel and overcame him at NIGHT.

AND IT CAME TO PASS AT MIDNIGHT!

You crushed the firstborn of Patros at MIDNIGHT.
They did not find their host upon arising at NIGHT.
The army of the prince of Charoshet You swept away with the stars of the NIGHT.

AND IT CAME TO PASS AT MIDNIGHT!

Embroidered cloth, Israel
The Wolfson Museum, Hechal Shlomo

יָעַץ מְחָרֵף לְנוֹפֵף אִוּוי, הוֹבַשְׁתָּ פְּגָרָיו בַּלַּיְלָה.
כָּרַע בֵּל וּמַצָּבוֹ בְּאִישׁוֹן לַיְלָה.
לְאִישׁ חֲמוּדוֹת נִגְלָה רָז חֲזוֹת לַיְלָה.
וַיְהִי בַּחֲצִי הַלַּיְלָה.

מִשְׁתַּכֵּר בִּכְלֵי קֹדֶשׁ נֶהֱרַג בּוֹ בַּלַּיְלָה.
נוֹשַׁע מִבּוֹר אֲרָיוֹת פּוֹתֵר בִּעֲתוּתֵי לַיְלָה.
שִׂנְאָה נָטַר אֲגָגִי וְכָתַב סְפָרִים בַּלַּיְלָה.
וַיְהִי בַּחֲצִי הַלַּיְלָה.

Torah Shield, 17th century, tin and golden brass
The Wolfson Museum, Hechal Shlomo

The blasphemer planned to raise his hand against the desired place (Jerusalem), but You made him into dry corpses in the NIGHT.
Bel, and the one who erected it, was overturned in the darkness of the NIGHT.
To the man You delighted in (Daniel) was revealed the secret of the visions of the NIGHT.

AND IT CAME TO PASS AT MIDNIGHT!

He who became drunk from the holy vessels was killed that very NIGHT.
Saved from the lion's den was he who interpreted the horrors of the NIGHT.
The Aggagi nursed hatred and wrote edicts by NIGHT.

AND IT CAME TO PASS AT MIDNIGHT!

---

to Lavan the Aramean in a dream of the night" (Genesis 31:24); "And God came to Avimelech in a dream of the night" (Genesis 20:3); "It came to pass at midnight" (Exodus 12:29); and it states, "there were the cloud and the darkness, and it illuminated the night" (Exodus 14:20); "he divided himself against them at night" (Genesis 14:15); and so with all of them.

It was on the basis of this midrash that the piyyut of "*az rov nissim*" was written. Why is it that these miracles were performed for Am Yisrael at night, as opposed to during the day? Why were the miracles performed for Am Yisrael specifically at night? It is possible that the meaning of this piyyut is that all occurred at midnight, as occurred in Egypt. This is the time when change begins, when the night begins to look towards the dawn, the good, and that is why it is a time of mercy and of favor (see Shulchan Aruch 1:2; and see more on this later in the piyyut, "*karev yom, asher hu lo yom velo laylah*").

One can also add that the night is the time of faith in God – "Your faith at night" (Psalms 92:3). The night is a time of doubt, the time when God's natural control of the world is not noticeable or open, and, therefore, one needs faith in God's existence. Yet, because of this, it is also a time that is appropriate for miracles, a time that is suitable for God's supervision in a

◂ supernatural

עוֹרַרְתָּ נִצְחֲךָ עָלָיו בְּנֶדֶד שְׁנַת לַיְלָה.
פּוּרָה תִדְרוֹךְ לְשׁוֹמֵר מַה מִלַּיְלָה.
צָרַח כַּשּׁוֹמֵר וְשָׂח: אָתָא בֹקֶר וְגַם לַיְלָה.
וַיְהִי בַּחֲצִי הַלַּיְלָה.

קָרֵב יוֹם אֲשֶׁר הוּא לֹא יוֹם וְלֹא לַיְלָה.
רָם הוֹדַע כִּי לְךָ הַיּוֹם אַף לְךָ הַלַּיְלָה.
שׁוֹמְרִים הַפְקֵד לְעִירְךָ כָּל הַיּוֹם וְכָל הַלַּיְלָה.
תָּאִיר כְּאוֹר יוֹם חֶשְׁכַת לַיְלָה.
וַיְהִי בַּחֲצִי הַלַּיְלָה.

---

supernatural way. From here we learn that it is only under conditions of God's "hiding Himself," when there is no natural way for a change in the situation, one may hope and wish for a Divine revolution and change – it is out of the darkness that we are granted a great light – "although I sit in darkness, the Lord is a light to me" (Micah 7:8). ▪

Food For Thought

Bring close the day that is neither day nor night

"*Trample the wine press for those who ask the watchman, 'What will come of the night?'*" This is a request and prayer for the future: just as grapes are trod in a wine press, we ask You to tread on our enemies. This sentence is based on the words of the prophet Isaiah in describing God's vengeance against Edom, "A wine press I trod alone, and from the peoples, none was with Me; and I trod them with My wrath, and I trampled them with My fury" (Isaiah 63:3).

He will shout like a watchman, and say, "Morning shall come and also night." God protects Am Yisrael, and He announces, "*Morning has come*," and Am Yisrael must be redeemed! (based on Isaiah 21:12: "Said the watchman, 'Morning has come, and also night').

Bring close the day that is neither

◂ *day*

You began Your victory over him with disturbing sleep at **NIGHT.**
Trample the wine press for those who ask the watchman, "What will come of the **NIGHT?"**
He will shout like a watchman, and say, "Morning shall come and also **NIGHT."**

AND IT CAME TO PASS AT MIDNIGHT!

Bring close the day that is neither day nor **NIGHT.**
Exalted One, make known that Yours is the day and Yours is also the **NIGHT.**
Appoint guards for Your city, all day and all **NIGHT.**
Brighten like the light of the day the darkness of **NIGHT.**

AND IT CAME TO PASS AT MIDNIGHT!

Riddles

89. Whose sleep was disturbed at night?
90. Who interpreted dreams of the night?
91. "Because you have commanding power with God and with men, and you have prevailed." Where is this alluded to in this piyyut?
92. Who was terrified at night?
93. Who blasphemed? What happened to his army?
94. Who was swept away?

day nor night. This alludes to the future redemption, as the prophet Zechariah said, "And it shall be one day that shall be known to the Lord, *neither day nor night*" (Zechariah 14:7).

Exalted One, make known that Yours is the day and Yours is also the night. God, let the world know that both day and night arc Yours – "Day is Yours, even night is Yours; You established the luminary and the sun" (Psalms 74:16).

Appoint guards for Your city, all day and all night. Protect us, appoint guards over Your nation and Your city – "On your walls, O Jerusalem, I have appointed watchmen; all day and all night…" (Isaiah 62:6).

Brighten like the light of the day the darkness of night. Am Yisrael, in the dark of exile, asks God, "*Make the day*

◂ *light,*

An ancient manuscript (Germany, 1331, Machzor Nuremberg, Part 1, Index 72), which includes the original piyyut in which there is the piyyut "az rov nissim" – courtesy of Dr. David and Jemima Jeselsohn.

light, bring the redemption." This we see in Exodus Rabbah (*Bo*, *Parashah* 18, 11):

> "It was a night of watching to the Lord" – In this world, Bnei Yisrael experienced a temporary miracle at night, but in the World to Come the night will become day, as it states, "And the light of the moon shall be like the light of the sun, and the light of the sun shall be sevenfold" (Isaiah 30:26), as the light that God first created and hid in the Garden of Eden.

What is the significance of the special times, "Morning shall come and also night," "neither day nor night," "Brighten like the light of the day the darkness of night?"

The piyyut of "*az rov nissim*" uses different definitions of time: "*Morning shall come and also night,*" "*neither day nor night,*" "*Brighten like the light*

◂ *of the*

of the day the darkness of night." What is the significance of this? Why is the redemption depicted as a mixture of day and night?

If we read the verses in the Torah that describe the redemption in Egypt closely, we see that the story itself is ambiguous as to the specific time of day involved. On the one hand, we are told that, "*on this very day* I have taken your legions out of the land of Egypt" (Exodus 12:17), but on the other hand it states that, "make the Pesach offering to the Lord, your God, for in the month of spring, the Lord, your God, brought you out of Egypt *at night*" (Deuteronomy 16:1). When did the Exodus from Egypt take place: during the the day or at night?

The Sages explain that the Egyptians wished to send out Am Yisrael already at night, but they left Egypt during the day (*Berachot* 9a). However, we can suggest a more profound answer.

The redemption from Egypt is characterized by the fact that it took place in haste, *chipazon* – Bnei Yisrael were obliged to eat the Pesach sacrifice in haste (Exodus 12:11), Egypt hastened to rid itself of Am Yisrael, and this haste resulted in their dough not being able to rise. Haste symbolizes the supernatural aspect of Am Yisrael's redemption, and, therefore, it could not be subject to the natural frameworks of time (see the section on "*Why in haste?*" on p. 114). The descriptions of the times of the Exodus from Egypt are vague because it was a redemption not bound by the limits of natural reality and time.

On the other hand, the future redemption will take place in an entirely different manner.

The prophet Zechariah describes the redemption with the words, "it shall come to pass that at evening it shall be light" (Zechariah 14:7). The future redemption will take place when the world is elevated to a level at which the light of the redemption will be visible with natural means. All will be purified, the evening will light up, and we will no longer need a time that is "neither day nor night." At that time we will merit that Godwill "Brighten like the light of the day the darkness of night," and we will merit the appearance of the Divine Presence within natural reality, until "God will be One and His name one" (Zechariah 14:9). ▪

וּבְכֵן, וַאֲמַרְתֶּם זֶבַח פֶּסַח.

אוֹמֶץ גְּבוּרוֹתֶיךָ הִפְלֵאתָ בַּפֶּסַח.
בְּרֹאשׁ כָּל מוֹעֲדוֹת נִשֵּׂאתָ פֶּסַח.
גִּלִּיתָ לְאֶזְרָחִי חֲצוֹת לֵיל פֶּסַח.
וַאֲמַרְתֶּם זֶבַח פֶּסַח.

דְּלָתָיו דָּפַקְתָּ כְּחוֹם הַיּוֹם בַּפֶּסַח.
הִסְעִיד נוֹצְצִים עֻגוֹת מַצּוֹת בַּפֶּסַח.
וְאֶל הַבָּקָר רָץ זֵכֶר לְשׁוֹר עֵרֶךְ פֶּסַח.
וַאֲמַרְתֶּם זֶבַח פֶּסַח.
זוֹעֲמוּ סְדוֹמִים וְלוֹהֲטוּ בָּאֵשׁ בַּפֶּסַח.
חֻלַּץ לוֹט מֵהֶם וּמַצּוֹת אָפָה בְּקֵץ פֶּסַח.
טִאטֵאתָ אַדְמַת מוֹף וְנוֹף בְּעָבְרְךָ בַּפֶּסַח.
וַאֲמַרְתֶּם זֶבַח פֶּסַח.

יָהּ רֹאשׁ כָּל אוֹן מָחַצְתָּ בְּלֵיל שִׁמּוּר פֶּסַח.
כַּבִּיר עַל בֵּן בְּכוֹר פָּסַחְתָּ בְּדַם פֶּסַח.
לְבִלְתִּי תֵּת מַשְׁחִית לָבֹא בִּפְתָחַי בַּפֶּסַח.
וַאֲמַרְתֶּם זֶבַח פֶּסַח.

Food For Thought

By virtue of the Pesach sacrifice
This piyyut, "*ometz gevurotecha*," resembles the previous one, "*az rov nissim*," and it also reviews miracles ◂ that

Outside Israel, this piyyut is said on the second Seder night.

THEREFORE, YOU SHALL SAY: THIS IS THE PESACH SACRIFICE.

You displayed Your mighty powers wondrously on PESACH.
Above all seasons of delight You elevated PESACH.
You revealed the Exodus to the Ezrachite at the midnight of PESACH.

AND YOU SHALL SAY: THIS IS THE PESACH SACRIFICE.

You knocked at his door in the heat of the day on PESACH.
He gave the angels cakes of matzah to dine on during PESACH.
He ran to the herd, harbinger of the sacrificial feast of the PESACH.

AND YOU SHALL SAY: THIS IS THE PESACH SACRIFICE.

The Sodomites provoked and were burned up with fire on PESACH.
Lot was rescued from them and he baked matzot at the end of PESACH.
You swept the ground of Moph and Noph when You passed through on PESACH.

AND YOU SHALL SAY: THIS IS THE PESACH SACRIFICE.

---

that were performed for Israel. One of the most obvious differences between them is the refrain at the end of each stanza: "And you shall say: This is the Pesach sacrifice" (Exodus 12:27). What is the significance of this?

This verse appears in the Torah as the answer to the *wicked son*. Mentioning it at the end of the seder teaches us that even the wicked son understands and acknowledges God's supervision over us throughout all the generations. However, this verse also teaches us the other side of God's supervision – Am Yisrael *is obligated* to serve God. Our special relationship with God and our closeness to Him are what preserve us, but they also obligate us to observe the mitzvot: "And you shall say: This is the Pesach sacrifice." God's rescue of us from Egypt, the way

◂ He passed

מְסֻגֶּרֶת סֻגָּרָה בְּעִתּוֹתֵי פֶּסַח.
נִשְׁמְדָה מִדְיָן בִּצְלִיל שְׂעוֹרֵי עֹמֶר פֶּסַח.
שׂוֹרְפוּ מִשְׁמַנֵּי פּוּל וְלוּד בִּיקַד יְקוֹד פֶּסַח.

וַאֲמַרְתֶּם זֶבַח פֶּסַח.

עוֹד הַיּוֹם בְּנוֹב לַעֲמוֹד עַד גָּעָה עוֹנַת פֶּסַח.
פַּס יָד כָּתְבָה לְקַעֲקֵעַ צוּל בַּפֶּסַח.
צָפֹה הַצָּפִית עָרוֹךְ הַשֻּׁלְחָן בַּפֶּסַח.

וַאֲמַרְתֶּם זֶבַח פֶּסַח.

קָהָל כִּנְּסָה הֲדַסָּה, צוֹם לְשַׁלֵּשׁ בַּפֶּסַח.
רֹאשׁ מִבֵּית רָשָׁע מָחַצְתָּ בְּעֵץ חֲמִשִּׁים בַּפֶּסַח.
שְׁתֵּי אֵלֶּה רֶגַע תָּבִיא לְעוּצִית בַּפֶּסַח.
תָּעֹז יָדְךָ וְתָרוּם יְמִינְךָ כְּלֵיל הִתְקַדֵּשׁ חַג פֶּסַח.

וַאֲמַרְתֶּם זֶבַח פֶּסַח.

He passed over our houses there, obligates us to observe the mitzvot when bringing the Pesach sacrifice.

We can also learn from this a lesson for subsequent generations – God looks after us, and we observe His mitzvot! Our commitment to halacha, to obeying God's wishes in the world, and to all the paragraphs of the Shulchan Aruch, are the expression of our recognition of God's supervision over us and the daily miracles He performs for us: "And you shall say: This is the Pesach sacrifice." ▪

God, You crushed the head of every firstborn on the watchful night of PESACH.

Powerful One, You skipped over Your firstborn by merit of the blood of PESACH.

So as not to let the Destroyer enter my threshold on PESACH.

AND YOU SHALL SAY: THIS IS THE PESACH SACRIFICE.

The besieged city was besieged at the time of PESACH.

Midian was destroyed through a barley cake, from the Omer of PESACH.

The mighty nobles of Pul and Lud were burnt in a great conflagration on PESACH.

AND YOU SHALL SAY: THIS IS THE PESACH SACRIFICE.

Still today would be standing at *Nov* until the time came for PESACH.

A hand inscribed the destruction of *Tzul* on PESACH.

As the watch and table were set on PESACH.

AND YOU SHALL SAY: THIS IS THE PESACH SACRIFICE.

Hadassah assembled a congregation for a three-day fast on PESACH.

The head of the wicked clan You crushed, through a gallows of fifty cubits, on PESACH.

Double will You bring in an instant upon Utsis on PESACH.

Let Your hand be strengthened and Your right arm be uplifted, as on that night when You made holy the festival of PESACH.

AND YOU SHALL SAY: THIS IS THE PESACH SACRIFICE.

כִּי לוֹ נָאֶה. כִּי לוֹ יָאֶה.

אַדִּיר בִּמְלוּכָה. בָּחוּר כַּהֲלָכָה. גְּדוּדָיו יֹאמְרוּ לוֹ:
לְךָ וּלְךָ. לְךָ כִּי לְךָ. לְךָ אַף לְךָ. לְךָ יְהֹוָה הַמַּמְלָכָה.
כִּי לוֹ נָאֶה. כִּי לוֹ יָאֶה.

דָּגוּל בִּמְלוּכָה. הָדוּר כַּהֲלָכָה. וָתִיקָיו יֹאמְרוּ לוֹ:
לְךָ וּלְךָ. לְךָ כִּי לְךָ. לְךָ אַף לְךָ. לְךָ יְהֹוָה הַמַּמְלָכָה.
כִּי לוֹ נָאֶה. כִּי לוֹ יָאֶה.

זַכַּאי בִּמְלוּכָה. חָסִין כַּהֲלָכָה. טַפְסְרָיו יֹאמְרוּ לוֹ:
לְךָ וּלְךָ. לְךָ כִּי לְךָ. לְךָ אַף לְךָ. לְךָ יְהֹוָה הַמַּמְלָכָה.
כִּי לוֹ נָאֶה. כִּי לוֹ יָאֶה.

Food For Thought

To Him praise is becoming – How many names does God have?

This piyyut was recited by the Rishonim of Ashkenaz, including Maharam of Rothenberg (*Tashbetz Kattan* 99). However, we do not know the identity of the author. This piyyut is composed of eight stanzas, each of which comprises three parts: the first and second relate to God (*mighty* in Kingship, perfectly *distinguished*), while the third relates to the angels or to the people who praise God (*His companies* say to Him).

We will explain a number of the unfamiliar expressions in the piyyut, and cite the sources to which they allude:

He is *distinguished* (*bachur*) – Song of Songs 5:15 – "chosen – *bachur* – as the cedars."

His *companies* (*gedudav*) – the angels (Job 25:3) – "Have His troops – gedudav – a number?"

Renowned (*dagul*) – Song of Songs 5:10 – "preeminent – dagul – among the myriads."

Glorious (*hadur*) – Isaiah 63:1 – "majestic – hadur – in His attire."

His *faithful* (*vatikav*) – His faithful ones.

◂ His

TO HIM PRAISE IS BECOMING;
TO HIM PRAISE IS FITTING.

Mighty in Kingship, perfectly distinguished,
His companies say to Him:
to You and to You;
to You, yes to You;
to You, only to You;
You, God, are the Sovereign.

TO HIM PRAISE IS BECOMING;
TO HIM PRAISE IS FITTING.

Renowned in kingship, perfectly glorious,
His faithful say to Him:
to You and to You;
to You, yes to You;
to You, only to You;
You, God, are the Sovereign.

TO HIM PRAISE IS BECOMING;
TO HIM PRAISE IS FITTING.

Worthy in kingship, perfectly immune,
His princes say to Him:
to You and to You;
to You, yes to You;
to You, only to You;
You, God, are the Sovereign.

TO HIM PRAISE IS BECOMING;
TO HIM PRAISE IS FITTING.

His *princes* (*tafserav*) – Jeremiah 51:27 – a marshal – tifsar.

His *learned ones* (*limudav*) – Am Yisrael, which studies His Torah (based on Isaiah 54:13).

His *surrounding ones* (*sevivav*) –

◂ Psalms

יָחִיד בִּמְלוּכָה. כַּבִּיר כַּהֲלָכָה. לִמּוּדָיו יֹאמְרוּ לוֹ:
לְךָ וּלְךָ. לְךָ כִּי לְךָ. לְךָ אַף לְךָ. לְךָ יְהוָֹה הַמַּמְלָכָה.
כִּי לוֹ נָאֶה. כִּי לוֹ יָאֶה.

מֶלֶךְ בִּמְלוּכָה. נוֹרָא כַּהֲלָכָה. סְבִיבָיו יֹאמְרוּ לוֹ:
לְךָ וּלְךָ. לְךָ כִּי לְךָ. לְךָ אַף לְךָ. לְךָ יְהוָֹה הַמַּמְלָכָה.
כִּי לוֹ נָאֶה. כִּי לוֹ יָאֶה.

Tablecloth for Pesach, Israel, 1981, gouache on paper,
artist: Shoshana Neuman
The Wolfson Museum, Hechal Shlomo

Unique in kingship, perfectly powerful,
His learned ones say to Him:
to You and to You;
to You, yes to You;
to You, only to You;
You, God, are the Sovereign.

TO HIM PRAISE IS BECOMING;
TO HIM PRAISE IS FITTING.

Commanding in Kingship, perfectly awesome,
His surrounding ones say to Him:
to You and to You;
to You, yes to You;
to You, only to You;
You, God, are the Sovereign.

TO HIM PRAISE IS BECOMING;
TO HIM PRAISE IS FITTING.

Psalms 89:8 – "in the great council of those surrounding Him" – *sevivav* – most probably His angels.

His *snow-white angels* (*shinanav*) – His angels (Psalms 68:18).

In general, we limit our descriptions of God. The Talmud in Tractate Megillah (25a) explains the problems involved in using numerous praises:

> A certain cantor went down to the ark in the presence of Rabbi Chanina and said: "The great, the mighty, the awesome, the majestic, the strong, the powerful God!" He said to him: "Have you finished the praises of your Master? Had it not been that Moshe wrote down the first three in the Torah, and had the Men of the Great Assembly not ordained them, we would not be permitted to recite (them); and you say all this! It is as if a man had thousands and thousands of gold dinars, and people, to praise his wealth, would say he had a thousand. Would it not be an insult to him?

One cannot praise God sufficiently, because we will never be able to utter even a small fraction of His praises. If that is the case, how is it that we say "the great, mighty, and awesome God" at the beginning of every amidah

◂ prayer?

עָנָיו בִּמְלוּכָה. פּוֹדֶה כַּהֲלָכָה. צַדִּיקָיו יֹאמְרוּ לוֹ:
לְךָ וּלְךָ. לְךָ כִּי לְךָ. לְךָ אַף לְךָ. לְךָ יְהוָה הַמַּמְלָכָה.
כִּי לוֹ נָאֶה. כִּי לוֹ יָאֶה.

קָדוֹשׁ בִּמְלוּכָה. רַחוּם כַּהֲלָכָה. שִׁנְאַנָּיו יֹאמְרוּ לוֹ:
לְךָ וּלְךָ. לְךָ כִּי לְךָ. לְךָ אַף לְךָ. לְךָ יְהוָה הַמַּמְלָכָה.
כִּי לוֹ נָאֶה. כִּי לוֹ יָאֶה.

תַּקִּיף בִּמְלוּכָה. תּוֹמֵךְ כַּהֲלָכָה. תְּמִימָיו יֹאמְרוּ לוֹ:
לְךָ וּלְךָ. לְךָ כִּי לְךָ. לְךָ אַף לְךָ. לְךָ יְהוָה הַמַּמְלָכָה.
כִּי לוֹ נָאֶה. כִּי לוֹ יָאֶה.

---

prayer? Rabbi Chanina explains that we may use these three terms only because they were written in the Torah by Moshe (Deuteronomy 10:17), and it was because of this that the Men of the Great Assembly instituted them in our prayers, as it states in Nehemiah (9:32), "Our God, the great, mighty, and awesome God."

Despite that, we find various piyyutim that list many attributes of God. For example, this can be found in the piyyut of "*mi'pi eil*," which is said on Simchat Torah, the piyyut of "*ha'aderet veha'emunah*," and many others.

It seems that there are special times when one may mention additional attributes of God. This is true during special joyous occasions such as the festival of Simchat Torah, and the end of the seder as well. We are now on a special plane of closeness to God. After we have clarified to others and to ourselves that there is no end to the praises that should be offered to God ("Were our mouths as full of song as the sea… we would still be unable to thank You Lord" – from *Nishmat*), and after we have thoroughly internalized that everything in this world comes

Riddles

95. How many times does the phrase "to You" appear in the piyyut? (try to work this out without actually counting the words)
96. Who is holy? Who is righteous?

◂ from

Modest in kingship, perfectly the
Redeemer, His legions say to Him:
to You and to You;
to You, yes to You;
to You, only to You;
You, God, are the Sovereign.

TO HIM PRAISE IS BECOMING;
TO HIM PRAISE IS FITTING.

Holy in kingship, perfectly merciful,
His snow-white angels say to Him:
to You and to You;
to You, yes to You;
to You, only to You;
You, God, are the Sovereign.

TO HIM PRAISE IS BECOMING;
TO HIM PRAISE IS FITTING.

Resolute in kingship, perfectly supportive,
His perfect ones say to Him:
to You and to You;
to You, yes to You;
to You, only to You;
You, God, are the Sovereign.

TO HIM PRAISE IS BECOMING;
TO HIM PRAISE IS FITTING.

---

from God, only now may we praise God in this way. We are now permitted to praise God and to say, "To Him praise is becoming; to Him praise is fitting." God is willing to accept these praises, "Halleluyah! For it is good to sing to our God; because He is pleasant, praise is fitting for Him" (Psalms 147:1), and, "among all the wise men of the nations and among all their kingdom there is none like You" (Jeremiah 10:7). ■

אַדִּיר הוּא, יִבְנֶה בֵיתוֹ בְּקָרוֹב.
בִּמְהֵרָה, בִּמְהֵרָה, בְּיָמֵינוּ בְּקָרוֹב.
אֵל בְּנֵה, אֵל בְּנֵה, בְּנֵה בֵיתְךָ בְּקָרוֹב.

בָּחוּר הוּא, גָּדוֹל הוּא, דָּגוּל הוּא, יִבְנֶה בֵיתוֹ בְּקָרוֹב.
בִּמְהֵרָה, בִּמְהֵרָה, בְּיָמֵינוּ בְּקָרוֹב.
אֵל בְּנֵה, אֵל בְּנֵה, בְּנֵה בֵיתְךָ בְּקָרוֹב.

הָדוּר הוּא, וָתִיק הוּא, זַכַּאי הוּא,
חָסִיד הוּא, יִבְנֶה בֵיתוֹ בְּקָרוֹב.
בִּמְהֵרָה, בִּמְהֵרָה, בְּיָמֵינוּ בְּקָרוֹב.
אֵל בְּנֵה, אֵל בְּנֵה, בְּנֵה בֵיתְךָ בְּקָרוֹב.

Food For Thought

He is mighty. May He soon rebuild His House, speedily

We do not know who wrote this piyyut. It is similar to the previous one, because it is also full of praises for God (this fits with the division of the piyyutim of the haggadah into pairs).

In this piyyut we again recite the praises of God, but this time we make a request of Him: "May He soon rebuild His House, speedily." We prayed earlier for "Next year in rebuilt Jerusalem," but this is more explicit – earlier, we only asked for rebuilt Jerusalem (although there is a hint there about the rebuilding of the Bet HaMikdash), but now we are bold enough to ask directly: "rebuild your House speedily."

The special link between the Exodus from Egypt and the building of the Bet HaMikdash was already revealed at the Song of the Sea:

> You shall bring them and plant them on the mount of Your heritage, directed toward Your habitation, which You made, O Lord (Exodus 15:17).

As soon as Am Yisrael is saved from its distress, it anticipates the final goal:

◄ *"the*

He is mighty
May He soon rebuild His House,
speedily, yes speedily, in our days, soon.

**GOD, REBUILD, GOD, REBUILD,
REBUILD YOUR HOUSE SOON!**

He is distinguished, He is great, He is renowned.
May He soon rebuild His House,
speedily, yes speedily, in our days, soon.

**GOD, REBUILD, GOD, REBUILD,
REBUILD YOUR HOUSE SOON!**

He is glorious, He is faithful, He is worthy, He is gracious.
May He soon rebuild His House,
speedily, yes speedily, in our days, soon.

GOD, REBUILD, GOD, REBUILD,

"the sanctuary, O Lord, [that] Your hands founded."

In the previous piyyutim, we spoke about God's special miracles that He performed for us throughout history. We mentioned God's unique descriptions and His sovereignty over us in the piyyut "*adir bimeluchah,*" but there the emphasis was on God's sovereignty as seen by the angels (His companies, His faithful, His princes), the righteous (His righteous ones), and maybe the Jewish People as well (His perfect ones).

Now we again mention God's praises, and ask that His praises and attributes be revealed through the building of the Bet HaMikdash. It should not only be revealed to His angels and to the righteous and perfect ones. *God's Presence should be revealed to all of Israel and to the entire world; the entire world should see and know that the Divine Presence rests upon Israel!*

At this stage, at the highest point of the Seder night, after all the preparations and stages that we have gone through, and after all the steps that we have ascended, we are not content to settle for any less. This is the time to request and pray for the Bet HaMikdash to be rebuilt and the Divine Presence to be revealed!

During this time of great joy we have faith that the Bet HaMikdash will be built speedily. However, this is also a time for introspection: are we doing

◂ *enough*

טָהוֹר הוּא, יָחִיד הוּא, כַּבִּיר הוּא, לָמוּד הוּא,
מֶלֶךְ הוּא, נוֹרָא הוּא, סַגִּיב הוּא, עִזּוּז הוּא,
פּוֹדֶה הוּא, צַדִּיק הוּא, יִבְנֶה בֵיתוֹ בְּקָרוֹב.
בִּמְהֵרָה, בִּמְהֵרָה, בְּיָמֵינוּ בְּקָרוֹב.
אֵל בְּנֵה, אֵל בְּנֵה, בְּנֵה בֵיתְךָ בְּקָרוֹב.

קָדוֹשׁ הוּא, רַחוּם הוּא, שַׁדַּי הוּא,
תַּקִּיף הוּא, יִבְנֶה בֵיתוֹ בְּקָרוֹב.
בִּמְהֵרָה, בִּמְהֵרָה, בְּיָמֵינוּ בְּקָרוֹב.
אֵל בְּנֵה, אֵל בְּנֵה, בְּנֵה בֵיתְךָ בְּקָרוֹב.

enough to reach the goal of rebuilding the Bet HaMikdash? Are we preparing ourselves in order to be worthy for the building of the Bet HaMikdash? Do we remember that it was destroyed because of unwarranted hatred (Yoma 9b) and will be rebuilt because of unwarranted love (based on Rav Avraham Yitzchak Kook in *Orot HaKodesh* 3, 324)? Are we willing to accept the yoke of the Kingdom of Heaven by observing God's mitzvot, with all that it involves? Do we truly feel the lack of the Bet HaMikdash, the lack of the Divine Presence? ▪

Wine goblet, Bohemian crystal and gold-plate, 20th century, artist: Iliya Shor
The Wolfson Museum, Hechal Shlomo

REBUILD YOUR HOUSE SOON!

He is pure, He is unique, He is powerful, He is majestic,
He is awesome, He is sublime, He is all-powerful,
He is the Redeemer, He is righteous.
May He soon rebuild His House,
speedily, yes speedily, in our days, soon.

GOD, REBUILD, GOD, REBUILD,
REBUILD YOUR HOUSE SOON!

He is holy, He is merciful, He is Almighty, He is forceful.
May He soon rebuild His House,
speedily, yes speedily, in our days, soon.

GOD, REBUILD, GOD, REBUILD,
REBUILD YOUR HOUSE SOON!

Topic for discussion

q. It is the custom to cover one's knife when reciting birkat hamazon (except on Shabbat and festivals – Shulchan Aruch 180:5). Why?

Rokeach (332) explains that a table is considered like an altar (Chagigah 27a), and regarding the altar it says: "You shall not wield any iron upon them." Shibolei HaLeket (155) explained that this custom was instituted because of one man who was reciting birkat hamazon, and, upon reaching the blessing about rebuilding Jerusalem, he was so upset about its destruction that he plunged a knife into his belly.

When we read the second explanation we feel better. There is no fear that any of us would, Heaven forbid, plunge a knife into our own stomachs – but is it because we understand the severity of the harm it would do to us, or because we are not sufficiently sensitive to the lack of the Bet HaMikdash? *Why do we not feel the lack of the Bet HaMikdash? What must we do to feel its absence? What can be done to make our prayers about the rebuilding of the Bet HaMikdash more sincere and truthful?*

אֶחָד מִי יוֹדֵעַ - אֶחָד אֲנִי יוֹדֵעַ: אֶחָד אֱלֹהֵינוּ שֶׁבַּשָּׁמַיִם וּבָאָרֶץ.

שְׁנַיִם מִי יוֹדֵעַ - שְׁנַיִם אֲנִי יוֹדֵעַ: שְׁנֵי לוּחוֹת הַבְּרִית, אֶחָד אֱלֹהֵינוּ שֶׁבַּשָּׁמַיִם וּבָאָרֶץ.

שְׁלֹשָׁה מִי יוֹדֵעַ - שְׁלֹשָׁה אֲנִי יוֹדֵעַ: שְׁלֹשָׁה אָבוֹת, שְׁנֵי לוּחוֹת הַבְּרִית, אֶחָד אֱלֹהֵינוּ שֶׁבַּשָּׁמַיִם וּבָאָרֶץ.

אַרְבַּע מִי יוֹדֵעַ - אַרְבַּע אֲנִי יוֹדֵעַ: אַרְבַּע אִמָּהוֹת, שְׁלֹשָׁה אָבוֹת, שְׁנֵי לוּחוֹת הַבְּרִית, אֶחָד אֱלֹהֵינוּ שֶׁבַּשָּׁמַיִם וּבָאָרֶץ.

חֲמִשָּׁה מִי יוֹדֵעַ - חֲמִשָּׁה אֲנִי יוֹדֵעַ: חֲמִשָּׁה חוּמְשֵׁי תוֹרָה, אַרְבַּע אִמָּהוֹת, שְׁלֹשָׁה אָבוֹת, שְׁנֵי לוּחוֹת הַבְּרִית, אֶחָד אֱלֹהֵינוּ שֶׁבַּשָּׁמַיִם וּבָאָרֶץ.

שִׁשָּׁה מִי יוֹדֵעַ - שִׁשָּׁה אֲנִי יוֹדֵעַ: שִׁשָּׁה סִדְרֵי מִשְׁנָה, חֲמִשָּׁה חוּמְשֵׁי תוֹרָה, אַרְבַּע אִמָּהוֹת, שְׁלֹשָׁה אָבוֹת, שְׁנֵי לוּחוֹת הַבְּרִית, אֶחָד אֱלֹהֵינוּ שֶׁבַּשָּׁמַיִם וּבָאָרֶץ.

Food For Thought

Who knows one?

This piyyut only appears in the haggadot of the last few hundred years, however, its origins are much older (see *Haggadat Chazal*, p. 193).

The Seder night opens with the Four Questions and ends with "Who knows one?" The first questions were related directly to the laws of Pesach: matzah, maror, two dippings, leaning, whereas the last questions do not relate to Pesach.

However, that is the greatness of this

◂ piyyut.

WHO KNOWS ONE? I know one: one is our God, in heaven and on earth.

WHO KNOWS TWO? I know two: two are the Tablets of the Covenant; one is our God, in heaven and on earth.

WHO KNOWS THREE? I know three: three are the Patriarchs; two are the Tablets of the Covenant; one is our God, in heaven and on earth.

WHO KNOWS FOUR? I know four: four are the matriarchs; three are the Patriarchs; two are the Tablets of the Covenant; one is our God, in heaven and on earth.

WHO KNOWS FIVE? I know five: five are the books of the Torah; four are the Matriarchs; three are the Patriarchs; two are the Tablets of the Covenant; one is our God, in heaven and on earth.

WHO KNOWS SIX? I know six: six are the orders of the Mishnah; five are the books of the Torah; four are the Matriarchs; three are the Patriarchs; two are the Tablets of the Covenant; one is our God, in heaven and on earth.

---

piyyut. Now that we have left Egypt, we look at the world around us, and see that everything stems from "Who knows one"; everything is because of the oneness and the Providence of God.

The poem includes well-known and elementary ideas. It is known that God is one; it is known that there were two Tablets of the Covenant. *What is innovative about the poem is not the information it contains; rather, it is the fact that we must internalize it! We sing it, and say repeatedly, "one is our God, in heaven and on earth," with the aim of allowing it to penetrate our hearts: God is the only power in the world; He alone controls everyone and everything in the world.* ▪

שִׁבְעָה מִי יוֹדֵעַ - שִׁבְעָה אֲנִי יוֹדֵעַ: שִׁבְעָה יְמֵי שַׁבַּתָּא, שִׁשָּׁה סִדְרֵי מִשְׁנָה, חֲמִשָּׁה חוּמְשֵׁי תוֹרָה, אַרְבַּע אִמָּהוֹת, שְׁלֹשָׁה אָבוֹת, שְׁנֵי לוּחוֹת הַבְּרִית, אֶחָד אֱלֹהֵינוּ שֶׁבַּשָּׁמַיִם וּבָאָרֶץ.

שְׁמוֹנָה מִי יוֹדֵעַ - שְׁמוֹנָה אֲנִי יוֹדֵעַ: שְׁמוֹנָה יְמֵי מִילָה, שִׁבְעָה יְמֵי שַׁבַּתָּא, שִׁשָּׁה סִדְרֵי מִשְׁנָה, חֲמִשָּׁה חוּמְשֵׁי תוֹרָה, אַרְבַּע אִמָּהוֹת, שְׁלֹשָׁה אָבוֹת, שְׁנֵי לוּחוֹת הַבְּרִית, אֶחָד אֱלֹהֵינוּ שֶׁבַּשָּׁמַיִם וּבָאָרֶץ.

תִּשְׁעָה מִי יוֹדֵעַ - תִּשְׁעָה אֲנִי יוֹדֵעַ: תִּשְׁעָה יַרְחֵי לֵידָה, שְׁמוֹנָה יְמֵי מִילָה, שִׁבְעָה יְמֵי שַׁבַּתָּא, שִׁשָּׁה סִדְרֵי מִשְׁנָה, חֲמִשָּׁה חוּמְשֵׁי תוֹרָה, אַרְבַּע אִמָּהוֹת, שְׁלֹשָׁה אָבוֹת, שְׁנֵי לוּחוֹת הַבְּרִית, אֶחָד אֱלֹהֵינוּ שֶׁבַּשָּׁמַיִם וּבָאָרֶץ.

עֲשָׂרָה מִי יוֹדֵעַ - עֲשָׂרָה אֲנִי יוֹדֵעַ: עֲשָׂרָה דִבְּרַיָּא, תִּשְׁעָה יַרְחֵי לֵידָה, שְׁמוֹנָה יְמֵי מִילָה, שִׁבְעָה יְמֵי שַׁבַּתָּא, שִׁשָּׁה סִדְרֵי מִשְׁנָה, חֲמִשָּׁה חוּמְשֵׁי תוֹרָה, אַרְבַּע אִמָּהוֹת, שְׁלֹשָׁה אָבוֹת, שְׁנֵי לוּחוֹת הַבְּרִית, אֶחָד אֱלֹהֵינוּ שֶׁבַּשָּׁמַיִם וּבָאָרֶץ.

אַחַד עָשָׂר מִי יוֹדֵעַ - אַחַד עָשָׂר אֲנִי יוֹדֵעַ: אַחַד עָשָׂר כּוֹכְבַיָּא. עֲשָׂרָה דִבְּרַיָּא, תִּשְׁעָה יַרְחֵי לֵידָה, שְׁמוֹנָה יְמֵי מִילָה, שִׁבְעָה יְמֵי שַׁבַּתָּא, שִׁשָּׁה סִדְרֵי מִשְׁנָה, חֲמִשָּׁה חוּמְשֵׁי תוֹרָה, אַרְבַּע אִמָּהוֹת, שְׁלֹשָׁה אָבוֹת, שְׁנֵי לוּחוֹת הַבְּרִית, אֶחָד אֱלֹהֵינוּ שֶׁבַּשָּׁמַיִם וּבָאָרֶץ.

WHO KNOWS SEVEN? I know seven: seven are the days of the week; six are the orders of the Mishnah; five are the books of the Torah; four are the Matriarchs; three are the Patriarchs; two are the Tablets of the Covenant; one is our God, in heaven and on earth.

WHO KNOWS EIGHT? I know eight: eight are the days to circumcision; seven are the days of the week; six are the orders of the Mishnah; five are the books of the Torah; four are the Matriarchs; three are the Patriarchs; two are the Tablets of the Covenant; one is our God, in heaven and on earth.

WHO KNOWS NINE? I know nine: nine are the months of the pregnancy; eight are the days to circumcision; seven are the days of the week; six are the orders of the Mishnah; five are the books of the Torah; four are the Matriarchs; three are the Patriarchs; two are the Tablets of the Covenant; one is our God, in heaven and on earth.

WHO KNOWS TEN? I know ten: ten are the Ten Mitzvot; nine are the months of the pregnancy; eight are the days to circumcision; seven are the days of the week; six are the orders of the Mishnah; five are the books of the Torah; four are the Matriarchs; three are the Patriarchs; two are the Tablets of the Covenant; one is our God, in heaven and on earth.

WHO KNOWS ELEVEN? I know eleven: eleven are the stars (in Joseph's dream); ten are the Ten Mitzvot; nine are the months of the pregnancy; eight are the days to circumcision; seven are the days of the week; six are the orders of the Mishnah; five are the books of the Torah; four are the Matriarchs; three are the Patriarchs; two are the Tablets of the Covenant; one is our God, in heaven and on earth.

שְׁנֵים עָשָׂר מִי יוֹדֵעַ - שְׁנֵים עָשָׂר אֲנִי יוֹדֵעַ: שְׁנֵים עָשָׂר שִׁבְטַיָּא, אַחַד עָשָׂר כּוֹכְבַיָּא, עֲשָׂרָה דִבְּרַיָּא, תִּשְׁעָה יַרְחֵי לֵידָה, שְׁמוֹנָה יְמֵי מִילָה, שִׁבְעָה יְמֵי שַׁבְּתָא, שִׁשָּׁה סִדְרֵי מִשְׁנָה, חֲמִשָּׁה חוּמְשֵׁי תוֹרָה, אַרְבַּע אִמָּהוֹת, שְׁלֹשָׁה אָבוֹת, שְׁנֵי לוּחוֹת הַבְּרִית, אֶחָד אֱלֹהֵינוּ שֶׁבַּשָּׁמַיִם וּבָאָרֶץ.

שְׁלֹשָׁה עָשָׂר מִי יוֹדֵעַ - שְׁלֹשָׁה עָשָׂר אֲנִי יוֹדֵעַ: שְׁלֹשָׁה עָשָׂר מִדַּיָּא, שְׁנֵים עָשָׂר שִׁבְטַיָּא, אַחַד עָשָׂר כּוֹכְבַיָּא, עֲשָׂרָה דִבְּרַיָּא, תִּשְׁעָה יַרְחֵי לֵידָה, שְׁמוֹנָה יְמֵי מִילָה, שִׁבְעָה יְמֵי שַׁבְּתָא, שִׁשָּׁה סִדְרֵי מִשְׁנָה, חֲמִשָּׁה חוּמְשֵׁי תוֹרָה, אַרְבַּע אִמָּהוֹת, שְׁלֹשָׁה אָבוֹת, שְׁנֵי לוּחוֹת הַבְּרִית, אֶחָד אֱלֹהֵינוּ שֶׁבַּשָּׁמַיִם וּבָאָרֶץ:

Prayer book cover, 18th century, silver
The Wolfson Museum, Hechal Shlomo

WHO KNOWS TWELVE? I know twelve: twelve are the tribes (of Israel); eleven are the stars (in Joseph's dream); ten are the Ten Mitzvot; nine are the months of the pregnancy; eight are the days to circumcision; seven are the days of the week; six are the orders of the Mishnah; five are the books of the Torah; four are the Matriarchs; three are the Patriarchs; two are the Tablets of the Covenant; one is our God, in heaven and on earth.

WHO KNOWS THIRTEEN? I know thirteen: thirteen are the attributes of God; twelve are the tribes (of Israel); eleven are the stars (in Joseph's dream); ten are the Ten Mitzvot; nine are the months of the pregnancy; eight are the days to circumcision; seven are the days of the week; six are the orders of the Mishnah; five are the books of the Torah; four are the Matriarchs; three are the Patriarchs; two are the Tablets of the Covenant; one is our God, in heaven and on earth.

Activity

In order to explore the piyyut's significance, make a quiz about the verses of the piyyut. For younger children, ask about the "seven days of the week," etc. For older children, ask about the "eleven stars" and the "thirteen attributes."

חַד גַּדְיָא, חַד גַּדְיָא, דְּזַבִּין אַבָּא בִּתְרֵי זוּזֵי. חַד גַּדְיָא, חַד גַּדְיָא. וְאָתָא שׁוּנְרָא, וְאָכְלָה לְגַדְיָא, דְּזַבִּין אַבָּא בִּתְרֵי זוּזֵי.

חַד גַּדְיָא, חַד גַּדְיָא. וְאָתָא כַלְבָּא, וְנָשַׁךְ לְשׁוּנְרָא, דְּאָכְלָה לְגַדְיָא, דְּזַבִּין אַבָּא בִּתְרֵי זוּזֵי.

חַד גַּדְיָא, חַד גַּדְיָא. וְאָתָא חוּטְרָא, וְהִכָּה לְכַלְבָּא, דְּנָשַׁךְ לְשׁוּנְרָא, דְּאָכְלָה לְגַדְיָא, דְּזַבִּין אַבָּא בִּתְרֵי זוּזֵי.

חַד גַּדְיָא, חַד גַּדְיָא. וְאָתָא נוּרָא, וְשָׂרַף לְחוּטְרָא, דְּהִכָּה לְכַלְבָּא, דְּנָשַׁךְ לְשׁוּנְרָא, דְּאָכְלָה לְגַדְיָא, דְּזַבִּין אַבָּא בִּתְרֵי זוּזֵי.

Food For Thought

One little goat – the significance of the piyyut

The story, in brief, of "One little goat" is as follows: the father bought a goat for two zuzim, a cat came and ate the goat, a dog came and bit the cat, a stick came and beat the dog, a fire came and burned the stick, water came and extinguished the fire, an ox came and drank the water, a slaughterer came and slaughtered the ox, the Angel of Death came and killed the slaughterer, God came and killed the Angel of Death.

What is the significance of all of this? Many of the kabbalist works have discussed this and offered various interpretations, but it seems that simply, this piyyut offers an important principle in God's supervision (this is based on the words of Ben Ish Chai in his commentary on the haggadah, in the section on "*baruch shomer havtachato*").

At first, as we follow the sequence of events in the piyyut, we are immediately faced with a problem:

◂ The

ONE LITTLE GOAT, ONE LITTLE GOAT, that father bought for two zuzim. One little goat, one little goat. And then came a cat and it ate the goat that father bought for two zuzim.

ONE LITTLE GOAT, ONE LITTLE GOAT. And then came a dog and it bit the cat, that ate the goat that father bought for two zuzim.

ONE LITTLE GOAT, ONE LITTLE GOAT. And then came a stick and it beat the dog, that bit the cat, that ate the goat that father bought for two zuzim.

ONE LITTLE GOAT, ONE LITTLE GOAT. And then came a fire and it burned the stick, that beat the dog, that bit the cat, that ate the goat that father bought for two zuzim.

The cat ate the goat, and that means that what the cat did was wrong – the goat was totally blameless.

The dog bit the cat, and that was the cat's punishment.

Now, if what the dog did was justified, the stick was wrong for having hit the dog.

If what the stick did was wrong, the fire was justified.

If the fire was justified, the water was wrong in extinguishing it.

If the water was wrong, the ox was justified in drinking it.

If the ox was justified, the slaughterer was wrong for killing it.

If the slaughterer was wrong, the Angel of Death was justified in killing him.

But according to that, God, who killed the Angel of Death, was – as it were – wrong in doing so, and was acting improperly.

Of course, the entire argument here is incorrect. The dog did not bite the cat because it was punishing the cat, but because it wanted to do so for its own personal benefit. The same was true for the other instances.

God is the One who acts and supervises everything, and it is He who makes sure that a person who acted sinfully will be suitably punished! That also happened at the Exodus from

◂ Egypt

חַד גַּדְיָא, חַד גַּדְיָא. וְאָתָא מַיָּא, וְכָבָה לְנוּרָא, דְּשָׂרַף לְחוּטְרָא, דְּהִכָּה לְכַלְבָּא, דְּנָשַׁךְ לְשׁוּנְרָא, דְּאָכְלָה לְגַדְיָא, דְּזַבִּין אַבָּא בִּתְרֵי זוּזֵי.

חַד גַּדְיָא, חַד גַּדְיָא. וְאָתָא תוֹרָא, וְשָׁתָה לְמַיָּא, דְּכָבָה לְנוּרָא, דְּשָׂרַף לְחוּטְרָא, דְּהִכָּה לְכַלְבָּא, דְּנָשַׁךְ לְשׁוּנְרָא, דְּאָכְלָה לְגַדְיָא, דְּזַבִּין אַבָּא בִּתְרֵי זוּזֵי.

חַד גַּדְיָא, חַד גַּדְיָא. וְאָתָא הַשּׁוֹחֵט, וְשָׁחַט לְתוֹרָא, דְּשָׁתָה לְמַיָּא, דְּכָבָה לְנוּרָא, דְּשָׂרַף לְחוּטְרָא, דְּהִכָּה לְכַלְבָּא, דְּנָשַׁךְ לְשׁוּנְרָא, דְּאָכְלָה לְגַדְיָא, דְּזַבִּין אַבָּא בִּתְרֵי זוּזֵי.

Egypt – Pharaoh was punished because his acts were monstrous and inspired by evil motives. However, God planned these events in advance, as was said to Abraham hundreds of years earlier: "they will enslave them and oppress them, for four hundred years" (Genesis 15:13). One cannot evaluate any one of the figures in the piyyut merely from what appears externally, and decide who is wicked and who is righteous – that is not within our power or ability. One must act in the best and most proper way, from within his world and from his perspective.

There are times when all we see is the world in a state of total upheaval. We witness world leaders attempting to control the world. However, we know: *there is a single Ruler, who supervises and directs the world. The feelings of various leaders that they are ruling the world are completely meaningless and inconsequential.* Each person must act in an honest and upright manner, knowing that if he acts in a wicked manner, he will be punished. One should not try to go above his station and attempt to rule the world. Everything is controlled by God and it is He who punishes the wicked ones and rewards the righteous ones. This knowledge is comforting, but it also obligates us to obey God's will.

It is God who looks after the little goat, Am Yisrael, and all the predators

◂ in the

ONE LITTLE GOAT, ONE LITTLE GOAT. And then came some water and it put out the fire, that burned the stick, that beat the dog, that bit the cat, that ate the goat that father bought for two zuzim.

ONE LITTLE GOAT, ONE LITTLE GOAT. And then came an ox and it drank the water, that put out the fire, that burned the stick, that beat the dog, that bit the cat, that ate the goat that father bought for two zuzim.

ONE LITTLE GOAT, ONE LITTLE GOAT. And then came a slaughterer and he slaughtered the ox, that drank the water, that put out the fire, that burned the stick, that beat the dog, that bit the cat, that ate the goat that father bought for two zuzim.

---

in the world who seek to destroy us will not succeed – *"the Holy One, Blessed be He, saves us from their hands."*

Pesach seder at the gates of hell

This was the first Pesach that I had to celebrate alone. On the previous Pesach I had still been with my parents in the ghetto. This year, I remain alone…

After the evening *appel* (roll call) and before we went into our hut to sleep, we were permitted to wander about a little between the huts. I went over to one of my friends and told him that tonight was the Seder night and we had to do something about it. We obviously did not have matzot, wine, or bitter herbs to eat, but there was one thing we could do – recite the haggadah. We did not have a haggadah, but there were passages we remembered by heart. And thus, as we paced back and forth in the clearing before the hut, we fulfilled the mitzvah of relating the story of the haggadah. We began with "this is the bread of affliction" and thought to ourselves that in Egypt our ancestors at least got to eat the bread of affliction. We had absolutely no bread to eat.

We also asked the Four Questions with special intensity. Could we say that "on this night we eat only matzah?" We had neither bread nor matzah. And could we say that on this night we all lean? "We were slaves to Pharaoh in Egypt." Were we only slaves in the past? Were we free now? Right then, we were slaves in even worse circumstances. The answer to all these questions was that

◂ while

חַד גַּדְיָא, חַד גַּדְיָא. וְאָתָא מַלְאַךְ הַמָּוֶת, וְשָׁחַט לְשׁוֹחֵט, דְּשָׁחַט לְתוֹרָא, דְּשָׁתָה לְמַיָּא, דְּכָבָה לְנוּרָא, דְּשָׂרַף לְחוּטְרָא, דְּהִכָּה לְכַלְבָּא, דְּנָשַׁךְ לְשׁוּנְרָא, דְּאָכְלָה לְגַדְיָא, דִּזְבַן אַבָּא בִּתְרֵי זוּזֵי.

חַד גַּדְיָא, חַד גַּדְיָא. וְאָתָא הַקָּדוֹשׁ בָּרוּךְ הוּא, וְשָׁחַט לְמַלְאַךְ הַמָּוֶת, דְּשָׁחַט לְשׁוֹחֵט, דְּשָׁחַט לְתוֹרָא, דְּשָׁתָה לְמַיָּא, דְּכָבָה לְנוּרָא, דְּשָׂרַף לְחוּטְרָא, דְּהִכָּה לְכַלְבָּא, דְּנָשַׁךְ לְשׁוּנְרָא, דְּאָכְלָה לְגַדְיָא, דִּזְבַן אַבָּא בִּתְרֵי זוּזֵי.

חַד גַּדְיָא, חַד גַּדְיָא.

---

while it is true that we were in worse conditions, when God took us out of Egypt, He granted us spiritual freedom. The Germans could enslave our bodies and destroy us, but it was impossible to enslave our spirit – that they could not break. At that moment, we were free. "In every generation they arise against us to destroy us." How deeply we felt these words! The Sages foresaw what would happen in the future in every generation, including what was happening in our generation, and yet in spite of that, the Sages proclaimed, "And the Holy One, Blessed be He, rescues us from their hand." We had no doubt that God would rescue us too and take us out of this hell on earth.

We continued to talk about the Exodus from Egypt as much as our memories served us, until we came to the last sentence of the haggadah, "Next year in Jerusalem." That was not only a prayer from the depths of our hearts, because we felt with all our might how much we needed Jerusalem, but it was also our greatest hope. "Our Father, merciful Father, take pity on us and take us out of this unspeakable exile and bring us to Jerusalem, Your city, and to Zion, Your holy city." This was a Seder night walking back and forth at the gates to hell, and possibly within it, the Seder night in Mauthausen.

[*BeGei Tzalmavet*, Rabbi Sinai Adler, pp. 88–89]

ONE LITTLE GOAT, ONE LITTLE GOAT. And then came the angel of death and he slew the slaughterer, who slaughtered the ox, that drank the water, that put out the fire, that burned the stick, that beat the dog, that bit the cat, that ate the goat that father bought for two zuzim.

ONE LITTLE GOAT, ONE LITTLE GOAT. And then came the Holy One, Blessed be He, and He killed the angel of death, who slew the slaughterer, who slaughtered the ox, that drank the water, that put out the fire, that burned the stick, that beat the dog, that bit the cat, that ate the goat that father bought for two zuzim.

ONE LITTLE GOAT, ONE LITTLE GOAT.

Riddles

97. Before "*chad gadya*" is sung, quiz the participants about the names mentioned in the piyyut in Aramaic, in order to remind everyone of who is who.

Activity

As the hour is late and everyone is tired, to keep everyone involved, everyone can take on the role of a different animal or object mentioned in the song. For example: the stick – banging on the table; fire – the sound of a crackling fire; water – the sound of running water; the cow – "moo, moo," the slaughterer – motioning in the air as with a knife; the Angel of Death – booing him; God – raising the hands to heaven.

קידוש (כנוסח ספרדים)

כולם מוזגים כוס ראשון, ומקדשים עליו.

יש נוהגים לומר לפני הקידוש:

הִנְנִי מוּכָן וּמְזֻמָּן לְקַיֵּם מִצְוַת קִדּוּשׁ וּמִצְוַת כּוֹס רִאשׁוֹן מֵאַרְבַּע כּוֹסוֹת. לְשֵׁם יִחוּד קוּדְשָׁא בְּרִיךְ הוּא וּשְׁכִינְתֵּיהּ עַל יְדֵי הַהוּא טָמִיר וְנֶעְלָם בְּשֵׁם כָּל יִשְׂרָאֵל. וִיהִי נֹעַם אֲדֹנָי אֱלֹהֵינוּ עָלֵינוּ וּמַעֲשֵׂה יָדֵינוּ כּוֹנְנָה עָלֵינוּ וּמַעֲשֵׂה יָדֵינוּ כּוֹנְנֵהוּ.

כשחל בשבת מתחילין כאן:

בלחש: **וַיְהִי עֶרֶב וַיְהִי בֹקֶר**

יוֹם הַשִּׁשִּׁי. וַיְכֻלּוּ הַשָּׁמַיִם וְהָאָרֶץ וְכָל צְבָאָם. וַיְכַל אֱלֹהִים בַּיּוֹם הַשְּׁבִיעִי מְלַאכְתּוֹ אֲשֶׁר עָשָׂה, וַיִּשְׁבֹּת בַּיּוֹם הַשְּׁבִיעִי מִכָּל מְלַאכְתּוֹ אֲשֶׁר עָשָׂה. וַיְבָרֶךְ אֱלֹהִים אֶת יוֹם הַשְּׁבִיעִי וַיְקַדֵּשׁ אֹתוֹ, כִּי בוֹ שָׁבַת מִכָּל מְלַאכְתּוֹ אֲשֶׁר בָּרָא אֱלֹהִים לַעֲשׂוֹת.

כשחל בחול מתחילין כאן:

(בשבת מוסיפים את המילים שבסוגריים)

סַבְרִי מָרָנָן וְרַבָּנָן וְרַבּוֹתַי:

אֵלֶּה מוֹעֲדֵי יְהֹוָה מִקְרָאֵי קֹדֶשׁ אֲשֶׁר־תִּקְרְאוּ אֹתָם בְּמוֹעֲדָם. וַיְדַבֵּר מֹשֶׁה אֶת מֹעֲדֵי יְהֹוָה אֶל בְּנֵי יִשְׂרָאֵל.

יכוון לפטור את הכוס השנייה בברכת בורא פרי הגפן.

בָּרוּךְ אַתָּה יְהֹוָה אֱלֹהֵינוּ מֶלֶךְ הָעוֹלָם, בּוֹרֵא פְּרִי הַגָּפֶן. בָּרוּךְ אַתָּה יְהֹוָה אֱלֹהֵינוּ מֶלֶךְ הָעוֹלָם, אֲשֶׁר בָּחַר בָּנוּ מִכָּל עָם וְרוֹמְמָנוּ מִכָּל לָשׁוֹן וְקִדְּשָׁנוּ בְּמִצְוֹתָיו, וַתִּתֶּן לָנוּ יְהֹוָה אֱלֹהֵינוּ בְּאַהֲבָה (שַׁבָּתוֹת לִמְנוּחָה וּ) מוֹעֲדִים לְשִׂמְחָה, חַגִּים וּזְמַנִּים לְשָׂשׂוֹן, (אֶת יוֹם הַשַּׁבָּת הַזֶּה וְ) אֶת יוֹם חַג הַמַּצּוֹת הַזֶּה, אֶת־יוֹם טוֹב מִקְרָא קֹדֶשׁ הַזֶּה, זְמַן חֵרוּתֵנוּ בְּאַהֲבָה כִּי בָנוּ בָחַרְתָּ וְאוֹתָנוּ קִדַּשְׁתָּ מִכָּל הָעַמִּים, (וְשַׁבָּת) וּמוֹעֲדֵי קָדְשְׁךָ (בְּאַהֲבָה וּבְרָצוֹן) בְּשִׂמְחָה וּבְשָׂשׂוֹן הִנְחַלְתָּנוּ. בָּרוּךְ אַתָּה יְהֹוָה, מְקַדֵּשׁ (הַשַּׁבָּת וְ) יִשְׂרָאֵל וְהַזְּמַנִּים.

בָּרוּךְ אַתָּה יְהֹוָה אֱלֹהֵינוּ מֶלֶךְ הָעוֹלָם, שֶׁהֶחֱיָנוּ וְקִיְּמָנוּ וְהִגִּיעָנוּ לַזְּמַן הַזֶּה.

שותים הכוס בהסבת שמאל ואין מברכים ברכה אחרונה.

KIDDUSH (SEPHARDI RITE)

The first cup is poured and kiddush is recited.
There are some who say before kiddush:

I am prepared and ready to recite kiddush and the mitzvah of the first cup of four cups. For the sake of the unification of the Holy One, Blessed be He, and His Presence, in the name of all Israel. And may the pleasantness of the Lord our God be upon us, and the work of our hands establish for us, and may the work of our hands establish it.

When the seder is on a Friday night, begin here:
Quietly: And it was evening and it was morning,

THE SIXTH DAY. And the heaven and the earth and all their hosts were completed. And on the seventh day, God finished His work that He had made, and He rested on the seventh day from all His work that He had made. And God blessed the seventh day and made it holy, for on it He rested from all His work that He, God, created to make.

When the Seder night is on a weekday night, one begins here:
(The sections in square brackets are added on Shabbat.)

With your permission, gentlemen, my masters and teachers:
There are the appointed seasons of the Lord, holy convocations, which you shall proclaim in their appointed season. Moses declared to the Children of Israel the appointed seasons of the Lord.

When making the blessing one should have in mind the blessing over the second cup.

BLESSED are You, Lord, our God, King of the universe, who creates the fruit of the vine. Blessed are You, Lord our God, King of the universe, who has chosen us from among all people, and exalted us above all tongues, and sanctified us through His mitzvot. You, Lord our God, have given us, with love, [Shabbat for rest and] festivals for happiness, festivals and seasons for joy: [this Shabbat and this] Festival of Matzot, season of our Freedom [in love], a holy convocation in remembrance of the Exodus from Egypt. This Festival of Matzot, this festival of a holy convocation, the season of our freedom, in love for You have chosen us and sanctified us from all the nations, and You gave us [the Shabbat and] Your holy festivals [with love and favor], in happiness and joy, as a heritage. Blessed are You, God, Who sanctifies [the Shabbat and] Israel and the festive seasons.

BLESSED are You, Lord our God, King of the universe, who has granted us life, sustained us, and enabled us to reach this season.

The wine is drunk while one leans to the left, and there is no concluding blessing after it.

בִּרְכַּת הַמָּזוֹן (בנוסח ספרדים)

לַמְנַצֵּחַ בִּנְגִינֹת מִזְמוֹר שִׁיר: אֱלֹהִים יְחָנֵּנוּ וִיבָרְכֵנוּ יָאֵר פָּנָיו אִתָּנוּ סֶלָה: לָדַעַת בָּאָרֶץ דַּרְכֶּךָ בְּכָל גּוֹיִם יְשׁוּעָתֶךָ: יוֹדוּךָ עַמִּים אֱלֹהִים יוֹדוּךָ עַמִּים כֻּלָּם: יִשְׂמְחוּ וִירַנְּנוּ לְאֻמִּים כִּי תִשְׁפֹּט עַמִּים מִישׁוֹר וּלְאֻמִּים בָּאָרֶץ תַּנְחֵם סֶלָה: יוֹדוּךָ עַמִּים אֱלֹהִים יוֹדוּךָ עַמִּים כֻּלָּם: אֶרֶץ נָתְנָה יְבוּלָהּ יְבָרְכֵנוּ אֱלֹהִים אֱלֹהֵינוּ: יְבָרְכֵנוּ אֱלֹהִים וְיִירְאוּ אֹתוֹ כָּל אַפְסֵי אָרֶץ:

אֲבָרְכָה אֶת יְהֹוָה בְּכָל עֵת תָּמִיד תְּהִלָּתוֹ בְּפִי: סוֹף דָּבָר הַכֹּל נִשְׁמָע אֶת הָאֱלֹהִים יְרָא וְאֶת מִצְוֹתָיו שְׁמוֹר כִּי זֶה כָּל הָאָדָם: תְּהִלַּת יְהֹוָה יְדַבֶּר פִּי וִיבָרֵךְ כָּל בָּשָׂר שֵׁם קָדְשׁוֹ לְעוֹלָם וָעֶד: וַאֲנַחְנוּ נְבָרֵךְ יָהּ מֵעַתָּה וְעַד עוֹלָם הַלְלוּיָהּ: וַיְדַבֵּר אֵלַי זֶה הַשֻּׁלְחָן אֲשֶׁר לִפְנֵי יְהֹוָה:

אם הם שלושה אומר המזמן:

המזמן: הַב לָן וְנִבְרִיךְ לְמַלְכָּא עִלָּאָה קַדִּישָׁא.

המסובים: שָׁמַיִם.

המזמן: בִּרְשׁוּת מַלְכָּא עִלָּאָה קַדִּישָׁא (בשבת: וּבִרְשׁוּת שַׁבָּת מַלְכְּתָא), וּבִרְשׁוּתְכֶם, נְבָרֵךְ (במניין: אֱלֹהֵינוּ) שֶׁאָכַלְנוּ מִשֶּׁלּוֹ.

המסובים: בָּרוּךְ (במניין: אֱלֹהֵינוּ) שֶׁאָכַלְנוּ מִשֶּׁלּוֹ וּבְטוּבוֹ חָיִינוּ.

המזמן: בָּרוּךְ (במניין: אֱלֹהֵינוּ) שֶׁאָכַלְנוּ מִשֶּׁלּוֹ וּבְטוּבוֹ חָיִינוּ.

BIRKAT HAMAZON (SEPHARDI RITE)

FOR THE CONDUCTOR, ON NEGINOT; A PSALM, a song. God will be gracious to us and bless us; He will cause His countenance to shine with us forever. That Your way should be known on earth, Your salvation among all nations. Peoples will thank You, O God; peoples will thank You, yea, all of them. Kingdoms will rejoice and sing praises, for You will judge peoples fairly, and the kingdoms –You will lead them on earth forever. Peoples will thank You, O God; peoples will thank You, yea, all of them. The earth gave forth its produce; God, our God, will bless us. God will bless us, and all the ends of the earth will fear Him

I WILL BLESS THE LORD AT ALL TIMES; HIS PRAISE is always in my mouth. The end of the matter, everything having been heard, fear God and keep His mitzvot, for this is the entire man. My mouth will speak the praise of the Lord, and all flesh will bless His holy name forever and ever. But we shall bless God from now until everlasting, Halleluyah! And he spoke to me, this is the table that is before the Lord.

If three adult men ate together, the Leader says:

LEADER: Let us bless the Supreme Holy King.

OTHERS: Heaven.

LEADER: With the permission of the Supreme Holy King (on Shabbat add: and with the permission of Shabbat Queen) and with your permission, let us bless (in a minyan: our God) from whose abundance we have eaten.

OTHERS: Blessed is (in a minyan: our God,) He from whose abundance we have eaten and through whose goodness we live.

LEADER: Blessed is (if ten or more men are present: our God,) He from whose abundance we have eaten and through whose goodness we live.

בָּרוּךְ אַתָּה יְהֹוָה, אֱלֹהֵינוּ מֶלֶךְ הָעוֹלָם, הָאֵל הַזָּן אוֹתָנוּ וְאֶת הָעוֹלָם כֻּלּוֹ בְּטוּבוֹ בְּחֵן בְּחֶסֶד בְּרֶוַח וּבְרַחֲמִים רַבִּים. נֹתֵן לֶחֶם לְכָל־בָּשָׂר. כִּי לְעוֹלָם חַסְדּוֹ: וּבְטוּבוֹ הַגָּדוֹל תָּמִיד לֹא חָסַר לָנוּ וְאַל יֶחְסַר לָנוּ מָזוֹן תָּמִיד לְעוֹלָם וָעֶד. כִּי הוּא אֵל זָן וּמְפַרְנֵס לַכֹּל וְשֻׁלְחָנוֹ עָרוּךְ לַכֹּל וְהִתְקִין מִחְיָה וּמָזוֹן לְכָל־בְּרִיּוֹתָיו אֲשֶׁר בָּרָא בְּרַחֲמָיו וּבְרוֹב חֲסָדָיו כָּאָמוּר: פּוֹתֵחַ אֶת־יָדֶךָ, וּמַשְׂבִּיעַ לְכָל־חַי רָצוֹן: בָּרוּךְ אַתָּה יְהֹוָה, הַזָּן אֶת הַכֹּל:

נוֹדֶה לְךָ יְהֹוָה אֱלֹהֵינוּ עַל שֶׁהִנְחַלְתָּ לַאֲבוֹתֵינוּ אֶרֶץ חֶמְדָּה טוֹבָה וּרְחָבָה, בְּרִית וְתוֹרָה, חַיִּים וּמָזוֹן. עַל שֶׁהוֹצֵאתָנוּ מֵאֶרֶץ מִצְרַיִם וּפְדִיתָנוּ מִבֵּית עֲבָדִים. וְעַל בְּרִיתְךָ שֶׁחָתַמְתָּ בִּבְשָׂרֵנוּ, וְעַל תּוֹרָתְךָ שֶׁלִּמַּדְתָּנוּ, וְעַל חֻקֵּי רְצוֹנָךְ שֶׁהוֹדַעְתָּנוּ, וְעַל חַיִּים וּמָזוֹן שֶׁאַתָּה זָן וּמְפַרְנֵס אוֹתָנוּ:

וְעַל הַכֹּל יְהֹוָה אֱלֹהֵינוּ אֲנַחְנוּ מוֹדִים לָךְ וּמְבָרְכִים אֶת שְׁמָךְ כָּאָמוּר וְאָכַלְתָּ וְשָׂבָעְתָּ. וּבֵרַכְתָּ אֶת־יְהֹוָה אֱלֹהֶיךָ עַל־הָאָרֶץ הַטּוֹבָה אֲשֶׁר נָתַן־לָךְ: בָּרוּךְ אַתָּה יְהֹוָה, עַל הָאָרֶץ וְעַל הַמָּזוֹן:

רַחֵם יְהֹוָה אֱלֹהֵינוּ עָלֵינוּ, וְעַל יִשְׂרָאֵל עַמָּךְ, וְעַל יְרוּשָׁלַיִם עִירָךְ, וְעַל הַר צִיּוֹן מִשְׁכַּן כְּבוֹדָךְ, וְעַל הֵיכָלָךְ, וְעַל מְעוֹנָךְ, וְעַל דְּבִירָךְ, וְעַל הַבַּיִת הַגָּדוֹל וְהַקָּדוֹשׁ שֶׁנִּקְרָא שִׁמְךָ עָלָיו. אָבִינוּ, רְעֵנוּ, זוּנֵנוּ, פַּרְנְסֵנוּ, כַּלְכְּלֵנוּ, הַרְוִיחֵנוּ,

BLESSED ARE YOU, LORD OUR GOD, KING of the universe, God, who, in His goodness, nourishes us and the whole world with His good, grace, kindness, abundance, and great compassion. He gives bread to all flesh, for His kindness is eternal. And through His great goodness we have never lacked, and may we never lack food forever and ever. For He is God who provides and sustains all, does good to all, and His table is set for all, and He has prepared nourishment and food for all His creatures whom He has created in His compassion and His great kindness, as it states: You open Your hand and satisfy every living thing with its desire. Blessed are You, Lord, who provides food for all.

WE THANK YOU, LORD OUR GOD, FOR having given as an inheritance to our fathers a desirable, good and spacious land; a covenant and Torah, life and food, for having brought us out from the land of Egypt and redeemed us from the house of slavery; for Your covenant that You have sealed in our flesh; for Your Torah that You have taught us; for Your statutes of Your will, which You have made known to us; for the life and food with which You feed and sustain us.

AND FOR ALL OF THIS, LORD, OUR GOD, WE give thanks to You, and bless Your name, as it is stated, "And you will eat and be satisfied, and you shall bless the Lord, your God, for the good land He has given you. Blessed are You, O Lord, for the land and for the food.

HAVE MERCY, LORD OUR GOD, UPON ISRAEL Your people, upon Jerusalem Your city, upon Zion the abode of Your glory, upon the kingship of the house of David, Your anointed; and upon the great and holy House upon which Your Name is called. Our God, our Father, our Shepherd, tend us, provide for us, sustain us, support us, and speedily grant us, Lord our God,

הָרְוַח לָנוּ מְהֵרָה מִכָּל־צָרוֹתֵינוּ. וְנָא אַל תַּצְרִיכֵנוּ יְהֹוָה אֱלֹהֵינוּ לִידֵי מַתְּנוֹת בָּשָׂר וָדָם, וְלֹא לִידֵי הַלְוָאָתָם, אֶלָּא לְיָדְךָ הַמְּלֵאָה וְהָרְחָבָה, הָעֲשִׁירָה וְהַפְּתוּחָה. יְהִי רָצוֹן שֶׁלֹּא נֵבוֹשׁ בָּעוֹלָם הַזֶּה, וְלֹא נִכָּלֵם לְעוֹלָם הַבָּא. וּמַלְכוּת בֵּית דָּוִד מְשִׁיחָךְ תַּחֲזִירֶנָּה לִמְקוֹמָהּ בִּמְהֵרָה בְיָמֵינוּ:

בשבת: **רְצֵה** וְהַחֲלִיצֵנוּ יְהֹוָה אֱלֹהֵינוּ בְּמִצְוֹתֶיךָ וּבְמִצְוַת יוֹם הַשְּׁבִיעִי הַשַּׁבָּת הַגָּדוֹל וְהַקָּדוֹשׁ הַזֶּה. כִּי יוֹם גָּדוֹל וְקָדוֹשׁ הוּא מִלְּפָנֶיךָ, נִשְׁבּוֹת בּוֹ וְנָנוּחַ בּוֹ וְנִתְעַנֵּג בּוֹ כְּמִצְוַת חֻקֵּי רְצוֹנָךְ, וְאַל תְּהִי צָרָה וְיָגוֹן בְּיוֹם מְנוּחָתֵנוּ, וְהַרְאֵנוּ בְּנֶחָמַת צִיּוֹן בִּמְהֵרָה בְיָמֵינוּ, כִּי אַתָּה הוּא בַּעַל הַנֶּחָמוֹת. וַהֲגַם שֶׁאָכַלְנוּ וְשָׁתִינוּ, חָרְבַּן בֵּיתְךָ הַגָּדוֹל וְהַקָּדוֹשׁ לֹא שָׁכַחְנוּ. אַל תִּשְׁכָּחֵנוּ לָנֶצַח וְאַל תִּזְנָחֵנוּ לָעַד, כִּי אֵל מֶלֶךְ גָּדוֹל וְקָדוֹשׁ אָתָּה:

אֱלֹהֵינוּ וֵאלֹהֵי אֲבוֹתֵינוּ, יַעֲלֶה וְיָבֹא וְיַגִּיעַ וְיֵרָאֶה וְיֵרָצֶה וְיִשָּׁמַע וְיִפָּקֵד וְיִזָּכֵר זִכְרוֹנֵנוּ וְזִכְרוֹן אֲבוֹתֵינוּ. זִכְרוֹן יְרוּשָׁלַיִם עִירָךְ, וְזִכְרוֹן מָשִׁיחַ בֶּן דָּוִד עַבְדָּךְ, וְזִכְרוֹן כָּל עַמְּךָ בֵּית יִשְׂרָאֵל לְפָנֶיךָ, לִפְלֵיטָה לְטוֹבָה, לְחֵן לְחֶסֶד וּלְרַחֲמִים, לְחַיִּים טוֹבִים וּלְשָׁלוֹם. בְּיוֹם חַג הַמַּצּוֹת הַזֶּה בְּיוֹם (ביום טוב: טוב) מִקְרָא קוֹדֶשׁ הַזֶּה לְרַחֵם בּוֹ עָלֵינוּ וּלְהוֹשִׁיעֵנוּ. זָכְרֵנוּ יְהֹוָה אֱלֹהֵינוּ בּוֹ לְטוֹבָה, וּפָקְדֵנוּ בוֹ לִבְרָכָה, וְהוֹשִׁיעֵנוּ בוֹ לְחַיִּים טוֹבִים, בִּדְבַר יְשׁוּעָה וְרַחֲמִים. חוּס וְחָנֵּנוּ וַחֲמוֹל וְרַחֵם עָלֵינוּ. וְהוֹשִׁיעֵנוּ כִּי אֵלֶיךָ עֵינֵינוּ. כִּי אֵל מֶלֶךְ חַנּוּן וְרַחוּם אָתָּה:

וְתִבְנֶה יְרוּשָׁלַיִם עִירָךְ בִּמְהֵרָה בְיָמֵינוּ: בָּרוּךְ אַתָּה יְהֹוָה, בּוֹנֵה יְרוּשָׁלָיִם. אָמֵן:

relief from all our troubles. Lord our God, please do not make us dependent upon the gifts of mortal men nor upon their loans, but only upon Your full, open, holy and generous hand. May it be Your will that we may not be shamed in this world or disgraced in the World to Come. And the kingdom of David, Your anointed one, return it to its place, speedily in our days.

On Shabbat: May it please You, God, our Lord, to give us rest, through Your mitzvot and through the mitzvah of the seventh day, this great and holy Shabbat. For this day is great and holy before You, to refrain from work on it and to rest on it with love, in accordance with Your will. May it be Your will, God our Lord, to grant us rest, that there shall be no distress, grief or moaning on this day of our rest. And show us God our Lord, the consolation of Zion Your city, and the rebuilding of Jerusalem Your holy city, for You are the Master of consolation, and even though we have eaten and we have drunk, the destruction of Your great and holy House we have not forgotten, and do not forget us eternally and do not abandon us forever, for You are God, King, great and holy.

OUR GOD AND GOD OF OUR FATHERS, MAY the remembrance of us; the remembrance of our fathers; the remembrance of Jerusalem, Your city; the remembrance of the Mashiach, son of David, Your servant; the remembrance of all your people, the House of Israel, ascend, come and reach, be seen and accepted, heard, and be considered, and be remembered before You, for deliverance, for goodness, for grace, for kindness, for compassion, for a good life, and for peace, on this Festival of Matzot, this (on the festival: good) day of convocation, to have pity on us and to save us. Remember us, Lord our God, on this day for goodness, consider us on it for blessing; and save us on it for a good life. And with Your word of salvation and mercy, pity us and be gracious and compassionate with us, and save us, for our eyes are turned to You, because You are a gracious and compassionate God and King.

MAY YOU REBUILD JERUSALEM, YOUR HOLY city, speedily in our days. Blessed are You, Lord, Who rebuilds Jerusalem. Amen.

בָּרוּךְ אַתָּה יְהֹוָה, אֱלֹהֵינוּ מֶלֶךְ הָעוֹלָם, לָעַד הָאֵל אָבִינוּ, מַלְכֵּנוּ, אַדִּירֵנוּ, בּוֹרְאֵנוּ, גּוֹאֲלֵנוּ, קְדוֹשֵׁנוּ, קְדוֹשׁ יַעֲקֹב, רוֹעֵנוּ, רוֹעֵה יִשְׂרָאֵל, הַמֶּלֶךְ הַטּוֹב וְהַמֵּטִיב לַכֹּל, שֶׁבְּכָל יוֹם וָיוֹם הוּא הֵטִיב לָנוּ, הוּא מֵטִיב לָנוּ, הוּא יֵיטִיב לָנוּ. הוּא גְמָלָנוּ, הוּא גוֹמְלֵנוּ, הוּא יִגְמְלֵנוּ לָעַד חֵן וָחֶסֶד וְרַחֲמִים וְרֵיוַח וְהַצָּלָה וְכָל-טוֹב:

הָרַחֲמָן הוּא יִשְׁתַּבַּח עַל כִּסֵּא כְבוֹדוֹ: הָרַחֲמָן הוּא יִשְׁתַּבַּח בַּשָּׁמַיִם וּבָאָרֶץ: הָרַחֲמָן הוּא יִשְׁתַּבַּח בָּנוּ לְדוֹר דּוֹרִים: הָרַחֲמָן הוּא קֶרֶן לְעַמּוֹ יָרִים: הָרַחֲמָן הוּא יִתְפָּאַר בָּנוּ לָנֶצַח נְצָחִים: הָרַחֲמָן הוּא יְפַרְנְסֵנוּ בְּכָבוֹד וְלֹא בְבִזּוּי בְּהֶתֵּר וְלֹא בְאִסּוּר בְּנַחַת וְלֹא בְצָעַר: הָרַחֲמָן הוּא יִתֵּן שָׁלוֹם בֵּינֵינוּ: הָרַחֲמָן הוּא יִשְׁלַח בְּרָכָה רְוָחָה וְהַצְלָחָה בְּכָל-מַעֲשֵׂה יָדֵינוּ: הָרַחֲמָן הוּא יַצְלִיחַ אֶת דְּרָכֵינוּ: הָרַחֲמָן הוּא יִשְׁבּוֹר עוֹל גָּלוּת מְהֵרָה מֵעַל צַוָּארֵנוּ: הָרַחֲמָן הוּא יוֹלִיכֵנוּ מְהֵרָה קוֹמְמִיּוּת לְאַרְצֵנוּ: הָרַחֲמָן הוּא יִרְפָּאֵנוּ רְפוּאָה שְׁלֵמָה רְפוּאַת הַנֶּפֶשׁ וּרְפוּאַת הַגּוּף: הָרַחֲמָן הוּא יִפְתַּח לָנוּ אֶת יָדוֹ הָרְחָבָה: הָרַחֲמָן הוּא יְבָרֵךְ כָּל אֶחָד וְאֶחָד מִמֶּנּוּ בִּשְׁמוֹ הַגָּדוֹל כְּמוֹ שֶׁנִּתְבָּרְכוּ אֲבוֹתֵינוּ אַבְרָהָם יִצְחָק וְיַעֲקֹב בַּכֹּל מִכֹּל כֹּל. כֵּן יְבָרֵךְ אוֹתָנוּ יַחַד בְּרָכָה שְׁלֵמָה. וְכֵן יְהִי רָצוֹן וְנֹאמַר אָמֵן: הָרַחֲמָן הוּא יִפְרוֹשׁ עָלֵינוּ סֻכַּת שְׁלוֹמוֹ:

בשבת: הָרַחֲמָן הוּא יַנְחִילֵנוּ עוֹלָם שֶׁכֻּלּוֹ שַׁבָּת וּמְנוּחָה לְחַיֵּי הָעוֹלָמִים:

BLESSED ARE YOU, LORD OUR GOD, KING OF THE Universe, God our Father, our King, our Sovereign, our Creator, our Redeemer, our Maker, our Holy One, the Holy One of Jacob, our Shepherd, the Shepherd of Israel, the King Who is good and Who continually does good to all. Each and every day He has done good for us, He does good for us, and He will [continue to] do good for us; He was bountiful to us, He is bountiful to us, and He will [continue to] be bountiful to us forever, with grace, kindness and with mercy, and with relief, salvation and success, blessing and help, consolation, sustenance and support, and with compassion and life and peace, and all goodness; and may He never deprive us of all good things.

MAY THE MERCIFUL ONE BE PRAISED UPON HIS glorious throne. May the Merciful One be blessed in heaven and on earth. May the Merciful One be praised for all generations. May the Merciful One uplift a horn for His people. May the Merciful One be glorified through all eternity. May the Merciful One sustain us in honor and not with shame, with that which is permitted and not with that which is prohibited, with comfort and not with pain. May the Merciful One grant peace among us. May the Merciful One send blessing, prosperity and success in all our undertakings. May the Merciful One bring success to our ways. May the Merciful One break the yoke of exile speedily from our neck. May the Merciful One speedily lead us upright to our land. May the Merciful One heal us completely, a cure for the soul and a cure for the body. May the Merciful One open for us His generous hand. May the Merciful One bless each and every one of us with His great name, as our patriarchs, Abraham, Isaac, and Jacob, were blessed in everything, from everything, and with everything, and so may He bless us all together with a perfect blessing. So may it be His will and let us say, Amen. May the Merciful One spread over us His protection of peace.

On Shabbat: May the Merciful One grant us to inherit a day that is entirely Shabbat and eternal rest.

הָרַחֲמָן הוּא יַגִּיעֵנוּ לְמוֹעֲדִים אֲחֵרִים הַבָּאִים לִקְרָאתֵנוּ לְשָׁלוֹם:
הָרַחֲמָן הוּא יַנְחִילֵנוּ לְיוֹם שֶׁכֻּלּוֹ טוֹב:

הָרַחֲמָן הוּא יִטַּע תּוֹרָתוֹ וְאַהֲבָתוֹ בְּלִבֵּנוּ וְתִהְיֶה יִרְאָתוֹ עַל פָּנֵינוּ לְבִלְתִּי נֶחֱטָא. וְיִהְיוּ כָל־מַעֲשֵׂינוּ לְשֵׁם שָׁמָיִם:

ברכת האורח: הָרַחֲמָן הוּא יְבָרֵךְ אֶת הַשֻּׁלְחָן הַזֶּה שֶׁאָכַלְנוּ עָלָיו, וִיסַדֵּר בּוֹ כָּל־מַעֲדַנֵּי עוֹלָם, וְיִהְיֶה כְּשֻׁלְחָנוֹ שֶׁל אַבְרָהָם אָבִינוּ עָלָיו הַשָּׁלוֹם, כָּל־רָעֵב מִמֶּנּוּ יֹאכַל, וְכָל־צָמֵא מִמֶּנּוּ יִשְׁתֶּה. וְאַל יֶחְסַר מִמֶּנּוּ כָּל־טוּב לָעַד וּלְעוֹלְמֵי עוֹלָמִים:

הָרַחֲמָן הוּא יְבָרֵךְ אֶת בַּעַל הַבַּיִת הַזֶּה וּבַעַל הַסְּעֻדָּה הַזֹּאת, הוּא וּבָנָיו וְאִשְׁתּוֹ וְכָל־אֲשֶׁר לוֹ, בְּבָנִים שֶׁיִּחְיוּ, וּבִנְכָסִים שֶׁיִּרְבּוּ. בָּרֵךְ יְהֹוָה חֵילוֹ וּפֹעַל יָדָיו תִּרְצֶה. וְיִהְיוּ נְכָסָיו וּנְכָסֵינוּ מֻצְלָחִים וּקְרוֹבִים לָעִיר, וְאַל יִזְדַּקֵּק לְפָנָיו וְלֹא לְפָנֵינוּ שׁוּם דְּבַר חֵטְא וְהִרְהוּר עָוֹן, שָׂשׂ וְשָׂמֵחַ כָּל־הַיָּמִים בְּעֹשֶׁר וְכָבוֹד מֵעַתָּה וְעַד עוֹלָם, לֹא יֵבוֹשׁ בָּעוֹלָם הַזֶּה וְלֹא יִכָּלֵם לָעוֹלָם הַבָּא, אָמֵן כֵּן יְהִי רָצוֹן:

הָרַחֲמָן הוּא יְחַיֵּינוּ וִיזַכֵּנוּ וִיקָרְבֵנוּ לִימוֹת הַמָּשִׁיחַ וּלְבִנְיַן בֵּית הַמִּקְדָּשׁ וּלְחַיֵּי הָעוֹלָם הַבָּא.

מִגְדּוֹל יְשׁוּעוֹת מַלְכּוֹ. וְעֹשֶׂה־חֶסֶד לִמְשִׁיחוֹ לְדָוִד וּלְזַרְעוֹ עַד־עוֹלָם: כְּפִירִים רָשׁוּ וְרָעֵבוּ. וְדֹרְשֵׁי יְהֹוָה לֹא־יַחְסְרוּ כָל־טוֹב: נַעַר הָיִיתִי גַּם־זָקַנְתִּי וְלֹא־

May the Merciful One enable us to other festivals coming to us in peace. May the Merciful One have us inherit a day that is all good.

May the Merciful One plant His Torah and love in our hearts, and may His fear be in our faces that we should not sin. And may all our actions be for the sake of Heaven.

The guest's blessing: May the Merciful One bless this table upon which we ate, and may He set upon it all the delicacies of the world. May it be like the table of our patriarch Abraham, may all who are hungry eat from it and all who are thirsty drink from it. May it never lack all that is good forever and for all eternity.

May the Merciful One bless the master of this house and the host of this meal – him, his children and his wife and all that is his – with children who shall live, and with possessions that shall increase. May God bless his wealth and favor the work of his hands. May his possessions and our possessions be successful and near the city, and may there not occur to him or to us any matter of transgression or sinful thought. May he be joyful and happy all the days, with wealth and with honor from now until eternity. May he not be ashamed in this world nor humiliated in the World to Come, Amen, and so be His will.

May the Merciful One grant us life and merit, and bring us near to the days of the Mashiach and the rebuilding of the Bet HaMikdash and life in the World to Come.

HE IS A TOWER OF SALVATION TO HIS KING, and bestows kindness upon His anointed, to David and his descendants forever. Young lions are in need and go hungry, but those who seek the Lord shall not lack any good. I was a youth and also have aged, and I have not seen a righteous man forsaken and his

רָאִיתִי צַדִּיק נֶעֱזָב. וְזַרְעוֹ מְבַקֶּשׁ־לָחֶם: כָּל־הַיּוֹם חוֹנֵן וּמַלְוֶה. וְזַרְעוֹ לִבְרָכָה: מַה שֶּׁאָכַלְנוּ יִהְיֶה לְשָׂבְעָה. וּמַה שֶּׁשָּׁתִינוּ יִהְיֶה לִרְפוּאָה. וּמַה שֶּׁהוֹתַרְנוּ יִהְיֶה לִבְרָכָה כְּדִכְתִיב וַיִּתֵּן לִפְנֵיהֶם וַיֹּאכְלוּ וַיּוֹתִירוּ כִּדְבַר יְהֹוָה: בְּרוּכִים אַתֶּם לַיהֹוָה. עוֹשֵׂה שָׁמַיִם וָאָרֶץ: בָּרוּךְ הַגֶּבֶר אֲשֶׁר יִבְטַח בַּיהֹוָה. וְהָיָה יְהֹוָה מִבְטַחוֹ: יְהֹוָה עֹז לְעַמּוֹ יִתֵּן. יְהֹוָה יְבָרֵךְ אֶת־עַמּוֹ בַשָּׁלוֹם:

עוֹשֶׂה שָׁלוֹם בִּמְרוֹמָיו הוּא בְּרַחֲמָיו יַעֲשֶׂה שָׁלוֹם עָלֵינוּ וְעַל כָּל־עַמּוֹ יִשְׂרָאֵל וְאִמְרוּ אָמֵן:

children begging for bread. All day he is gracious and lends, and his children are a blessing. May what we ate satisfy and what we drank be for health, and what we left over for a blessing, as it is written, "He placed it before them and they ate and left over as the Lord had spoken." Blessed are you to the Lord, Maker of heaven and earth. Blessed is the man who trusts in the Lord, and the Lord will be his trust. God will give strength to His people, God will bless His people with peace.

He who makes peace in His heights, may He make peace for us and for all Israel; and say, Amen.

Answers to the riddles
Sources and expansions of various topics for discussion
Who is free? (a general discussion)

Answers and Further Discussion

Answers to the riddles

1. By saying kiddush on Seder night we fulfill two mitzvot: saying kiddush and drinking the first of the four cups of wine.

2. Generally, we make sure to eat shortly after kiddush. There is a principle that "one should only make kiddush in a place where there is a meal" (Shulchan Aruch 273:3). However, on *Seder* night there is a considerable gap between the time we say kiddush and the time we eat.

   There are a number of reasons this is not a problem:

   a. Interruptions for matters that are integral to the meal are not considered interruptions. Therefore, reciting the haggadah and relating the Exodus from Egypt are not considered interruptions, as they are integral aspects of the meal. After all, matzah is described as "bread over which many words are recited" (Pesachim 36a. For a more detailed explanation see Ritva on the haggadah; *Mikra'ei Kodesh* by Rav Tzvi Pesach Frank, II:37; Responsa *Chazon Ovadyah* I:11 p. 171). This is also why we start maggid with "this is the bread of affliction"; we want to show that what follows during this section is related to matzah (Rav Shlomo Zalman Auerbach, in *Pa'amei Kol Torah*).

   b. Drinking a *revi'it* of wine from kiddush is considered to be like a meal, and on the Seder night everyone drinks this amount. Therefore, we consider it as if kiddush really was followed by a meal (see *Shulchan Gavoah*, 473:27, and *Halachah MiMekorah – Kinor David, Kaddesh* p. 39, note 7).

   c. Reciting the haggadah is considered like one long kiddush. Therefore, there is really no gap between kiddush and the meal. After all, whenever we say kiddush the main point is to mention the theme of the day and the Exodus from Egypt. Reading the haggadah on the Seder night can be considered the same, just in a longer and more detailed way (Rav Chaim Falaji, *Chaim LeRosh* 41b). Moreover, since the primary purpose of reciting the haggadah is to sanctify the night, the entire seder can be considered a continuation of kiddush (Rav Shlomo Zalman Auerbach, *Kuntres Seder HaPesach*).

3. On every other festival only the one who recites kiddush is obligated to drink the wine (although it is customary that everyone drinks a small amount to show our love for the mitzvah). However, on the Seder night everyone is obligated to drink because this is the first of the four cups of wine. It is proper for all to hold their cups of wine when kiddush is recited on the Seder

◂ night,

night, so that all will feel that this is also a cup of kiddush in addition to being one of the four cups (Rav Shlomo Zalman Auerbach, *Shemirat Shabbat Kehilchatah*, II: 47, Note 26). Furthermore, on every other festival, if there is no wine one may recite kiddush on bread. However, on the Seder night one must recite kiddush on wine because it represents the first of the four cups (when one has no wine, he may recite kiddush on another proper beverage – see *Halachah MiMekorah – Kinor David, Kaddesh* p. 42, note 9).

4. One must wash one's hands before eating any vegetable that has moisture on it, but without reciting a blessing (see *Halachah MiMekorah – Kinor David, Urchatz* p. 57, and the table of this volume on p. 109).
5. If a person wishes to eat food that is wet or moist with any one of seven specific liquids, he must first wash his hands without reciting a blessing, as we do with karpas. The seven liquids are wine, honey (from bees), oil (from olives), milk, dew, blood, and water (Shulchan Aruch 158:4).
6. One does not recite a blessing on it.
7. One may use any vegetable for karpas. Therefore, one may even use a cucumber. However, it is customary to use celery or a potato.
8. The vegetable referred to as karpas is presumably parsley or celery. Karpas is not mentioned in the Talmud in regard to the seder. It is mentioned by the Rishonim as the ideal vegetable for the Seder night, because they rearranged the four letters of karpas, *chaf, resh, peh, samekh*, to stand for *samekh* (sixty) *ribo* (ten thousand = 600,000) worked *befarech* (*peh, resh, chaf*) in hard labor. This is only a hint, and by Jewish Law one can use any vegetable, and that is why many use potatoes or other vegetables.
9. The reason for this is there is a doubt whether to recite a concluding blessing on it. Therefore, if one eats less than an olive-sized portion, there is no doubt that one does not recite a concluding blessing. There are those, though, who hold that one must eat an olive-sized portion (and not recite the concluding blessing after it) and, therefore, one who is hungry can eat now, and can recite the haggadah at his leisure (for more on this, see *Halachah MiMekorah – Kinor David, Karpas* p. 72).
10. One breaks matzah as a poor person would, for a poor person usually eats only a portion of bread rather than a whole loaf, and it is not just to facilitate having afikoman later (Berachot 39b). However, the reason matzah is broken now, well before the start of the meal, is in order to recite the haggadah over a broken matzah, as well as to save half of the matzah for afikoman, to ensure that it is not consumed accidentally (both explanations are found in *Kol Bo* 50).

◂ There

11. There are those who hold that one must eat a portion the size of two *kezaitim* of afikoman (one as a remembrance of the Pesach sacrifice and one as a remembrance of the matzah that was eaten along with the Pesach sacrifice), and that is why the bigger piece is put away (*Chok Ya'akov*, 475:26).

    However, it is possible that the reason the larger piece is set aside as afikoman is not because of afikoman but because we want to keep only a small piece with us. When we eat matzah at the beginning of the seder, we want to eat the way a poor person would eat, and that is why we leave a small piece, as a poor person does.

12. According to the Torah, there are two mitzvot on the Seder night: maggid – relating the story of the Exodus from Egypt – and eating matzah. In Rabbinic Law, there are several more: kiddush, the four cups, maror (in our times this is rabbinic, because there is no Pesach sacrifice), hallel, and leaning. There are also things we do as a remembrance of mitzvot we are unable to fulfill nowadays: korech (in remembrance of how Hillel, at the time the Bet HaMikdash stood, would eat the Pesach sacrifice along with matzah), afikoman (a remembrance of the Pesach sacrifice or of the matzah eaten along with the Pesach sacrifice).

13. One can find a detailed answer to this in the diagram in maggid, p. 28.

14. The words literally mean "he will come and bring a Pesach sacrifice." The problem with this is that nowadays we are unable to bring a Pesach sacrifice so why do we say this? One possible answer is that we still have this phrase in our haggadah as a remnant of an older haggadah. Perhaps another answer is that this is an expression of our hope for redemption in the coming year and that next year we will indeed bring a Pesach sacrifice. Alternatively, we might not be referring to the Pesach sacrifice but to all the mitzvot of Pesach (the four cups, matzah, etc.).

    There is another problem with this phrase: the Pesach sacrifice was only supposed to be eaten by people who had joined together in advance to slaughter a particular lamb, and one cannot invite a person to join the group after the slaughter. So how can we invite others at this point? For this reason Tosafot Rid left this sentence out of his haggadah (see *HaManhig, Hilchot Pesach* 72).

15. The translation of the term is "flour for Pesach." It refers to the collection of money for the poor so that they will be able to buy the needs of the festival. In the past, the primary concern was to ensure that people had flour so that they could bake matzot, and that is the source of the term.

◄ Most

16. Most people, due to the melody, place a question mark after "What makes this night different from all other nights?" We answer accordingly, that we eat matzah and maror, etc. According to this, we do not expect any answer later on, because the answer has already been supplied.

However, it is more logical to understand this passage differently. The question mark is at the end of the first question: "Why is this night different from all other nights, that while on all other nights we eat chametz or matzah, on this night we eat only matzah? If that is the case, the entire passage consists of four questions, for which no answers are supplied. This is evidently the way the Rishonim understood this passage. Based on this understanding, we do not ask how this night is different, but why it is different (see Rashbam Pesachim 115b, *patartan*, who explains that all these questions are about various changes, and the next passage of "We were slaves" answers them).

17. Four questions, four sons, four cups of wine, four verbs of redemption, four parts of the Seder night (kiddush, maggid, the mitzvot regarding eating, hallel).

18. There is an obligation to eat a kezayit of matzah on the Seder night. There is no such obligation during the other days of Pesach, though it is still a mitzvah. There is a minority opinion that there is not even a mitzvah to eat matzah on the rest of Pesach, and the only reason we do so is because we are not allowed to eat chametz (see *Halachah MiMekorah – Kinor David, Motzi Matzah* p. 154).

19. The Mishnah's rite of Mah Nishtanah asks why on this night we eat only roasted meat. The Pesach sacrifice had to be eaten roasted, and not cooked. We do not include this in our rite today because we no longer offer the Pesach sacrifice (Rashbam Pesachim 116a, *ha'lailah*; Rambam *Hilchot Chametz U'Matzah* 8:3).

Our rite has a question about leaning. This question does not appear in the Mishnah. The rabbis may have wished to maintain the structure of the four questions, because the number four is an important element of the Seder night (however, the Mishnah in the Jerusalem Talmud 10:4 only has three questions – dipping, matzah, roast). It is, however, possible that there is another reason: at the time of the Bet HaMikdash they were accustomed to lean throughout the year, so leaning on Seder night was not a change (Gra in his commentary on the haggadah). However, Rambam's (8:2) rite of Mah Nishtanah is that there were *five questions* when the Bet HaMikdash stood – including both questions, on leaning and roast meat.

◄ In Deuteronomy

20. In Deuteronomy 6:21, it states, "You shall say to your son, 'We were slaves to Pharaoh in Egypt, and the Lord took us out of Egypt with a strong hand.'" The editor of the haggadah omitted the beginning, "You shall say to your son." It is possible that the haggadah did not intend to quote the verse and only used it as a guideline. Proof of this is that while the verse itself only mentions "the Lord," the haggadah adds "our God." In the verse it speaks of "the strong hand," whereas the editor added "and an outstretched arm" (the words appear in the Ten Mitzvot in Deuteronomy 5:14 – "you shall remember that you were a slave in the land of Egypt, and that the Lord your God took you out from there *with a strong hand and with an outstretched arm*," and so too in Deuteronomy 26:8).

    Another reason why the haggadah omitted the first part of the verse may be that the verse tells a father how to tell the story of the Exodus from Egypt to his son. So when the father actually tells the story to his son it is not necessary to mention the introduction of "You shall say to your son," rather just the story itself – "We were slaves..." (*Imrei Emet* of Gur).

    Why didn't the editor of the haggadah use the verse of the Ten Mitzvot? It is possible that he preferred our verse because it contains, "He took us out of Egypt," a statement that includes all of us, all of the generations. Alternatively, in our verse the Torah gives us an example of how to relate the story, "You shall say to your son, 'We were slaves to Pharaoh in Egypt.'"

21. We were supposed to be slaves for 400 years – "You shall surely know that your seed will be strangers in a land that is not theirs, and they will enslave them and oppress them, for four hundred years" (Genesis 15:13). However, the Sages explain that we were only slaves for 210 years, and the 400 years are to be calculated from the birth of Isaac.

22. With Rabbi Akiva, who lived in Bnei Brak.

23. Only the first name of each rabbi is mentioned, except for Rabbi Elazar ben Azaryah, whose father is mentioned too. The reason may be that in regard to the others, the name itself is enough to know to whom we refer. However, "Rabbi Elazar" can also refer to Rabbi Elazar ben Shamu'a (see *Rashi Yevamot* 72b, *ra'iti*).

24. In the Talmud Berachot (28a) it states that the sages wished to appoint Rabbi Elazar ben Azaryah as nasi (the head of all the Jews at the time) when he was only eighteen years old. A miracle occurred where eighteen rows of hair in his beard turned white, giving him the appearance that he was much older and more worthy of being nasi.

◄ Rambam

Rambam in his commentary on the Mishnah (*Berachot*, end of Chapter 1) explains that since he had learned so much in his youth, he became weak and his beard turned white, as if he were seventy years old.

The Jerusalem Talmud (Berachot 1:6) implies that he really did live until the age of seventy. According to this, *he was around seventy years old* at the time he said his statement and that is why he said "like (that is, about) seventy years old." (This is in accordance with the explanation of *Sefer Charedim* (ibid.). It is possible that he was young when he was appointed nasi, as the Babylonian Talmud states, but he made this statement years later, when he actually was about seventy years old).

25. The verse that speaks of the wise son states, "When your son asks," as a question expecting an answer. However, the verse that speaks of the wicked son states, "when your son says to you," a statement that does not require an answer. For more on this topic, see "The Four Sons – a comparative study between the haggadah and verses in the Torah," p. 55.

26. It is generally assumed that the midrash ends after "the one who does not know how to ask," with the words, "when I left Egypt." However, the truth is that the paragraph of "One might think that from the beginning of the month" is also part of the Four Sons section, because that is the commentary on the one who does not know how to ask: "It is because of this that the Lord did [all these miracles] for me when I left Egypt." It is true that the latter is an independent commentary, but it is connected to the answer to the one who does not know how to ask. See in "Source of the Haggadah" on p. 71.

27. Our forefather Abraham is known as "Abraham the *Ivri*" – "the Hebrew" (Genesis 14:13). Rashi (ibid.) explains, based on the Sages, that Abraham came "from across ("*mei'eiver*") the river, as is stated in the verse from Joshua quoted in the haggadah. That is why the Hebrew language is called "*Ivrit*," from "Abraham the *Ivri*." There are other explanations for the term "Abraham the *Ivri*": Abraham was on one side (God's), while all the rest of the world was on the other (*me'ever*) side; Abraham brought (*he'evir*) the entire world over to the side of God; Abraham was a descendant of Ever.

28. Verses 2–4 are quoted in the haggadah, even though these verses do not deal with the Exodus from Egypt. Verses 5–6 deal with the Exodus and are not quoted in the haggadah:

5. And I sent Moshe and Aaron, and I plagued the Egyptians, according to that which I did in their midst; and afterward I brought you out.

6. And I brought your fathers out of

◂ Egypt,

Egypt, and you came to the sea; and the Egyptians pursued your fathers with chariots and horsemen to the Red Sea.

It is not clear why this is so. It is possible that the aim was to show the Exodus from Egypt from the standpoint of spiritual servitude, and that is why only these verses are quoted. It is also possible that there was a different aim here – not to mention Moshe in the haggadah, and in verse 5 he is mentioned (see also the haggadah of Goldschmidt, p. 18; *HaSeder HaAruch*, 3, p. 163. For an explanation why Moshe does not appear in the haggadah, see the section on "Why doesn't Moshe appear in the haggadah?" p. 103).

29. Nachor was Abraham's brother, the son of Terach.

30. Esau was called "*se'ir,*" because when he was born his body "was completely like a coat of hair" – *ke'aderet sei'ar.*

31. According to the Sages, Am Yisrael was not enslaved for 400 years, but only for 210 years. The gematria of *resh, dalet, vav* (200+4+6) is 210. This fits with the verse "go down (*redoo*) there" (Genesis 42:2). According to this interpretation, God's promise that "they will enslave them and oppress them, for four hundred years" refers to the years from the birth of Isaac (see Sotah 12a; Rashi Genesis 15:13; *Seder Olam* ch. 3; *Yalkut Shimoni Bereishit*, section 77).

32. Yocheved was born as Bnei Yisrael were going down to Egypt, between the walls (and that is why there were 69 people who went down, as can be seen in the list in Genesis 46, and she was the 70th person). Yocheved was 130 years old when she gave birth to Moshe (as is known in our tradition). Moshe was 80 years old at the time of the Exodus from Egypt (Exodus 7:7); 130+80=210.

33. To this figure of 210 one must add 60 years from the birth of Isaac to the birth of Jacob (Genesis 25:26 – "and Isaac was 60 years old at the time of their [Jacob and Esau's] birth"), and there were 130 years from the birth of Jacob until he went down to Egypt (Genesis 47:9).

    One can also see based on the simple meaning of the verses that Am Yisrael could not have been enslaved in Egypt for 400 years:

    Kehat was among those who went down to Egypt (Genesis 46:11), and he lived 133 years (Exodus 6:18); his son, Amram, lived 137 years (Exodus 6:20); and Moshe, Amram's son, was 80 years old when he appeared before Pharaoh.

    Even if we add all the years of the life of Kehat, Amram, and Moshe, we will not reach 400 years, but 350 years (133+137+80=350). It is clear that the number must be lower, for one must subtract the years from the birth of

◄ Kehat

Kehat until the descent to Egypt, as well as Amram's age when Moshe was born.

34. Am Yisrael borrowed "silver and gold vessels" from the Egyptians and thereby accumulated "great wealth." The Torah states that God granted the favor of the nation in the eyes of the Egyptians, and that is why they lend these vessels to them. The Sages add that during the plague of darkness, Am Yisrael entered the homes of the Egyptians and saw where the silver and gold vessels of Egypt were hidden. Thus, when they later asked the Egyptians to borrow their vessels, the Egyptians could not say to them that they didn't have any, as Am Yisrael knew where their vessels were!

35. The Rishonim and Acharonim differ about the meaning of this phrase, and there are many explanations. We will note the main ones: a. Avudraham (*Seder HaHaggadah*) explains that *the promise* that God made to Abraham at the Covenant between the Pieces, that God would redeem Am Yisrael after 400 years, was the merit whereby our fathers were redeemed. b. One can explain this in a similar fashion, and say that the word "it" refers to the *Covenant between the Pieces*, and was that which sustained our fathers.

c. Shibolei HaLeket (on the haggadah, 218) explains that this phrase refers to all our exiles. The promise that God gave, that "Also the nation that they will serve will I judge" at the Covenant between the Pieces refers to *all the exiles* (the additions in the verse of the letter *vav* in the word *vegam* comes to include all the exiles), and it is this promise that has sustained us to rescue us throughout all our exiles.

36. We can see that he wrote it by memory because he wrote "*brit bein habesarim*" (with the Hebrew letter *sin*), rather than "*brit bein habetarim*" (with the Hebrew letter *taf*).

37. It is clear that he was Ashkenazic, and that he spoke Hebrew with an Ashkenazic pronunciation, which pronounces the letter *taf* like the letter *samech* or *sin* (which in the Ashkenazic pronunciation can be "s"). That was why he wrote the letter *sin* rather than the letter *taf*.

38. From the paragraph on the first fruits in *Parashat Ki Tavo*, Deuteronomy 26:5–8.

39. "Israel was distinctive there" tells us that they kept their religion and their identity (see the section on "He became there a nation," p. 77. One can find other interpretations in Ritva on the haggadah).

40. "Great and numerous" – at the sin of the golden calf, when God wanted to destroy Am Yisrael and to make Moshe a great and mighty nation [rather than Am Yisrael] – "Leave Me alone, and I will destroy them and obliterate their name from

◂ beneath

beneath the heavens, and I will make you into a nation *greater and more numerous* than they" (Deuteronomy 9:14). "Numerous and great" – in the description of Pharaoh's fear of Am Yisrael, which was growing: "Behold, the people of Bnei Yisrael are more *numerous and greater* than we are" (Exodus 1:9); and so too in Joel (2:2), "A day of darkness and gloom, a day of cloud and thick darkness, like the dawn spread over the mountains; a *numerous and great* people, the like of which has never been, and after it there shall be no more for many generations."

41. The editor of the haggadah deduces it from a verse in Deuteronomy (10:22), even though there is a parallel verse in Genesis (46:27). One might think it would be preferable to quote the verse in Genesis, which talks about the descent to Egypt. However, the editor of the haggadah evidently made a point of using the verse in Deuteronomy, because this verse states that in the past we were "seventy souls" and now God has made us like "the stars in the heavens in number." From here we learn that the "seventy" is "a small number" in comparison to our number now.

42. The exposition with the "two hundred and fifty plagues." The editor of the haggadah first uses this verse to expound upon the *types of plagues* (pestilence, the sword) and afterwards about the quantity of plagues ("with an outstretched arm – two," etc.). As part of the exposition regarding the *quantity of plagues*, he quotes the views of Tanna'im that also deal with the quantity of plagues.

43. Pharaoh's heart was hard.

44. BLOOD: the river turned into blood. According to the Sages, all the water that the Egyptians had anywhere in their possession also turned into blood. The fish in the river died, and it made the river smell.

    FROGS: Frogs appeared throughout all of Egypt – in the houses, in the bedrooms, and in the ovens. In the end, they all died and made the entire country smell.

    LICE: The earth of Egypt turned into lice, which infested both men and animals.

    WILD BEASTS: Ravenous animals filled Egypt. These animals also harmed humans [the Hebrew word used here, *arov*, evidently derived from the word *irbuv* – a mixture, in that it was a mixture of different kinds of wild animals – Ibn Ezra, Abarbanel and others].

    PESTILENCE: A disease that affected animals and killed them.

    BOILS: A kind of boil that affected both people and animals.

    HAIL: Heavy hail fell on Egypt, which brought down trees and destroyed the crop (except for young plants, which had just begun to grow: Exodus 9:32) and injured people and

◂ animals

animals that had remained outside. The hail itself was miraculous, with fire in the midst of the hail.

LOCUSTS: These invaded Egypt and ate all the remaining crops.

DARKNESS: A heavy darkness descended on Egypt for three days, a darkness that prevented people from moving from their places. According to the Sages, it was not just an absence of light, but a thick and tangible fog-like darkness (Exodus 10:21).

THE KILLING OF THE FIRSTBORN: All the Egyptian firstborn died at midnight of the 15th of Nissan. Am Yisrael placed blood on their doorposts and they were saved.

45. This refers to the plague of frogs. The Egyptians gathered the dead frogs into mounds.

46. In *Parashat Va'Eira* there are seven plagues, and in *Parashat Bo* there are the remaining three plagues. A hint at this division is that the first two letters of *Va'Eira* are *vav* and *alef*, which add up (in gematria) to 7 (6+1), while the word *Bo* consists of the letters *bet* and *alef*, adding up to 3 (2+1).

47. The plague of locusts – "and the land was darkened, and the locusts ate all the produce of the land" (Exodus 10:15).

48. So that he would see all of God's plagues and to enhance God's prestige in the plagues of Egypt (in the end, he would die at the sea), as it says, "Because this time, I am sending all My plagues into your heart and into your servants and into your people, in order that you know that there is none like Me in the entire earth. For if now I had stretched forth My hand, and I had smitten you and your people with pestilence, you would have been annihilated from the earth. But, for this [reason] I have allowed you to stand, in order to show you My strength and in order to declare My name all over the earth" (Exodus 9:14–16).

49. Lice.

50. Wild beasts, pestilence, killing of the firstborn.

51. Wild beasts, pestilence, killing of the firstborn.

52. Regarding the quails – "those who collected little collected ten piles" – Numbers 11:32.

53. Lice, boils, and darkness. In each case it is the third plague of the sequence: *DeTzaCh, ADaSh, BeAChaV* (the plague of the killing of the firstborn is considered to be a general plague, and is independent of the others).

54. The plague of locusts (Exodus 10:17).

55. The plague of darkness – "the darkness will become tangible" (Exodus 10:21). The Sages explain that the darkness was tangible, and had a substance to it (Midrash Rabbah, Exodus 14:1).

◂ The

56. The plague of hail: "And Pharaoh saw that the rain, the hail, and the thunder had ceased; so he continued to sin, and he *hardened his heart and so did his servants*" (Exodus 9:34); "The Lord said to Moshe: 'Come to Pharaoh, for *I have hardened his heart and the heart of his servants*'" (Exodus 10:1).

57. The transforming of the staff into a snake – Exodus 7:11; the changing of water to blood – Exodus 7:22; bringing up frogs on the Land of Egypt – Exodus 8:3.

58. Aaron's staff swallowed their staffs – Exodus 7:12; they were unable to produce lice – Exodus 8:14; they were unable to stand before Moshe because of the lice, because they were also affected by it – Exodus 9:11.

59. Frogs – "Entreat the Lord" – Exodus 8:4; Wild beasts – "entreat on my behalf" – Exodus 8:24; hail – "Entreat the Lord" – Exodus 9:27; locusts – "forgive now my sin only this time, and entreat the Lord your God" – Exodus 10:17. Pharaoh said that he had sinned during the plagues of hail and locusts.

60. Blood.

61. On the Philistines, after they captured the Ark of the Covenant, the Philistine ministers said that the Ark had to be returned in a respectable way: "And why should you make your heart hard as the Egyptians and Pharaoh made their hearts hard? Will it not be, just as He mocked them, and they sent them away, and they departed?… And you shall take the Ark of the Lord, and you shall place it on the cart" (1 Samuel 6:6–8).

62. Those struck by the killing of the firstborn were the firstborn of animals, as well as the gods of Egypt – "upon all *the gods of Egypt* will I wreak judgments" (Exodus 12:12 – and see Ramban as to why there is no mention of the gods of Egypt in Exodus 12:29).

63. About the locusts in the plagues on Egypt (Exodus 10:5), and so too in *Parashat Balak* on Am Yisrael (Numbers 22:5).

64. The plague of pestilence, so that the Egyptians would not die and continue to see the hand of God in the plagues of Egypt: "Because this time, I am sending all My plagues into your heart and into your servants and into your people, in order that you know that there is none like Me in the entire earth. For if now I had stretched forth My hand, and I had smitten you and your people with pestilence, you would have been annihilated from the earth. But, for this [reason] I have allowed you to stand, in order to show you My strength and in order to declare My name all over the earth" (Exodus 9:14–16).

65. Pharaoh said this after the plague of darkness – Exodus 10:28; Pharaoh again called Moshe and Aaron

◂ after

after the plague of the killing of the firstborn – Exodus 12:31.

66. The locusts and the splitting of the sea.

67. The wild beasts – Exodus 8:18; pestilence – Exodus 9:4; hail – Exodus 9:26; darkness – Exodus 10:23; plague of the firstborn – Exodus 11:7.

68. The trees had not been affected until then, but they were affected by the hail, "it broke all the trees of the field" – Exodus 9:25. The young plants (wheat and spelt) were not affected by the hail – "The wheat and the spelt, however, were not broken, because they ripen late" – Exodus 9:32. They were eaten by the locusts, Exodus 10:5 and Exodus 10:15.

69. In Joel (2:2) it states that the locusts were such as had never happened before or ever thereafter: "A day of darkness and gloom, a day of cloud and thick darkness, like the dawn spread over the mountains; a numerous and great people, the like of which has never been, and after it there shall be no more for many generations." Rashi reconciles this based on a verse in Joel 1:4, that there was one type of locust in Egypt, whereas in Joel there were a number of different kinds of locusts. What the Torah tells us is that in the plague of locusts there had never been as dense a plague of one kind of locust as there was in Egypt. (Ramban (ibid.) answers that there was never again that heavy a plague of locusts in Egypt, but in other places there were).

70. Generally, the praises are arranged in historical order. However, there are a number of differences: a. the Exodus from Egypt is listed here before the execution of judgments against the Egyptians and their gods, before the slaying of the firstborn, before acquiring their money, whereas it actually took place after all of them. b. The acquiring of their money was before the slaying of the firstborn, and here it is listed after (however, it is possible that Am Yisrael only took these gifts as they were leaving Egypt, and acquired the rest of their money later). c. The manna is before Shabbat, but the Sages explain that Shabbat was given in Marah (Sanhedrin 56b; and Rashi Exodus 15:25), and if so Shabbat preceded the manna. It is true that there is a dispute about this is the Jerusalem Talmud (Beitzah 2:1): according to Rabbi Eliezer, they were commanded about Shabbat at Marah, whereas according to Rabbi Yehoshua they were commanded about it at Alush (after the manna). Ramban (Exodus 15:25) suggests a middle way: indeed Shabbat was given at Marah, but that was only theoretical, to learn about it and to teach them the laws of Shabbat, but they were only commanded to observe it later on.

It thus appears that the main difficulty is with the Exodus from Egypt, which certainly took place

◂ before

before these events. It is logical to say that the Exodus from Egypt was listed first here because all the miracles and all the benefits were brought about because of it. The Exodus from Egypt was the culmination of all the previous stages, and in its wake we were granted the subsequent stages (the Torah, Eretz Yisrael, and the Bet HaMikdash).

71. Fifteen stages, as we see in the Mishnah in Sukkah (5:4) that there were fifteen steps in the Bet HaMikdash on which the Levites would stand with their musical instruments, and as we see in Psalms (120–134) that there are fifteen Psalms beginning with *shir ha'ma'alot* – "a song of ascents."

72. Matzah that was guarded from an early stage in the process of preparing it (reaping the grain or grinding it), to ensure that it does not come into contact with water, and was prepared with the specific intention of the mitzvah (that while reaping it and preparing matzah, they said: "this is for matzah of the mitzvah").

73. Matzah that was kneaded with fruit juice rather than with water. Sefardim permit this to be eaten on Pesach (but many forbid the matzah cakes of our days), whereas Ashkenazim forbid this, because they fear that fruit juice can cause the flour to ferment, and further, a little water might have gotten into the dough, and then it would certainly ferment.

74. Water that has been drawn and left overnight, and, therefore, it is somewhat cooler and is suitable for baking matzah (so that the dough should not ferment).

75. Zero'a.

76. At first, it seems that Rabban Gamliel of Yavneh was the one who said this, because it states, "the Pesach sacrifice that our forefathers ate *when the Bet HaMikdash still stood*," which would imply that now it no longer existed (Rashbatz, *Pesach she'hayu*). However, it is possible that the original rite did not contain that sentence, and it was added later on, after the Bet HaMikdash had been destroyed (the rite of Rambam does not have that sentence, but look at *Hilchot Chametz U'Matzah*, 8:4, where Rambam does mention something along these lines).

77. He brings on Pesach Sheni, the "second Pesach," a month later, on 14 Iyar.

78. Matzah and maror.

79. PESACH OF EGYPT: the Pesach sacrifice that Am Yisrael offered in Egypt, before they left for freedom. PESACH FOR ALL GENERATIONS: The Pesach sacrifice that Am Yisrael must offer each year.

80. BLOOD ON THE DOORPOST: blood of the Pesach sacrifice was placed on both doorposts and on the lintel by

◂ means

means of hyssop (to understand the significance of this, see the section of "What blood?" on p. 86) – Exodus 12:7 (in Pesach for all generations, one sprinkled the blood on the altar – one sprinkle at the base of the altar).

EATING IN HASTE: the Pesach sacrifice had to be eaten hastily, in one's clothes – Exodus 12:11 (on Pesach for all generations, one eats at one's leisure, leaning, as free people).

PROHIBITION AGAINST GOING OUT: one was forbidden to leave the house until the morning – Exodus 12:11 (on Pesach for all generations one may leave one's home, but is not permitted to take the Pesach sacrifice outside the house – Exodus 12:46. There is a dispute whether one's "house" means one's group, and whether one is ever permitted to transfer it from place to place within the home – see Rashi's commentary).

THE TIME TO TAKE THE LAMB: on Pesach in Egypt, they took the lamb for the sacrifice on the 10th of Nissan (according to the midrash, so that the Egyptians would see the taking of their god). This law does not exist for the Pesach for all generations (it is true that for Pesach of all generations one must check the sacrifice for blemishes four days before the sacrifice, but one is not required to set aside a specific lamb already on that date, and one can even set it aside on the 14th of Nissan) – Exodus 12:3, and also in the Mishnah Pesachim 9:5.

THE PLACE OF THE SLAUGHTER: On the Pesach in Egypt one could sacrifice it any place in Egypt. On Pesach for all generations – only in the Bet HaMikdash, any place in the courtyard – Deuteronomy 16:2.

THE PROHIBITION AGAINST CHAMETZ: was only obligatory on the Pesach of Egypt on the 15th of Nissan – Exodus 13:3–4. On Pesach for all generations, it applies to all seven days – Exodus 12:15. See Mishnah Pesachim 9:5.

One should note that the prohibition against eating chametz on Pesach of Egypt was complex: From the words of the Talmud in Pesachim (90b) it appears that on Pesach in Egypt the prohibition against chametz lasted for the night and the following day. However, according to Shibolei HaLeket (on the haggadah, 218), it appears that the prohibition was only at night and not during the day. Another opinion, Ran on Pesachim (116b), writes that it was forbidden at night and in the day, but the prohibition was only against eating, but not against possessing chametz.

One can argue on his words, because the Torah states specifically regarding Pesach in Egypt that "leaven shall not be found in your homes" – Exodus 12:19 – i.e., that the prohibition against owning chametz also applied to Pesach in Egypt. However, it is

◂ possible

possible that these verses refer to "the festival of Matzot" and not "the festival of Pesach."

Tzlach in Pesachim (116b) discusses these questions, and, according to him, during that first Pesach in Egypt the prohibition of chametz only applied to the night, because for *kodashim* – animal sacrifices – the morning is considered to be a new day (and so too, before the giving of the Torah, the night followed its day). Indeed on the morning of the 15th they prepared their dough in order to bake chametz, but the dough did not have a chance to rise, "because they were driven out of Egypt." If so, it means that the night of the 15th they did not eat chametz because they were commanded not to, and in the morning they did not eat chametz because their dough did not have enough time to ferment.

81. The laws they have in common:

The sacrifice must be an unblemished animal, a male born that year, from the sheep or the goats – Exodus 12:5.

The time of the slaughter: the 14th of Nissan in the afternoon – Exodus 12:6.

It is to be eaten *with matzah and maror* – Exodus 12:8.

It must be roasted, *with the entire animal roasted whole* ("its head with its legs and with its innards") – Exodus 12:9 (one may not eat it cooked).

One is forbidden to break any bone – Exodus 12:46.

One must eat it by the morning – and whatever is left over must be burned – Exodus 12:10.

One must be registered to eat this particular sacrifice: A number of people register for a single sacrifice. Here there is a difference: in Pesach of Egypt, the entire family was party to a single sacrifice – Exodus 12:3; whereas in the case of Pesach for all generations each person can in advance join any group and be part of that sacrifice (and not necessarily join with his family) – Exodus 12:47, and see Rashi.

82. Tzafun.

83. God pours out His wrath. In other words, He shows His anger at them and punishes them.

84. Each person waits for and longs for God – "every eye will await you" (from the Sefardi rite of *Nishmat*).

85. "You save the poor from one stronger than he [is]" – You save the poor from those who would rob him; You hear the cry of the poor, and You hearken to and save the destitute who cry out.

86. "The great, mighty, awesome God" – as in the first blessing of the amidah prayer, and in Magen Avot (recited on Friday night) it quotes from Nishmat even further and it adds another phrase – "Possessor of heaven and earth!"

◂ Our

87. Our mouths – as full of song as the sea; our tongues – full with joyous singing; our lips – full with praise; our hands – spread out [in prayer] like eagles; our feet – swift like deer [to run and praise God]; our limbs and tongue – shall thank and praise – "Therefore, the limbs... and the tongue..."; every tongue should swear to accept God – "every tongue shall swear loyalty to You"; eye – "every eye shall await you"; knee – shall bend; bones – will say "Lord, who is like You" (possibly by swaying back and forth – that is the ruling of Rama, *Orach Chaim* 48:1). In the continuation (beginning with "He who dwells for eternity"): the mouths exalt God "By the mouth of the upright You shall be exalted"; the lips bless Him "and by the lips of the righteous You shall be blessed"; and the tongues sanctify Him "and by the the tongue of the devout You shall be sanctified."

88. The Exodus from Egypt: "You redeemed us from Egypt, O Lord our God, You have freed us from the house of bondage."

89. King Ahasuerus.

90. Daniel.

91. Our patriarch Jacob struggled with the angel and emerged victorious.

92. God terrified Lavan the Aramean at night.

93. Sennacherib cursed God and in the end his army all became corpses.

94. The army of Sisera was swept away.

95. The word "to you" appears seven times in the chorus. There are eight stanzas (so the chorus is recited eight times). Thus, it appears a total of 56 times.

96. God is holy, Am Yisrael is righteous.

97. *Gadya* – a goat; *shunra* – a cat; *kalba* – a dog; *chutra* – a stick; *nura* – fire; *maya* – water; *tora* – an ox.

Sources and expansions for discussion topics

a. The nature of freedom:

What is the definition of freedom? Is a free person one who does whatever he wants? Does freedom mean that a person is not subject to any entity in the world?

The great philosopher, John Locke, writes in his Treatise on Government:

The natural liberty of man is to be free from any superior power on earth, and not to be under the will or legislative authority of man.

According to him, freedom means being free of any superior power, not subject to any authority. Does Judaism accept that definition? Let us look at the words of Rabbi Yehudah HaLevi, in his treatise, Kuzari (third article, 2–5), on the definition of freedom:

> The righteous man is the one who rules his country... This righteous man is the ruler, for all his senses and spiritual and physical powers are obedient to his discipline, and he rules it with true political leadership... He is the one worthy of leading... for he harnesses the contending forces... and he prevents them from straying beyond the boundaries... and so too does he harness the angry forces...

Rabbi Yehudah HaLevi explains that freedom does not mean that the person does whatever he feels like, but that the person knows how to privilege the spiritual over the physical. Every person is composed of a body and a soul; the soul is the more important, more spiritual and central. The body has urges and desires. Which of the two dictates to the other what to do? If a person acts in accordance with his urges, without any restraint, the body emerges triumphant – it controls the soul and enslaves it. However, if the person succeeds in harnessing his body – not to get angry, to refrain from eating foods that are bad for him, to force the body to act in accordance with the feelings of his soul – then his soul controls his body, and the soul returns to its freedom.

A free person is one who succeeds in doing what he believes in, and not what he desires!

The Seder night is the season of our freedom, the time when we allow our souls to be in full control. The ability to sit at the table, to smell the food, but not to eat right away, but to deal with the spiritual for a considerable amount of time, also expresses this freedom.

Subjecting one's body to God is subjecting one's body to the spirit, to the soul, to God's wishes. The soul wishes to do the will of God, but the physical body drags it downward. The ability to permit the soul to triumph, to allow it to fulfill God's

◂ will

will in the world, enables us to be free men.

We do not seek to do "whatever we feel like"; that type of life is slavery – the triumph of the body over the soul. We seek to do that which is moral, that which is good and upright; to be subject to God's will, to bend the body to the will of God, and thereby to bring our soul to complete freedom.

The idea of freedom is discussed in many places in the haggadah. It is worth studying what we wrote about the significance of inviting guests (p. 34) and on "'This matzah' – Why do we eat matzot on Pesach?" (p. 112) and the table of freedom below (p. 285).

b. On the one hand, matzah symbolizes freedom. In Exodus we are commanded to eat matzah in preparation for God's revelation: "It is because our fathers' dough did not have time to rise before the King of kings that the Holy One, Blessed be He, revealed Himself to them and redeemed them" (for more on this topic, see Likutei Torah by Rabbi Shneur Zalman of Liadi, *Parashat Tzav, sheshet yamim*). Similarly, Rishonim write, among them HaManhig (*Hilchot Pesach* 79), that matzah symbolizes freedom.

On the other hand, in Deuteronomy matzah is referred to as "the bread of affliction" (16:3), and in the haggadah we also mention "this bread of affliction," and we break the matzah because a poor person does not eat a whole loaf.

In addition, on the Seder night itself there are things that symbolize freedom: leaning, four cups, eating karpas before the meal; and there are others that symbolize slavery: maror, charoset (a reminder of the clay that was used).

It would appear that both elements have to be emphasized on the Seder night: both freedom and bitterness. This idea is reinforced by the view of Rambam (*Hilchot Chametz U'Matzah* 8:8), who writes that "one dips matzah into charoset and eats it." Ra'avad disagrees with this and says about it, "this has no basis whatsoever." Rabbenu Mano'ach (on Rambam ibid.) explains the problem that Ra'avad felt about this custom, in that there is a contradiction in it: matzah is the symbol of freedom, while charoset is the symbol of slavery! It is true that on the Seder night there is a tendency to link the slavery and the freedom. This is especially so as expressed in hallel, which is interrupted by matzah and maror. Why does one join the two concepts of freedom and slavery?

1) Abarbanel (in his commentary, Zevach Pesach, on the haggadah, p. 34) states that this is the question of the child in the Four Questions: why do we have symbols of freedom (leaning, dipping food) and symbols of slavery (maror, and – according to him – matzah)? And

◂ the

the answer is that "we were slaves to Pharaoh in Egypt and the Lord our God took us out of there" – we went out from slavery to freedom, and, therefore, we have symbols of slavery and symbols of freedom (although, according to this we would have expected the first part of the seder to have only symbols of slavery and thereafter only symbols of freedom).

2) After a person learns and understands something new, one must remind him of the old things he has learned, so that he can see the difference – "the advantage of light over darkness" (Ecclesiastes 2:13). After a person is given an answer to a question, one must repeat the question, to show how the answer is appropriate. It is by contrasting freedom and slavery that we will understand better what freedom is. Therefore, we need both these symbols at the seder, in order to deepen our understanding of freedom (see *Michtav Mei'Eliyahu*, 4, p. 218).

3) On the Seder night we mention and think about the slavery as well, out of our belief that everything is from God and that all is part of the Divine plan. Our patriarch Abraham, at the Covenant between the Pieces, received a promise both about the slavery and the freedom. This teaches us that slavery also has a role, because the slavery here was a preparation and consolidation of Am Yisrael before the redemption. No one wants to have difficult periods in life. However, when we undergo trying times – both in our personal lives and in regard to Am Yisrael – we must remember that *difficulties have a role to play, and the beginning of the redemption lies within these difficulties themselves.* One can extract from these difficulties the impetus and guidance toward the rectification that is needed and the redemption.

c. *Study the section on "What is so special about the story of the Exodus from Egypt?"* on p. 30, the tables on maggid on p. 26, and in *Halachah MiMekorah – Kinor David, Maggid* p. 95. In brief: what is special about this night? 1) The story of the Exodus from Egypt in the form of questions and answers. 2) One must also relate the process, which began with slavery, and not only the results (and one does so at length). 3) One is to tell it through the mitzvot of the night: Pesach, matzah, and maror (these three answers are by Rav Chaim of Brisk). 4) The mitzvah is not only to tell, but also to praise and thank God (Rav Yosef Dov Soloveitchik). 5) One is not only to tell about the past but to literally feel that we are leaving Egypt right now.

d. It is important to remember that when the Bet HaMikdash existed, the Seder night was substantively different from the festival with which we are familiar. That night revolved

◄ entirely

entirely on the Pesach sacrifice, with its special laws. The Pesach sacrifice is characterized by the sacrifice itself, a sacrifice that must be eaten in a group. The eating of the Pesach sacrifice expresses the gathering together for a meal that serves as service of God at the highest level.

The sacrifices in general serve as a factor in *drawing Am Yisrael close to God, as well as for atoning* for Am Yisrael (Ketubot 10b: "the altar removes and feeds, makes beloved, and atones"). The Bet HaMikdash was the place where the Divine Presence was at its highest level, and it created *a direct link between God and Am Yisrael. Our difficulties today in connecting ourselves to serving God and to expressing fully our ties with God are part of the problem of the lack of the Bet HaMikdash and sacrifices in our lives.*

e. 1) A person who remembers his slavery will see to it to take care of the rights of others. 2) When we understand the slavery that we experienced, we can understand better the significance of going out to freedom. 3) When we know that we were slaves and nevertheless went out to freedom, we know that even in the most difficult circumstances God helps us, and from this we will find encouragement even in trying times for Am Yisrael in different eras (Rav Avraham Yitzchak Kook, *Olat Re'iyah*, on *ha lachma anya*).

f. See the section on "Why retell the story each year if we already know it?" on p. 46.

g. See the section on "Do we exclude the wicked son from Am Yisrael?" on p. 55.

h. There are a number of messages that emerge if we study the midrash of the Four Sons:

1) One must teach and educate each individual child based on the method most suitable for that child – see what we wrote on "Teach a child according to his nature" on p. 56. 2) There are different people in Am Yisrael as well, and all must remain united, around a single table – see the section on "Do we exclude the wicked son from Am Yisrael?" on p. 55. 3) Each of us has some elements of the Four Sons, and we all have to deal with these characteristics – see the section on "The four sons within each of us," on p. 58.

i. 1) We want to start with shame, in that our forefathers were idolaters, and, therefore, we begin with Terach, who was an idolater, and Abraham rejected idolatry. 2) Our strength is derived from our forefathers. One cannot speak of processes of the redemption of Israel without understanding that the process had already begun in the time of Abraham. Our tradition passes via our forefathers to us, and is based on them. If a person is called up to

◂ the

the Torah, he is called as "so-and-so the son of so-and-so," as his identity is also composed of the fact that he traces back to the generation of the forefathers. On the one hand, each generation has its own identity. On the other hand, our might is built on the foundation of the earlier generations. It is from them that we draw the strength, and from them that we draw our principles. 2) Abraham serves as a figure to emulate for all generations, and, therefore, we begin the story of the creation of nation with Abraham. d. It is possible that what is emphasized is that the selection of Abraham was a special act, one not dependent on anything, and is not dependent on our actions.

j. *Responsa Mi'ma'amakim* (III, 6) brings questions and answers from the Holocaust era:

> In the valley of murder, prisoners of poverty and steel in darkness and the valley of death, in the ghetto of Kovno in Lithuania...
>
> And at the time of the morning prayer, the cantor, Reb Abraham Joseph, may God avenge his death, began to say the morning blessings with total concentration. When he got to "who has not made me a slave" he cried out in a bitter voice to the Lord of all lords: "How can I recite this blessing at a time when we are under curfew and captivity... How can a slave pronounce the blessing of a free man when a metal bar is on his throat ..."
>
> Answer: The primary intention of this blessing is not on the slavery of the body but on the slavery of the soul, which is expressed by the law that a Canaanite slave, who is not obligated to perform the mitzvot [does not recite this blessing]... but a Jew, who is obligated to perform the mitzvot, even if he is in captivity... does recite this blessing...

A person can be a slave, but his spirit is that of a free man. Alternatively, a person can be free and be enslaved to the passions of this world, to fashion, and to his lusts. This was expressed well by Rav Avraham Yitzchak Kook (*Ma'amarei Re'iyah*, p. 157):

> The difference between a slave and a free man is not only a difference of status in that one is indentured and the other is not. We can find an educated slave whose spirit is free and the reverse, a free man whose spirit is that of a slave. This freedom is the lofty spirit of the person, and so too the entire nation is raised up by its faith to its internal freedom, to its spiritual character of being in the image of God within it.

One who is enslaved to things that

◂ others

others perceive as beautiful, one who is led by his desires – is considered to be like a slave, even if externally he is a free man. One who is faithful to his independence, to the spirit of God in him, is a free man, even when he is totally subject to the whim of others, with his body enslaved completely.

k. Study "Why do we expound on verses from Deuteronomy and not from Exodus?" (p. 72).

l. The Exodus from Egypt was significant not only because the Egyptians were punished and Bnei Yisrael were redeemed, but for all future generations. There is significance in terms of the honor of God that was revealed in Egypt, and, therefore, this had to be carried out by God Himself (for more on this, see the section on "Why not through an angel?" on p. 84). One may add that at first, it appears that this was carried out through a messenger, for the Torah states: "He will not permit the Destroyer to enter your houses to smite [you]" (Exodus 12:23), which would imply that the Egyptians were smitten by the "destroyer" angel! However, it seems that this means that the plague itself was what destroyed them, as stated in "there will be no plague to destroy [you] when I smite the [people of the] land of Egypt" (Exodus 12:13) – Shibolei HaLeket and Avudraham on the haggadah. And there are other interpretations.

m. See the section on "Why couldn't they have had only a single plague – blood?" on p. 88.

n. See the section on "Why did God harden Pharaoh's heart?" on p. 97.

o. There are three answers: 1) It means that we were not worthy of the next stage. 2) Each stage is individually worthy of our thanks to God. 3) Each stage has its own independent significance, and each stage advanced Am Yisrael, including even just standing at Mount Sinai.

p. For more on this and the sources on the topic, see the answer to discussion "j" above, p. 282.

q. The more a person's desire to come closer to God increases, the more keenly he will feel the absence of the Bet HaMikdash. The Bet HaMikdash was the holiest of all places, the place where one could physically feel close to God. Does the fact that we do not feel the lack of the Bet HaMikdash keenly enough teach us that our desire to draw close to God is also lacking?

18. The Bet HaMikdash is the place where the Divine Presence "resides." The existence of the Divine Presence is not only a spiritual experience, but it creates obligations! Life in the shadow of the Divine Presence teaches a person that the human is not the center, not his personal desires, but those of God. Are we ready for this? Maybe our present

◂ circumstances

circumstances are preferable? Maybe we are not sufficiently prepared to do God's will in full, to accept Him as our King, to steer our lives in accordance with our mission and our obligations to Am Yisrael and to God, and not only in terms of what we find convenient and our desires.

Shulchan Aruch (Orach Chaim 1:3) writes that it is proper for a person to mourn for the Bet HaMikdash. He must feel the loss in the past but must also feel that without the Bet HaMikdash there is something basic missing. The great light of the Divine Presence does not shine in the same way.

IN SUMMARY: in order to draw closer to God and to prepare ourselves for the building of the Bet HaMikdash, we must strive to feel what is lacking, to intensify our desire for the Divine Presence's return, to be prepared to wholeheartedly do whatever God's will demands of us, and act in a more humane manner in order to prepare the ground for the rebuilding of our Bet HaMikdash. We must know that no private association or segment of Am Yisrael can build the Bet HaMikdash, but only the entire nation, and we must therefore be united in order to be prepare for its rebuilding, which will, God willing, take place soon.

Who is free?

A GENERAL SUMMARY

Slave	Free man	Passages that deal with this in our haggadah:
Seeks to receive	Seeks to give	Rav Yosef Dov Soloveitchik, "What is the significance of inviting guests when no one hears the invitation?" p. 34.
Pleasures dictate to the body what to do	The soul, profound values, the spirit – all these dictate to the body how to act; a person who acts in accordance with his beliefs, and not based on what he desires to do	"This [promise] has sustained us" – topic for discussion "j" – see the end of the haggadah, in the words of Rav Avraham Yitzchak Kook, p. 282. "Why drink four cups of wine?" on p. 5. Karpas – Discussion topic "a," on p. 278. Korech – the words of Rav Avraham Yitzchak Kook, p. 155.
Pursues instant gratification	Has the ability to wait, is able to postpone instant gratification for the sake of a higher, more complex process	"Why do we eat karpas?" p. 18.
I am in the center!	God is in the center – a sense of mission, idealism – that is the true "I"	The words of Maharal in the section on "'This matzah' – Why do we eat matzot on Pesach?" p. 112. "Lavan wanted to uproot everyone?" p. 72. *"Returning to the inner self – Afikoman"* p. 160.

A person's environment dictates how to act	A person's inner truth dictates how to act	The desire to be true to oneself and to truth, as opposed to the desire to imitate others – see the previous item on "I am in the center," and in our words: "'This matzah' – Why do we eat matzot on Pesach?" p. 112 and p. 160.
A desire for unlimited freedom	The desire for discipline and significance	"This [promise] has sustained us" – topic for discussion "j" – see the end of the haggadah, in the words of Rav Avraham Yitzchak Kook, p. 282. "Why do we eat karpas?" See discussion "a" above, on p. 278. "This night we are going free!" see p. 43.
A material life	Sanctifies reality	"Kaddesh or Kiddush?" p. 10.
In bondage to time	Is not even a slave of time	
Remains the way he was, is unable to change	The power to change and be changed	"Why ask questions?" p. 36.

Basic guidelines for the second day of festival, outside of Israel

a. It is best to minimize the consumption of matzah during the daytime of the first festival day. This will facilitate eating matzah with proper appetite during the second seder (Rama 471:2).

b. It is forbidden to prepare items for the second festival day on the first festival day. The reason is that the first day's sanctity is written in the Torah, while the second day's sanctity is only of rabbinical standing. This would be tantamount to preparing on a festival for a weekday (Mishnah Berurah 503:1, 502:11, and 495:23).

c. It is forbidden to prepare on the first festival day for the second festival day, even items that are only rabbinically forbidden. This includes activities that are forbidden only due to concerns about working too hard on the festival (Mishnah Berurah *ibid.*).

d. It is permissible to begin preparation for the second festival day only once it is clearly nighttime, after the stars have come out. However, already at sunset, it is permissible to perform activities whose prohibition is only rabbinic (Responsa Rabbi Akiva Eiger, Hagahot Rabbi Akiva Eiger 473, and Ginzei Rabbi Akiva Eiger 21). This is also the consensus of the authorities, that at that time we refrain from performing activities that are biblically prohibited, but we do perform activities that are only rabbinically prohibited (Rav Shlomo Zalman Auerbach, Rav Shalom Yosef Elyashiv, Rav Shmuel Wosner in *Yom Tov Sheini KeHilchato* 1, note 21).

e. The evening prayer service (*ma'ariv*) on the second festival day is the same as on the first festival day. It is proper to wait until it is definitely nightfall before beginning (*Levush* 488). At the conclusion of ma'ariv we recite sefirat ha'omer (Shulchan Aruch 489:1. Some have the custom to recite it at the seder itself).

f. Candle lighting is performed on the second festival day in the same manner as on the first festival day. Therefore, women who recite the shehechiyanu blessing when lighting candles on the first festival day (see Hagahot Rabbi Akiva Eiger 263:5 and Mishnah Berurah note 23) should also recite it when lighting candles on the second festival day (Shabbat 23a, Mishnah Berurah 662:2 and 473:1). It is proper to wear a new garment before lighting candles, or at least to have in mind a new fruit that will be eaten (in the latter case, it is proper to light the candles as close to kiddush as possible, so the shehechiyanu blessing can immediately precede the eating of the fruit). However, even if a woman does not have a new garment or a new fruit, she may recite the shehechiyanu blessing (Shulchan Aruch 600:2).

g. We light candles on the second festival day only after nightfall (notes

◄ of the

of the wife of Sma, quoted by her son in his introduction to *Tur Yoreh De'ah 'Hakdamah MiBen HaDerishah'*; *Dagul MiRevavah* 263). Some are lenient and permit lighting candles before nightfall on the second festival day, but only once it has started to get dark. That way we can at least derive some benefit from the candles on the first festival day (Mishnah Berurah 514:33), but it is still preferable to wait for nightfall (especially in modern times when we have electric lights, giving less incentive to rely on this leniency).

h. We recite kiddush at the second seder, and we recite *shehechiyanu* and any other blessings that we recited on the first night (Rama 481:2). The Sages established this as a rule to prevent anyone from belittling, or being overly lenient on the second festival day (Shabbat 23a, *Bi'ur HaGra* 539:11, Mishnah Berurah 662:2 and 473:1, and *Minchat Shlomo* 19).

i. We eat matzah, maror, and korech on the second festival day as on the first festival day, but it is permissible to follow the most lenient opinion for the kezayit (this is logical. Since we are actually fulfilling all the mitzvot, just using the minimal size, this does not diminish the standing of the second festival day; rather, it shows that the day is a rabbinic festival. This is also the view of Rav Shlomo Zalman Auerbach, quoted in *Yom Tov Sheini KeHilchato* 1:197. See there how this is not similar to *Bi'ur Halachah* 475 *lo yatza*, where he states that one must have the intention to fulfill the mitzvah while eating matzah on the second festival day; that is fundamental to fulfilling a mitzvah – knowing what one is doing and why one is doing it).